MW00642054

Cross Vision

Cross Vision

How the Crucifixion of Jesus Makes Sense of Old Testament Violence

Gregory A. Boyd

Fortress Press
Minneapolis

CROSS VISION
How the Crucifixion of Jesus Makes Sense of Old Testament Violence

Cover design: Brad Norr
Author photo: Paul Weaver

Hardcover ISBN: 978-1-5064-2073-8
eBook ISBN: 978-1-5064-2074-5

The paper used in this publication meets the minimum requirements of American National Standard for Information Sciences — Permanence of Paper for Printed Library Materials, ANSI Z329.48-1984.
Manufactured in the U.S.A.

To the staff and congregation of Woodland Hills Church,
the passionate-yet-open-minded church
that I've had the honor of pastoring
for the last twenty-five years.
Thank you!

Contents

Introduction: Something Else Must Be Going On

> I'll tell you all my ideas about Looking-glass House.
> First, there's the room you can see through the
> glass that's just the same as our drawing room,
> only the things go the other way . . .
> the books are something like our books,
> only the words go the wrong way . . .
> —Alice, *Through the Looking-Glass*

A Tale of My Strangely Behaving Wife

My wife, Shelley, is as kind, gentle, and compassionate a person as you'll ever meet. (She's obviously also exceptionally wise since she decided to marry *me* thirty-seven years ago!)

Having established these facts, I'd like you to imagine a story.[1]

Suppose I am walking downtown one sunny day and I spot Shelley walking on the other side of a busy street. I shout her name and wave my hand in the air, but the noise of the heavy traffic drowns out my voice and the traffic makes it impossible to jaywalk across the street to greet her. I try to call her on my phone, but she apparently isn't carrying her phone or has it silenced. So I decide to keep pace with her until I arrive at the corner crosswalk.

As we both approach the intersection, I see Shelley come upon a

1. Pay attention to the details in this hypothetical story. They will become significant at various points in this book.

panhandler in a wheelchair. He appears to suffer from mental illness since he's muttering to himself and rocking back and forth while holding out his can for donations. His tattered baseball cap seems to be his most prized possession, for he clings to it as people pass by, apparently afraid that someone might try to steal it. Knowing how compassionate Shelley is, I anticipate that she'll probably put a five- or ten-dollar bill in this poor man's can and start up a conversation with him.

But suppose that, instead of showing compassion, my lovely wife suddenly screams at this man at the top of her lungs, knocks his donation can out of his hand, grabs his cap, kicks over his wheelchair, and takes off running down the street!

Obviously, witnessing this would horrify me. But without an opportunity to talk to my wife, how should I understand what I just witnessed?

I could consider the possibility that Shelley had a Jekyll-and-Hyde sort of split personality that she'd somehow kept hidden from me for thirty-seven years. But for me to question my wife's character after all our years together feels dishonoring to her and to our marriage. I *know* my wife, and I have to trust that, despite what I had just witnessed, she has the kind and compassionate character I've come to know and love over the years.

The only remaining alternative for me is to reinterpret the horrifying event I just witnessed in light of what I know about Shelley's true, compassionate character. Since the cruelty Shelley appeared to display cannot be true, I have to assume that *something else must be going on* that I am not aware of.

For example, maybe Shelley had volunteered to be part of a sociological experiment to test how people respond when witnessing a shocking assault. Or maybe Shelley and the panhandler had agreed to play roles for *Candid Camera*, or *Punk'd*, or some other reality TV show that pulls pranks on people. Indeed, I might suspect that I am the one being punk'd! Each of these ideas may seem pretty far-fetched, but they're far more plausible than the suggestion that my compassionate wife actually could be capable of engaging in such cruel behavior.

Further, the plausibility of each of these hypothetical scenarios could be increased or diminished by other considerations. For example, suppose that earlier in the day Shelley had insisted, without explanation, that I meet her downtown on that exact street and at that exact time. This would increase the likelihood that I was the victim of a carefully orchestrated prank and decrease the likelihood that Shelley was part of a sociological experiment. If I had seen a mischievous look in Shelley's eye as she implored me to meet her at that time and place, the plausibility of the prank scenario would be increased even further and the experiment scenario even less. On the other hand, if I happened to be downtown on a whim and/or if I noticed several official-looking people taking notes in the area of the panhandler, the converse would be true.

Our Dilemma

The situation in which I found myself in the above story is somewhat like the predicament we Christians find ourselves in when we witness Yahweh seeming to act in cruel ways in the Old Testament (OT).[2] Christians have always affirmed that Jesus Christ, and especially Jesus Christ crucified, is the full and complete revelation of God.[3] From him we learn that God's nature is love—the kind of self-sacrificial love that led God to become a human and to offer himself up for us when we were yet enemies.[4]

But what are we to think when we find Yahweh acting in surprisingly sub-Christlike ways in the OT? For example, what are we to make of God commanding the Israelites to mercilessly slaughter "anything that breathes" in certain areas within Canaan (e.g., Deut 20:16)? That command certainly doesn't seem to reflect self-sacrificial love!

One option that some people take is to simply reject passages that depict God in violent ways.[5] This solves our dilemma, but it conflicts with the fact that Jesus repeatedly endorsed the OT as the inspired word of God.[6] If we confess Jesus as Lord, I don't see how we can reserve for ourselves the right to correct his theology. I thus don't feel I'm free to simply reject anything I find in Scripture.

2. "Yahweh" is the primary name of God in the OT.
3. I will defend this claim in chapter 2.
4. 1 John 4:8; 1 John 3:16; Rom 5:10.
5. For example, E. Seibert, *Disturbing Divine Behavior: Troubling Old Testament Images of God* (Minneapolis: Fortress Press, 2009), and C. S. Cowles, "The Case for Radical Discontinuity," in *Show Them No Mercy: 4 Views on God and Canaanite Genocide*, ed. S. Gundry (Grand Rapids: Zondervan, 2003), 13–44.
6. See, for example, Matt 15:4; 21:42; 22:29, 31; 26:54. On Jesus's high view of Scripture, see e.g., J. H. Wenham, *Christ and the Bible* (Grand Rapids: Baker, 1994).

So we're in a tricky spot. We cannot deny that God sometimes appears violent and cruel in the OT. At the same time, just as it would be unfaithful for me to question the compassionate character of my wife after thirty-seven years of marriage, it seems unfaithful for us to question the altogether loving character of God that is revealed in the crucified Christ. In fact, we'll later see that the New Testament (NT) presents the crucified Christ not as one revelation among others, but as the revelation that culminates and supersedes all others. And this rules out allowing any OT portrait of God to compromise the beauty of the God who is revealed on the cross.

This leaves us with only one remaining possibility: If we believe that Jesus fully reveals what God is *really* like, we have no choice but to suspect that *something else must be going on* when God appears to act violently in the OT. And until we have the opportunity to sit down with God face-to-face, our job is to try to imagine what this *something else* might be.

***

In Lewis Carroll's 1871 sequel to *Alice in Wonderland*, titled *Through the Looking-Glass*, Alice steps through her looking-glass (a mirror) into an alternate reality.[7] There she finds that everything is reversed—the way things appear in a mirror. Similarly, we will later discover that, when we interpret the OT's violent portrayals of God while fully trusting that God's *true* character is revealed on the cross, the cross begins to function along the lines of Alice's looking-glass.

We shall see that this looking-glass cross allows us to see *what else is going on* in a way that completely reverses the violent dimension of these portraits. In fact, when interpreted through the looking-glass cross, the violence that OT authors sometimes ascribe to God no longer bears witness to a violent God; it rather bears witness to the self-sacrificial, nonviolent God who was supremely revealed on the cross.

7. L. Carroll, *Through the Looking-Glass* (New York: Dover, 1999 [1871]).

PART I

The Problem and a Looking-Glass Cross Solution

1

The Elephant

> The God of the Old Testament is arguably
> the most unpleasant character in all fiction:
> jealous and proud of it; a petty, unjust, unforgiving control-freak;
> a vindictive, bloodthirsty, ethnic cleanser;
> a misogynistic, homophobic, racist, infanticidal, genocidal,
> filicidal, pestilential, megalomaniacal, sadomasochistic,
> capriciously malevolent bully.
> —Richard Dawkins[1]

Sixteen years into our marriage, Shelley and I had to name the proverbial elephant that was in the room of our relationship. And it was an *ugly* elephant! A void had grown between us almost from the start of our marriage. We loved each other and loved our three children, and we got along reasonably well and had memorable times together. But Shelley and I are wired about as differently as two people can be. Because of this, we never found a way to get deeply inside each other's heart and mind, and at some point rather early on in our marriage, we gave up trying. Consequently, as the years rolled on, we both increasingly felt alone in our marriage. At the core of our being—our soul—we didn't feel fully known, loved, or appreciated by the other.

For the first sixteen years of our marriage, the business of raising three children, finishing grad school, supporting the family, engaging in ministry, and everything else that life requires made it pretty easy to suppress our inner pain and ignore the growing gulf. But our kids

1. R. Dawkins, *The God Delusion* (Boston: Houghton Mifflin, 2006), 31.

were growing older, and we each had begun to wonder what our life together would look like without the children in the home.

The elephant became impossible to ignore. We had to finally get real with the fact that we felt like aliens to one another.

***

Acknowledging the elephant unleashed sixteen years' worth of suppressed loneliness, resentment, and pain, and the ensuing six months were, frankly, pure hell. Only our commitment before God to stay married "for better or for worse" kept us in the game. And truth be told, even that was at times stretched almost to the breaking point.

Thankfully, with the help of some excellent counseling, something beautiful began to emerge out of this hell, and it has continued ever since. It took a lot of work, but Shelley and I slowly discovered ways of getting into each other's alien inner worlds. And by doing so, we discovered a profound mutual love and friendship we previously never dreamed was possible.

This scary, painful, but transformative period of our marriage illustrates an important truth: The only way to discover the beauty that lies on the other side of a mountain of ugliness is to courageously confront and work through it.

Calling It What It Is

Brothers and sisters who follow Jesus, we have an elephant in our room. We believe that God is altogether beautiful, loving, compassionate, and just. And this belief is well founded, for this is how the Bible generally portrays God. Most importantly, this is the God who is revealed in Jesus Christ. What we tend to ignore, however, is that there are some portraits of God in the OT, which we rightly confess to be "God-breathed" (2 Tim 3:16), that are most definitely *not* beautiful, loving, compassionate, or just.

In fact, though it may sound irreverent to say it, some portraits of God in the OT are, quite frankly, *really ugly*! How else can you honestly describe a depiction of God, for example, ordering his people to mercilessly annihilate every member of the Midianites except for the virgin girls, whom Israelite soldiers were allowed to keep alive to enjoy as spoils of war (Num 31:1–17)?

Suppose you came upon a depiction of a god like this while

reading an ancient pagan religious text. Would you hesitate to call it ugly? Of course not. But isn't it disingenuous to refrain from calling this same depiction "ugly" simply because it's found in *your* holy book rather than in someone else's?

At the same time, admitting that a biblical depiction of God is ugly seems to conflict with the Christian belief that God is beautiful and that everything in the Bible is divinely inspired. So, not knowing what else to do, most Christians go on professing that God is beautiful while trying to ignore the biblical depictions of God that are ugly. Whether we do it consciously or not, we subject the OT to a "textual cleansing" in order to create "an acceptable Bible Lite" for ourselves.[2]

This is not a helpful strategy. Among other things, even if we rarely think about them, Scripture's violent portraits of God will continue to pollute our mental images of God until we find a way to reconcile them with Jesus's supreme revelation of God. And the thing about polluted mental images of God is that they inevitably compromise the vibrancy of our relationship with God, which in turn compromises the passion with which we live out our faith in God.

On top of this, numerous studies have shown that violent depictions of God in literature that is regarded as sacred make believers more inclined toward violence.[3] Given the rising fear surrounding religiously motivated violence since 9/11, this makes many people understandably concerned about the OT's violent representations of God.

These divine portraits also give plenty of ammunition to critics of the Bible, and I have met far too many former Christians, and even former pastors, whose faith was destroyed because they found they could no longer defend these ugly portraits against these critics.[4]

The time for us to name the large and very ugly elephant in our

2. P. Jenkins, *Laying Down the Sword: Why We Can't Ignore the Bible's Violent Verses* (New York: HarperOne, 2011), 15.

3. M. Beier, *A Violent God-Image: An Introduction to the Work of Eugen Drewermann* (New York: Continuum, 2004); D. Daschke and A. Kille, eds., *A Cry Instead of Justice: The Bible and Cultures of Violence in Psychological Perspective* (New York: T&T Clark, 2010); R. S. Hess and E. A. Martens, eds., *War in the Bible and Terrorism in the Twenty-First Century* (Winona Lake, IN: Eisenbrauns, 2008), and Jenkins, *Laying Down the Sword*, 15.

4. See Dawkins, *God Delusion*; C. Hitchens, *God Is Not Great: How Religion Poisons Everything* (New York: Twelve, 2009); D. Barker, *God, the Most Unpleasant Character in All Fiction* (New York: Sterling, 2016). It's worth noting that Dan Barker, the author of this last book, was a Christian evangelist for sixteen years before losing his faith and becoming an atheist. And one of the main reasons is that he concluded there was no way to defend the immoral character of God in many narratives of the OT.

room is long past due. We have to honestly deal with the awful violence that some OT authors ascribe to God.[5]

The Book I Couldn't Write

Ten years ago I set out to write a book that attempted to tackle the OT's violent portraits of God. Like other Evangelical books on this topic, my plan was to put forth the best arguments I had accumulated over the years that attempt to justify the violence of God in the OT.

After writing about fifty pages, I had to quit. My arguments frankly struck me as woefully inadequate. Even if they succeeded in justifying the violence that God commanded or enacted—which they usually didn't—none of them came close to showing how these portraits were compatible with Jesus's cross-centered revelation of God.

Even more problematic, however, was that I had come to understand that, according to Jesus, all Scripture is supposed to *point to him*, and especially to his sacrificial suffering on the cross.[6] While my best explanations might make the violently behaving God of the OT look a little less nasty, and perhaps sometimes even ethical, they did absolutely nothing to show how these violent divine portraits *point to Christ crucified*.

Admitting that I could no longer justify the OT's violent portraits of God put me in a serious dilemma. On the authority of Jesus, I had to affirm that the whole OT is divinely inspired. But also on the authority of Jesus, I could no longer accept the violence that some narratives within this divinely inspired book ascribe to God.

I struggled with this inner conflict for several months. But then something unexpected and wonderful began to happen. I actually began to see how even the most offensively violent portraits of God in the OT reflect and point toward the self-sacrificial and nonviolent character of God that is revealed on the cross.

Most surprisingly of all, I found that the thing that enabled me to see this was that I was *no longer trying to justify these offensive pictures*! As paradoxical as it sounds, it was only by acknowledging that the

5. I should note that some allege that the NT also contains violent portraits of God. I have not addressed these allegations in this book because, in my opinion, others have already adequately accomplished this. Two excellent examples are T. Yoder Neufeld, *Killing Enmity* (Grand Rapids: Baker Academic, 2011) and M. Strauss, *Jesus Behaving Badly* (Downers Grove, IL: InterVarsity, 2015).
6. John 5:38–40, 45–47; Luke 24:25–27, 45–46; cf. 1 Cor 15:3. We will discuss this in depth in the following chapter.

violent portraits of God in the OT were *not* compatible with the God who is fully revealed on the cross that I came to see how these portraits actually *point to* the God who is fully revealed on the cross!

Well, this set me off on a ten-year reading and writing adventure that resulted in a highly academic, two-volume, 1445-page book called *The Crucifixion of the Warrior God*.[7] Obviously, few nonacademics are going to try to tackle a book like that, which is why this much more reasonably sized book was written.

But it all began when I stopped trying to justify the violence that some OT authors ascribe to God while continuing to believe that all Scripture, including its most violent portraits of God, are divinely inspired for the ultimate purpose of pointing people to the crucified Christ, who is the very "life" of Scripture (John 5:38–47).

Embracing the Problem

For this reason, readers should be forewarned that I am not going to try to minimize the moral awfulness or put the best possible spin on the OT's violent depictions of God, as Evangelical apologists typically do.[8] If a biblical author ascribes an action to God that we would normally consider morally awful, I will not hesitate to admit that the action is, in fact, morally awful.

Taking a ruthlessly honest look at this material is going to create some cognitive dissonance in the minds of some readers, for it will challenge assumptions about what it means to confess that all Scripture is divinely inspired, or, as Paul puts it, "God-breathed" (2 Tim 3:16). The first step in this journey is to suspend this concern and simply embrace whatever inner conflict you experience as we review this material. We have to honestly confront and work through this mountain of ugliness if we are to eventually find the beauty on the other side.

Remember, God is not offended or angry with our questions. The major heroes of faith in the Bible were brutally honest in voicing

7. Gregory Boyd, *The Crucifixion of the Warrior God: Interpreting the Old Testament's Violent Portraits of God in Light of the Cross*, 2 vols. (Minneapolis: Fortress Press, 2017). I will frequently refer readers who are interested in my sources and/or who want a more scholarly and extensive treatment of a given topic to this work, which I will henceforth abbreviate as *CWG*.

8. H. Wettstein, "God's Struggles," in *Divine Evil?: The Moral Character of the God of Abraham*, ed. M. Bergmann, M. J. Murray, and M. C. Rea (New York: Oxford University Press, 2011), 321–33 (322).

objections to God when it seemed that God was acting out of character.[9] In fact, the Lord changed Jacob's name to "Israel" precisely because he was willing to wrestle with God (Gen 32:24–32)! So, honestly wrestling with God actually lies at the foundation of the Bible's understanding of faith. As I have argued elsewhere, not only is God not offended or angered by our honest questioning, God applauds it![10]

Bearing this in mind, let's go to the mat.

Genocidal Worship[11]

It's a few thousand years ago. A young Canaanite couple is enjoying an afternoon with their newborn infant. Like everybody else in their small town, this couple has heard rumors of a warring nomadic tribe called the Hebrews who worshiped a mighty warrior god named Yahweh. But the people of their town had prayed and made sacrifices to their chief god, Baal. And since Baal had protected them from other warring tribes and deities in the past, they had hope that the Hebrews would not attack their town.

On this day, however, their prayers and sacrifices prove futile. This couple hears the battle horns and war cries of an approaching army. They see and hear neighbors screaming and frantically running down the dirt path outside their tiny hut. Their hearts pound as they stare at each other for a brief bewildered and terrified moment. Suddenly realizing what is taking place, the teenage mother sweeps up her newborn, the husband grabs his sword, and they turn to run out the door.

Unfortunately, they're too late. Before they reach the door, two sword-wielding Hebrew soldiers appear before them screaming, "Praise Yahweh! Yahweh is great!" The terrified husband raises his weapon, but the soldiers quickly run their swords through him. Seeing the hopelessness of her situation, the petrified mother curls up in

9. Look, for example, at the honest objections and complaints to God raised by Abraham (Gen 18:23–33), Moses (Exod 32:9–14; 33:12–16), the psalmist (Ps 89:19–44), Habakkuk (Hab 1:3–4, 13), and, of course, Job (Job 9:17, 22–24; 10:3, 8, 16–20; 16:12–14; 24:12).

10. See G. Boyd, *Benefit of the Doubt: Breaking the Idol of Certainty* (Grand Rapids: Baker, 2013), 75–90. In this book I share the story of how I learned that getting raw with God can open us up to receive more insightful revelations from God (see ibid., 91–111).

11. For a more comprehensive and in-depth review of the OT's violent portraits of God, see *CWG*, vol. 1, ch. 6.

the corner of her hut, crying and shaking as she clutches her wailing infant.

As the two Hebrew soldiers approach her with their bloodied swords raised above their heads, she holds up her baby, begging the soldiers to at least have mercy on her infant. One of the soldiers is moved and hesitates for a moment as he thinks about his own young wife and newborn daughter. His comrade notices his hesitation and reminds him that Yahweh had specifically commanded Moses to have his people worship him by *showing no mercy* toward anyone or anything. "The mother and baby must also be offered up to Yahweh," he says.

The first soldier reluctantly nods his head, closes his eyes, and shouts, "Praise be to Yahweh!" as he puts his full weight and strength into his falling sword. Both soldiers are splattered with blood as the sword splits the young mother's skull. The other soldier then shouts the same praise as he bludgeons the crying infant to death.

***

When you imagine this story, how does it make you feel? The revulsion I experienced when I first vividly imagined this scene was one of the factors that caused me to abandon any hope or desire that I had to justify violent portraits of God such and this one. For, as disturbing as it is, this fictionalized story represents the biblical account of what took place thousands and thousands of times when Israel invaded the land of Canaan.

Scripture says that Yahweh told Moses to destroy the lands' inhabitants totally, adding that the Israelites were to "make no treaty with them, and show them no mercy" (Deut 7:2–3). At another point Yahweh is depicted as telling Moses:

> In the cities of the nations the Lord your God is giving you as an inheritance, do not leave alive anything that breathes. Completely destroy them—the Hittites, Amorites, Canaanites, Perizzites, Hivites and Jebusites—as the Lord your God has commanded you. (Deut 20:16–17)

We find variations of this frightful command being given or carried out *thirty-seven times* in the OT![12]

12. See the informative table of the "Most Disturbing Conquest Texts" in Jenkins, *Laying Down the Sword*, 36–39. For an excellent overview of the brutality of the conquest narrative, see ibid., 29–47.

What makes these commands even more horrific is that the Hebrew word for "total destruction" is *hērem*, meaning to "set apart" or "devote" to Yahweh a people group "for destruction." In other words, when the Israelites engaged in wholesale genocide against various populations, they believed they were doing it as an *act of devotion to Yahweh.*

If our wrestling with these disturbing divine portraits is to be authentic, we must allow their gruesome character to affect us. We need to concretely imagine the *hērem* command being carried out on mothers with their children and newborn babies. And we need to do the same with the multitude of other horrifically violent portraits of God in the OT.

Other Accounts of God Commanding Violence

Moses came down from Mount Sinai just after he had received the Ten Commandments. During the forty days he was gone, the children of Israel had fallen into idolatry. Yahweh is depicted as telling Moses to have each of the Levites "strap a sword to his side." Then they were to "go back and forth through the camp from one end to the other, each killing his brother and friend and neighbor" (Exod 32:27).

The Levites obeyed Moses, with the result that "about three thousand" people were slain (v. 28). Moses then congratulated the Levites for doing such a thorough job while reminding them that the people they had slaughtered had been "set . . . apart to the Lord" (v. 29). In other words, as with the *hērem* command, Moses understood this bloodbath to be an act of worship.

***

Other things that Moses believed Yahweh had told him to do are no less disturbing. For example, at one point Scripture reports that Yahweh told Moses to send out troops to "take vengeance" upon the Midianites, as I mentioned above (Num 31:1–3). The Israelites obeyed Moses and proceeded to slaughter every Midianite man and burn all the Midianites' cities to the ground (vv. 7, 10). However, the soldiers "captured the Midianite women and children and took all the Midianite herds, flocks and goods as plunder" (v. 9).

That was apparently a bad idea. When Moses found out that his troops had shown mercy on the noncombatants, he was furious (v. 15). Apparently still believing he was following Yahweh's command, Moses instructed his warriors to "kill all the boys" as well as all the women who were not virgins. However, he permitted the troops to "save for yourselves every girl who has never slept with a man" (vv. 17–18). These virgins became spoils of war for the soldiers.

Notice that Moses didn't stipulate that these soldiers had to marry a virgin captive before having sex with her. Throughout the Ancient Near East (ANE), and, unfortunately, throughout much of history, raping the women of a conquered people group was assumed to be a soldier's reward for victory. But even if we assume marriage was implied, imagine having to spend the rest of your life sexually gratifying the soldier who helped murder your family and tribe.[13]

***

David's fame began with his courageous killing and decapitation of the giant Goliath (1 Sam 17:48–51). Before long he was revered for killing not just thousands, as Saul had done, but *tens of thousands*.[14] David's divinely sanctioned military campaigns are frequently celebrated in Scripture, affirming that it was his practice never to "leave a man or woman alive."[15]

This tells us a little bit about the violent mindset of God's people at the time. As was true throughout the ANE, it was a badge of honor for kings and warriors as well as for warrior-deities to be credited with mercilessly wiping out entire populations. And in this light, it's not surprising that the Psalmist believed he was complimenting Yahweh when he credited him with training his "hands for war" and his "fingers for battle."[16] Nor is it surprising that biblical authors believed they were complimenting God when they proclaimed that "the Lord

13. Elsewhere Moses states that if a soldier notices "a beautiful woman" and is "attracted to her" from among virgins who have been spared, he can marry her and then, after she's had a time to mourn the loss of her family and kin, have sex with her (Deut 21:10–13). Oddly enough, however, Moses adds that if at some point this soldier "is not pleased with her," he may "let her go" (v.14). Since the instructions about who Israelite soldiers were allowed to keep alive and what they were allowed to do with them vary throughout Deuteronomy and Joshua, we can't assume that marriage, even on a trial basis, was assumed in Numbers 31 or any other account where soldiers are allowed to "save for yourselves" virgins (Num 31:18).
14. 1 Sam 18:7–8; 21:11, 29:5.
15. 1 Sam 27:9–11; see also 1 Sam 23:2–5; 1 Chron 14:10–17.
16. Ps 144:1; see also Ps 18:34; 2 Sam 22:35.

gave David victory wherever he went" (2 Sam 8:14), which meant leaving no man or woman alive.

***

Other depictions of Yahweh commanding violence are found in the law of the OT. According to the biblical record, God instructed the Israelites to execute adulterers (Lev 20:10), fornicators (Lev 21:9), homosexuals (Lev 20:13), as well as people who had sex with their siblings (Lev 20:14), their daughters-in-law (Lev 20:16), or animals (Lev 20:15–16). Also to be executed were any son and mother (or stepmother) who had sex together, for they dishonored the father/husband (Lev 20:11).[17] Similarly, if the daughter of a priest "defiles herself by becoming a prostitute . . . she must be burned in the fire," not so much because of her prostitution, but because "she has disgraced her father" (Lev 21:9).

Other capital offenses were associated with religious violations. For example, we find capital punishment prescribed for anyone who cursed God (Lev 24:16) or who worshiped or sacrificed to an idol (Exod 22:20). In fact, entire Israelite towns were devoted to destruction if they turned to idols.[18] Persons who practiced witchcraft, sorcery, divination, or other occult activities were also condemned to die, as was any false prophet.[19] So was anyone who so much as looked upon "holy furnishings" in the "tent of meeting," as well as anyone who worked on the Sabbath, even merely gathering sticks.[20] This was the same fate priests met if they entered the tabernacle with their hair disheveled, their clothes torn, or after they had drunk any alcohol (Lev 10:6–10).

But the most disturbing laws are those that required the execution of children. Children who were stubborn, lazy, drunkards, gluttonous, or who struck their parents were to be stoned to death.[21]

Walter Kaiser, a renowned Evangelical OT scholar and apologist, attempts to defend the reasonableness of these laws by stressing their importance in preserving strong families in ancient Israel.[22] This is a

17. See also Deut 22:30.
18. Deut 13:15; cf. 7:4; 28:63.
19. Exod 22:18; Lev 20:27; Deut 18:20; cf. 13:1–5.
20. Exod 19:12–13; 33:20–21; 31:14; 35:2–3; Num 4:15–20; 18:3, 22, 32; 15:32–36.
21. Deut 21:18–21; Exod 21:15, 17; Lev 20:9.
22. W. Kaiser Jr., *Hard Sayings of the Old Testament* (Downers Grove, IL: InterVarsity, 1988), 95–97.

troubling defense. If these laws actually reflect the wisdom of God on how to preserve strong families, should we not be enforcing them *today*? In fact, couldn't Kaiser's argument be applied to *all* of the OT's capital offenses, since they all presumably reflect the wisdom of God?

I hope you agree that it's not wise to try to preserve strong families by killing disobedient children! And so I hope you're beginning to suspect that *something else was going on* when God breathed these barbarically violent laws into his written word.

God Engaging in Violence

Yahweh not only commands violence in the OT, he sometimes is portrayed as actively engaging in it. The most famous example is the Genesis Flood that wiped out every living thing upon the earth with the exception of those few humans and animals that found refuge on the Ark (Genesis 6–8). Only slightly less famous is Yahweh's ferocious rain of fire that incinerated all the inhabitants of Sodom and Gomorrah (Genesis 19).

Then there's the well-known account of Yahweh slaying the firstborn son of every family that did not have blood on its doorposts in Egypt, which was followed by him drowning Pharaoh's army in the Red Sea.[23] The Israelites responded to this massacre by praising Yahweh as a mighty warrior who dashes his enemies to pieces (Exod 15:3, 6).

Some time later, when the Israelites were journeying in the wilderness, an ill-advised fellow named Korah led a group of complainers in a rebellion against Moses's leadership (Numbers 16). Some of these rebels were judged when the earth opened up and they "fell alive into Sheol" (v. 32), while others were incinerated by fire that fell from the sky (v. 35). Unfortunately, these violent judgments only succeeded in causing many other Israelites to start complaining, at which point "wrath [came] out from the Lord" and 14,700 Israelites were slaughtered by a plague (vv. 42, 46, 49).

***

Some biblical portraits depict God engaging in violence that seems, quite frankly, capricious. The most famous example of this concerns

23. Exod 11:4–6; 12:12, 29–30; 14:23–28.

a "devoted servant" named Uzzah. This poor fellow was struck dead simply because he touched "the ark of God" in an attempt to keep it from falling off its cart while it was being transported to Jerusalem (2 Sam 6:6–7).

David was understandably angry at Yahweh about this, but he was also a little freaked out. He decided he didn't want the ark to reside anywhere near him (vv. 8–10). Since the ark had been killing just about everyone it had come in contact with, including seventy Israelites (1 Sam 6:19), David's decision to have it sent to the home of Obed-Edom the Gittite instead of having it dwell in Jerusalem, where he lived, seems wise—though I suspect that Obed-Edom might not have agreed.[24]

***

Some of the most brutal violence that's ascribed to Yahweh in the OT is found in portraits of him using nations as instruments of judgment. For example, as Babylon was planning an attack on Israel, Yahweh is depicted as telling his people, "I am against you. I will draw my sword from its sheath and cut off from you both the righteous and the wicked . . . my sword will be unsheathed against everyone from south to north" (Ezek 21:3–4). As the Catholic priest and theologian Raymond Schwager notes, the indiscriminate killing of "both the righteous and the wicked . . . everyone from south to north," gives the impression that Yahweh is "so blinded in bloody intoxication" that he "ignores the difference between the guilty and the innocent."[25]

Other depictions of Yahweh using nations to judge his people are even more macabre. For example, Jeremiah depicts Yahweh declaring his commitment not to allow his compassion and mercy to influence him as he mercilessly slaughters families by smashing together parents and children, using Babylon as his servant (Jer 13:14). Later, the prophet quotes Yahweh saying to Israelite women that "he will pull up your skirts over your face," a euphemism for a sexual assault.[26]

As challenging as it is to accept, I see no way of avoiding the con-

24. For other accounts of the ark's violence, see 1 Sam 5:6–6:4. I address the problematic aspects of the ark of the covenant in *CWG*, vol. 2, ch. 25.
25. R. Schwager, *Must There Be Scapegoats? Violence and Redemption in the Bible*, 3rd ed. (New York: Crossroad, 2000), 54.
26. Jer 13:26, cf. v. 22; Nah 3:5.

clusions that these passages depict Yahweh as a warrior who planned on raping the women of the city he was about to conquer!

Along similar lines, Yahweh is portrayed as planning to trample his own "Virgin Daughter Judah" like one crushes grapes in a winepress (Lam 1:15). Try to imagine Israelite men, women, children, and infants being crushed by Yahweh like grapes being squashed in a winepress.

Other passages depict Yahweh declaring that, as judgment for the Israelites' rebellion, parents would have to witness their babies being dashed to the ground, while pregnant women would have their unborn babies ripped out of their wombs.[27] And, perhaps the grisliest of all are the OT's portraits of Yahweh causing parents to "eat their children" and children to "eat their parents."[28]

***

As morally revolting as these portraits of God are, if we confess Jesus to be Lord, I believe we are obliged to confess that all of them, together with the entire canon, are God-breathed. But at the same time, if we confess Jesus to be Lord, we also should feel obliged to insist that *something else is going on* when God's breathing results in biblical authors ascribing such atrocities to God, for these depictions of God contradict what we learn about God in Jesus's cross-centered life and ministry.

And whatever this *something else* turns out to be, it must make clear how these ghastly divine portraits are signs that point to the self-sacrificial love of God revealed on Calvary.

***

There you have it! The ugly elephant in our Christian room.

At this point in our exploration, I want to encourage you to embrace whatever cognitive dissonance you may be experiencing. For reasons that will become clear over the next several chapters, embracing this dissonance will actually help you discern *what else is going* on behind the scenes of the OT's ugly portraits of God.

On this note, I'd like to bring this chapter to a close by sharing a word of advice from a thinker in the early church named Origen

27. Hos 13:16; cf. Isa 13:16.
28. Exod 5:9–10; Lev 26:28–29; Jer 19:7, 9; Lam 2:20.

whom I have found very helpful on this journey. In fact, his words contributed to my epiphany about how the OT's violent depictions of God bear witness to the crucified Christ.

Origen taught that when we come upon a biblical passage that seems unworthy of God, we must humble ourselves before God and ask the Spirit to help us find a deeper meaning in the passage that *is* worthy of God. He sometimes referred to this as a treasure buried in the depth of a passage. Origen believed that God intentionally buried treasures beneath the ugly and "unworthy" surface meaning of various passages to force us to mature spiritually as we humbly wrestle with Scripture and become more dependent on the Spirit.[29]

Like many other Christian thinkers in the first several centuries of church history, Origen considered all the violent portraits of God in the OT to be unworthy of God. Yet these thinkers didn't feel free to dismiss these portraits, for they firmly believed that *all* Scripture is inspired by God. These thinkers rather believed that *something else was going on* when Scripture represents God in ways that are inconsistent with what is revealed in Christ, and they patiently waited on the Holy Spirit and contemplated what this *something else* might be.

As a result, they believed the Spirit helped them discover the Christ-centered, God-glorifying treasure that was buried in the depths of this unworthy material.

I encourage you to heed Origen's advice: As you contemplate the unworthy yet divinely inspired material that we've just reviewed, surrender whatever cognitive dissonance you're experiencing to God. Humbly ask the Spirit to open and illuminate your mind. And be assured that Jesus was telling the truth when he taught that *all* Scripture is inspired by God for the purpose of pointing to him. We just need the ability to see it.

And as we shall now see, the key that opens up our eyes is Jesus himself.

29. For an extensive discussion on Origen's approach to Scripture's violent divine portraits, see *CWG*, vol. 1, ch. 10.

2

The Unveiling

God is Christlike, and in him is no un-Christlikeness at all.
—A. M. Ramsey[1]

For Jesus, the key to understanding the Old Testament
was located in his own life and work,
for everything pointed to himself.
—David Dockery[2]

As soon as I said "Amen" in the closing prayer of my sermon, I noticed an agitated, middle-aged fellow making his way to the front of our church auditorium. He clearly had a bone to pick with me. "You're twisting the Scripture!" he shouted as he approached.

"And your name is . . . ?" I asked with a smile as I held out my hand to greet him.

He introduced himself as Micah, gave my hand a dismissive single shake, and picked up where he'd left off.[3] "You cherry pick verses you like and then privilege them over the rest of the Bible!" he said.

"I do?" I asked.

Micah's eyes squinted in anger as he pointed his finger at me and said, "Yes you do, like when you claim Christians should base their mental picture of God solely on Jesus!" Then raising his Bible in the air, he proclaimed, "The *whole* Bible is the inspired word of God, so

1. Michael Ramsey, *God, Christ, and the World: A Study in Contemporary Theology* (London: SCM, 1969), 9.
2. David S. Dockery, *Biblical Interpretation Then and Now: Contemporary Hermeneutics in the Light of the Early Church* (Grand Rapids: Baker, 1992), 26.
3. I have altered the names of people who have not given me permission to cite them in this book.

our view of God must be based on the *whole* Bible, not just on the parts you like!"

"So Micah," I asked, "do you believe everything in the Bible should be given equal weight?"

"Absolutely!" he snapped. "It's all from God!"

I then asked if he thought that children who are disobedient and slothful should be stoned to death, since this is what the law of the OT requires. Micah just stared at me with an angry and agitated gaze. "Look," I continued, "I readily admit that I privilege Jesus over previous revelations in the OT. But this isn't because I happen to like Jesus more. It's because Jesus himself did this."

Micah didn't believe me, so I asked him to open his well-worn Bible and read John 5:36: "But I have a greater witness than that of John." He studied the passage for a moment and then said, "What's this got to do with anything? Jesus is talking about John the Baptist, but John didn't write any part of the Bible."

"True," I said. "But what's interesting is that in Matthew, Jesus claimed that John the Baptist was the greatest of all the prophets leading up to himself."

Micah again didn't believe me, so I had him turn to Matthew 11:11 and read it for himself. "Do you see the point?" I asked. "If John is greater than all the prophets leading up to Jesus, yet Jesus's teaching carries more weight than John's, doesn't it follow that Jesus's teaching should carry more weight than everything the prophets taught prior to him?"

In a slightly humbler tone of voice, Micah admitted he'd never connected those verses together. Our discussion ended with him saying he would think about my suggestion and get back to me—which, to date, he has not done.

The All-Too-Common Montage God

How do you picture God? I'm not asking about your theology of God. I'm inquiring about what mental images automatically pop into your head when you think about God. I've known many people who had sound *beliefs about* God but who, without being aware of it, nevertheless had horrendous *mental representations of* God.

It's impossible to exaggerate the importance of a believer's mental representation of God, for the way you imagine God largely determines the quality of your relationship with God. The intensity of your love for God will never outrun the beauty of the God you envision. Related to this, the depth of your transformation into the likeness of Christ will never outrun the Christlikeness of your mental representation of God.

As Paul says, when you turn to the Lord, the veil over your mind is removed, allowing you to behold the glory of God in the face of Jesus Christ and thereby to be "transformed into the same image from one degree of glory to another" (2 Cor 3:16–4:6). No wonder the first thing the serpent did to seduce humanity was pollute Eve's mental picture of God (Gen 3:1–5).

In fact, there is mounting neurological evidence that a person's mental representation of God significantly affects their quality of life, for better or for worse. For example, it's a neurological fact that people who have a loving mental representation of God tend to have a greater capacity to think objectively about controversial matters and to make rational decisions than do people who have a threatening mental representation of God.[4]

***

Thirty-five years of ministry and teaching in churches and at a Christian university, combined with a whole lot of reading, has persuaded me that most Evangelical Christians embrace something like Micah's view of the Bible. If all Scripture is divinely inspired, they think, it must all carry the same level of divine authority. In this view, which some refer to as "the flat view of the Bible," Jesus's revelation of God is placed on the same level as all other biblical depictions of God, creating a montage mental conception of God. That is, *part* of the God these Christians envision is Christlike, but *other parts* are vengeful and jealous and capable of doing horrible things like commanding genocide and causing parents to cannibalize their children.

No wonder so many believers have trouble feeling passionate love for God.

I totally understand the logic behind this approach to the Bible, for it's what I was taught when I first became a Christian. But I'm now convinced that this approach is fundamentally and tragically misguided. While I continue to affirm that the whole Bible is inspired by

4. See T. R. Jennings, *The God-Shaped Brain: How Changing Your View of God Transforms Your Life* (Downers Grove, IL: InterVarsity, 2013); V. Copan, *Changing Your Mind: The Bible, the Brain, and Spiritual Growth* (Eugene, OR: Cascade, 2016).

God, I'm now persuaded that the Bible itself instructs us to *base our mental representation of God solely on Jesus Christ*. Other biblical portraits of God may nuance our Christ-centered picture, but only to the degree that they cohere with what we learn about God in Christ.

As Jesus himself taught, everything else in Scripture is to be interpreted in a way that *points to him*. Thus nothing in Scripture should ever be interpreted in a way that *qualifies or competes with* his revelation of God. And as we'll now see, this all-important conviction permeates the NT.[5]

The Only Exact Representation

Listen carefully to what the author of Hebrews says about the revelation of God in Christ:

> In the past God spoke to our ancestors through the prophets at many times and in various ways, but in these last days he has spoken to us by his Son, whom he appointed heir of all things, and through whom also he made the universe. The Son is the radiance of God's glory and the exact representation of his being, sustaining all things by his powerful word. (Heb 1:1–3)

Mark Buchanan captures the gist of this passage as well as the central theme of Hebrews when he notes that the author of Hebrews

> draws a vivid contrast between past and present, Moses and Jesus, the Old Testament and the New. In every way, Jesus . . . is superior to whoever and whatever has come before him. The past is a mere shadow of Christ's present reality and of his glory.[6]

This stark contrast is reflected in several ways in this passage. First, Jesus alone is God's own Son. As is true throughout the NT, when the author of Hebrews speaks of God's Son, he is referring to *God himself* in the flesh.[7] Hebrews is thus declaring that, in contrast to past

5. For a more comprehensive and in-depth treatment of this theme, see *CWG*, vol. 2, chs. 2–3.
6. M. Buchanan, "Can We Trust the God of Genocide?," *CT* (July/August 2013), 20–24 (23).
7. The divinity of the Son in Hebrews is evident, for example, in the fact that angels are commanded to "worship him" (1:6) as well as in the fact that he is referred to as "God" (1:8) and as the Creator (1:10). On the high Christology of Hebrews, see R. Bauckham, *Jesus and the God of Israel: God Crucified and Other Studies on the New Testament's Christology of Divine Identity* (Grand Rapids: Eerdmans, 2008), 233–53. For several good defenses of the full deity of Christ in the NT, see M. J. Harris, *Jesus as God: The New Testament Use of* Theos *in Reference to Jesus*

revelations that were mediated through ancestors and prophets, God himself gave us this culminating revelation "in these last days."

Second, the author says that previous revelations came in "various ways." The Greek word for this is *polymerōs*, which can be translated as "diverse portions" (ASV) or as "glimpses of truth" (J. B. Phillips). By contrast, the Son is the very "radiance of God's glory," which basically means that Jesus is to God's glory what light and heat are to the sun. When God shines, in other words, it looks like Jesus. So, insofar as people in the OT caught authentic "glimpses of truth," they were seeing the same Son that we see. It's just that they also had clouds that obstructed their vision.

Not only this, but while people in the past got "glimpses of truth," the Son is the *truth itself*. Jesus claimed to be "the way and the *truth* and the life" (John 14:6, emphasis added). The Greek word for "truth" (*aleithia*) literally means "uncovered," or "unveiled." So, in contrast to the "glimpses of truth" that people in the OT were given, in the Son we have the full unveiling of the true God. Jesus is what God looks like when there are no clouds in the way.

This is why this author goes on to say that the Son is the one and only *exact representation* of God's *very being*, or *essence* (*hypostasis*). Jesus is the perfect revelation of everything that makes God *God*. As Michael Ramsey put it, "God is Christlike, and in him is no un-Christlikeness at all."[8] Or, as C. S. Lewis once said, "Jesus is what the Father has to say to us."[9] Jesus is not *part of* what the Father has to say or even the *main thing* the Father has to say. As the one and only Word of God (John 1:1), Jesus is the *total content* of the Father's revelation to us. For this reason, Jesus must be our sole criterion to assess the degree to which previous prophets were catching genuine glimpses of truth and the degree to which they were seeing clouds.

Please note: I'm not suggesting that Jesus is the criterion for assessing the degree to which previous prophets were and were not *divinely inspired*, for their writings are *completely* inspired. But as we'll explain later on, to say that a passage is divinely inspired is not to say that it necessarily reflects an unclouded vision of God.

In any case, the clear implication of the teaching in Hebrews is that

(Grand Rapids: Baker, 1992) and R. M. Bowman Jr. and J. E. Komoszewski, *Putting Jesus in His Place* (Grand Rapids: Kregel, 2007).

8. Ramsey, *God, Christ, and the World*, 98.
9. C. S. Lewis, *Mere Christianity* (San Francisco: HarperCollins, 2001), 17.

the revelation of God in his Son should never be regarded as one revelation among others. He is rather the revelation that culminates and surpasses all previous revelations. And, just as Micah learned when he consulted the Scriptures, Jesus himself confirms this perspective.

The Life and Subject Matter of All Scripture

Not only does Jesus ascribe more authority to himself than the OT, but he had the audacity to present himself as the one whom all previous revelations *are about* and the one who *gives life to them*! In a debate with some Pharisees, Jesus said, "You study the Scriptures diligently because you think that in them you possess eternal life. These are the very Scriptures that testify *about me*, yet you refuse to come *to me* to have life." And a moment later he added: "If you believed Moses, you would believe me, for *he wrote about me*" (5:39–40, 45–46, emphasis added).

That's quite an astonishing claim! Jesus is talking specifically about the first five books of the Bible, but elsewhere he applied this same teaching to the whole OT. After his resurrection, Jesus explained to his disciples why he had to suffer and die. He told them that everything that was written about him in the Law of Moses, the Prophets, and the Psalms had to be fulfilled. And in this way, Luke writes, Jesus "opened their minds so they could understand the Scriptures."[10]

In Jesus's day, "the Law, Prophets, and Psalms" was a shorthand way of referring to the entire Hebrew Bible.[11] Vern Poythress and others are thus on the mark when they conclude that Jesus is claiming that "the whole Old Testament . . . speaks of Christ."[12] Hence, the only proper way to "study the Scripture diligently" is to study it in a way that discloses how *all* of it is about Jesus and thus in a way that leads us to the *life* of Scripture.

This is also the clear implication of Paul's teaching that "there is . . . one mediator between God and humankind, Christ Jesus" (1 Tim 2:5, NRSV).[13] This means that Jesus alone mediates every aspect of

10. Luke 24:25–27; cf. vv. 44–45.

11. V. Poythress, *God-Centered Biblical Interpretation* (Phillipsburg, NJ: Presbyterian and Reformed, 1999), 59–60.

12. Ibid., 59; S. Swain, *Trinity, Revelation and Reading: A Theological Introduction to the Bible and Its Interpretation* (New York: T&T Clark, 2011), 60; A. Wolters, "History of Old Testament Interpretation: An Anecdotal Survey," in *Hearing the Old Testament: Listening for God's Address*, ed. C. Bartholomew and D. Beldman (Grand Rapids: Eerdmans, 2012), 23–44 (23–25).

13. Many NT scholars argue that 1 Timothy along with several other epistles attributed to Paul

our relationship with God, including our knowledge of God. So we should not treat the Bible as an independent source of information about God. It rather should be considered to be a source of information about God only insofar as it points us to Jesus Christ.

We should therefore regard Jesus as the key that unlocks the revelatory content of every passage of Scripture, as numerous scholars have argued.[14] In the words of Graeme Goldsworthy, Jesus is "the central subject matter of the Hebrew Scripture" as well as its "goal and fulfillment." We must therefore read Scripture with the firm conviction that "all texts in the whole Bible bear a discernible relationship to Christ and are primarily intended as a testimony to Christ." And so, he concludes, the most important question we must ask while reading any part of the Bible is: "How does this passage of Scripture . . . testify to Christ?"[15]

To return to my favorite metaphor, Goldsworthy is claiming that Jesus is the looking-glass through which all Scripture must be interpreted. And we can only see how all Scripture "testifies to Christ" when we read Scripture through this lens. This is what I'm doing to the OT's violent portraits of God: I'm asking, how do these sometimes horrifically ugly portraits testify to Christ when interpreted through the looking-glass of Jesus's life, and especially of his sacrificial death?

Yet, the very fact that we're trying to see how these violent divine portraits *point to* Christ rules out treating these portraits as though they were supplementary revelations *alongside of* Christ.

It's All in Christ

We can also see a reflection of Paul's view of Jesus as the full revelation of God when he declares that Christ is "the mystery of God . . . in whom are hidden all the treasures of wisdom and knowledge" (Col

were written by a disciple of Paul's, not Paul himself. Because I consider this debate to be irrelevant when we are reading Scripture as God's word (as opposed to studying it from a historical-critical perspective), I will follow the church tradition and ascribe to Paul all the epistles that bear his name. I'll do the same for all other works whose authorship is disputed.

14. See T. Torrance, *Atonement: The Person and Work of Christ*, ed. R. T. Walker (Downers Grove, IL: InterVarsity, 2009), 75–77, 161–62, 167–68; Dockery, *Biblical Interpretation Then and Now*, 23–26; Poythress, *God-Centered Biblical Interpretation*, 59–60.
15. G. Goldsworthy, *Christ-Centered Biblical Theology: Hermeneutical Foundation and Principles* (Downers Grove, IL: IVP Academic, 2012), 45; G. Goldsworthy, *Preaching the Whole Bible as Christian Scripture* (Grand Rapids: Eerdmans, 2000), 33, 21.

2:2–3). If all the treasures of wisdom and knowledge about God are found in Christ, then we clearly have no business treating the Bible as an independent source of wisdom and knowledge to supplement what we find in Christ.

In this same letter, Paul teaches that Christ is not only the embodiment of all God's wisdom and knowledge, he is the full embodiment of *God himself*! In the process of refuting false teachers who taught that Jesus was merely the best among many distinct manifestations of God—which, by the way, is pretty much what Christians inadvertently do when they treat all portraits of God in the Bible as equal—Paul declared that "in Christ all the fullness of the Deity lives in bodily form" (Col 2:9; cf. 1:19).

This statement could not be more emphatic. *All* (not some) of the *fullness* (not a part or an aspect) of the *Deity* (not a lesser divine being) is embodied in Christ! Paul is in essence claiming that "all the attributes and activities of God—his spirit, word, wisdom and glory—are disclosed in [Christ]."[16] And if *all* the *fullness* of *Deity* is embodied and disclosed in Christ, we are misguided to think we need to supplement what we find in Christ with what we find in the OT or in any other source. *Everything* we need to know and can know about God is found *in Christ*.

The Only One Who Knows and Reveals the Father

Once I quit trying to justify the violence ascribed to God in the OT, I found that a large number of passages that I previously hadn't given much consideration to acquired great significance. One of the first to catch my eye was a passage in which Jesus said to his disciples: "All things have been committed to me by my Father." The "all things" caught my attention, but it's what Jesus said next that floored me: "No one knows the Son except the Father, and *no one knows the Father except the Son and those to whom the Son chooses to reveal him*" (Matt 11:27, emphasis added).

I have to assume that Jesus was speaking somewhat hyperbolically here, for if we interpreted his statement literally, it would mean that literally "no one"—including all the authors of the OT!—had *any*

16. F. F. Bruce, *The Epistles to the Colossians, Philemon and to the Ephesians*, NICNT (Grand Rapids: Eerdmans, 1984), 207. Similarly, see G. A. F. Knight, *Christ the Center* (Maryknoll, NY: Orbis, 2004), 36.

knowledge of the Father. But Jesus clearly didn't believe that, for he often quoted the OT.

In ancient Jewish culture, hyperbolic language was often used to draw an extreme contrast. For example, when Jesus told his disciples they must "hate" their family members if they were going to follow him (Luke 14:26), he didn't mean this literally. After all, this is the same Jesus who commanded disciples to love everyone, including our worst enemies (Luke 6:27–36). Jesus was using hyperbole to communicate that our allegiance to him must be incomparably greater than our allegiance to our family members or to anyone else.

So too, in Matthew 11:27 Jesus is using hyperbole to claim that his knowledge and revelation of the Father is so much greater than all others that it's *as though* they didn't know God at all. While we certainly catch glimpses of truth in the God-breathed writings of the OT, God committed *all things* to Jesus alone, including the capacity to fully and perfectly know and reveal the Father.

The Reality and Its Shadow

The radical superiority of Jesus's revelation over all previous revelations is captured in a different way when Paul and the author of Hebrews utilize an analogy of a shadow-versus-reality. Paul instructs his disciples not to "let anyone judge you by what you eat or drink, or with regard to a religious festival, a New Moon celebration or a Sabbath day," because "these are a shadow of the things that were to come; the reality, however, is found in Christ" (Col 2:16–17). Similarly, the author of Hebrews says that the law and sacrificial system of the OT were "only a shadow of the good things that are coming—not the realities themselves" (Heb 10:1).[17] As with Paul, the "realities" are all found in Christ.

These two authors see Christ, the reality, casting a shadow back in time, and this shadow takes the form of the first covenant, with its law and sacrificial system. While there were certainly "glimpses of truth" in the OT's law and sacrificial system, the revelation we are given in Christ is as superior to them as, for example, the *real you is superior to your shadow*.

No wonder the author of Hebrews says there was something "wrong" with the first covenant (Heb 8:7). And, he adds, now that

17. See also Heb 8:5.

the reality of Christ has come, the shadowy covenant has become "obsolete" (v. 13).

This doesn't mean that the OT is any less inspired than the NT, or that the OT is no longer vitally important for us. To the contrary, the story of Jesus only makes sense when it is understood as the culmination of the broader story of God's first covenant with Israel. This is the most basic way the OT points toward Jesus.

Yet, precisely because the function of this story is to point people to the reality—Christ—the way a shadow points to the real object it is a shadow of, the OT should never be treated as though its purpose was to supplement or in any way qualify what we learn about God from Christ. When you have the real object, you don't need to supplement what you know about it by examining the shadow it casts!

In other words, the OT's revelatory authority for us is found in its Christ-pointing function, period. Like Jesus said, the OT is all about *him*, and he is the *life* that it is intended to point to.

Seeing the Father in the Son

At one point in Jesus's ministry, Philip asked him, "Show us the Father." Jesus responded by saying: "Have I been with you all this time, Philip, and you still do not know me? Whoever has seen me has seen the Father. How can you say, 'Show us the Father'?" (John 14:9). Jesus is claiming that to know what God is like; we only need to look *at him*.[18]

Jesus obviously isn't suggesting that we can know how tall God is, how much God weighs, or what gender God is, by looking at him. He was rather claiming that to know God's *character*, we need not, and should not, look anywhere other than to him.

The same point is made when John presents Jesus as "the Word of God" (John 1:1).[19] In John, the "Word" (*logos*) signifies God revealing himself—and notice the definite article in front of it. Jesus isn't one Word among many words. He is the one and only Word, which is why Jesus elsewhere claims to be *the* way to the Father, *the* truth of the Father, and *the* life that the Father offers (John 14:6).[20]

Similarly, a number of times John presents Jesus as "*the* light of the

18. See also 1 John 2:23; 4:15; 2 John 9.
19. See also Rev 19:13.
20. See also John 5:17–26; 6:44–46, 57; 8:19, 28; 17:3.

world."[21] There isn't an assortment of different sources of light that reveal God, each complementing or competing with the others. No, there is only one true light, and he "gives light to everyone" (John 1:9). In other words, insofar as anyone has ever received light, it is *this* light that they were receiving. It's the same point we earlier saw the author of Hebrews make when he said that the Son was "the radiance of God's glory." So, to the extent that previous authors, or anyone else for that matter, caught glimpses of light, they were seeing Jesus.

The Revelation without Rivals

After his general introduction of the Word that was always with God and is himself God, John declares that the Word "became flesh and made his dwelling among us," adding that "we have seen his glory, the glory of the one and only Son, who came from the Father, full of grace and truth" (1:14). And then John "virtually reiterates the whole Old Testament witness" when he goes on to proclaim, "No one has ever seen God, but the one and only Son, who is himself God and is in closest relationship with the Father, has made him known" (John 1:18).[22]

John frequently uses *seeing* as a metaphor for knowing or experiencing.[23] This is what he's doing when he contrasts the *invisibility* of God with the "one and only Son" who now makes him *known.* Similar to the astonishing claim that Jesus made in Matthew 11:27, John is using hyperbole to claim that the revelation of God in Christ is so superior to all that preceded him that it's *as though* no one had any knowledge of God before the Son made him known. And this is why John refers to the Son as the "one and only." He is utterly unique in his capacity to reveal God.[24]

This also explains why John contrasts the "grace and *truth*" that came through Jesus Christ with "the law" that was given through Moses in the preceding verse (1:17, emphasis added). While we can

21. John 1:4–9; 3:19–21; 8:12; 9:5 (emphasis added).
22. Knight, *Christ the Center*, 37.
23. We do the same thing, as when we say things like: "I *see* what you mean" or "Do you *see* what it's like to feel this way?" On "seeing" as a metaphor for "knowing" and "experiencing" in John, see John 6:46; 8:51; 11:9; 12:40, 45; 14:7, 9, 17; 16:30. For a discussion, see H. C. Waetjen, *The Gospel of the Beloved Disciple* (New York: T&T Clark, 2005), 127–40.
24. A. J. Köstenberger, *John* (Grand Rapids: Baker Academic, 2004), 43; D. Moody, "God's Only Son: The Translation of John 3:16 in the Revised Standard Version," *JBL* 72 (1953): 213–19.

certainly find glimpses of the true God in the divinely inspired writings of Moses, John's contrast requires us to accept that these writings lacked an element of truth as well as grace that was given only in the Son.

As Gary Burge argues, this means that "Jesus does not have a relative superiority, but an absolute superiority" over all revelations that preceded him. Hence, Burge rightly concludes, "[T]he Son's revelation cannot . . . have any rivals."[25]

Jesus's Repudiation of Aspects of the Old Testament

One of the most striking illustrations of the superiority of Jesus over all that preceded him is the way Jesus sometimes taught things that "blatantly contradict and overturn multiple Old Testament passages and principles."[26] For example, while the law taught that people were defiled if they ate "unclean" animals (Leviticus 11), Jesus taught that "nothing going into a man from the outside can defile him," thereby making "all food clean" (Mark 7:19).

Similarly, the law stipulated that any woman who bled was "unclean" and that anyone she touched became "unclean," which meant they were not to touch anyone else until they had purified themselves (Lev 15:25–27). Yet when a woman with a bleeding disorder touched Jesus, hoping to be healed, Jesus praised her faith instead of rebuking her as a lawbreaker (Luke 8:43–48). Moreover, Jesus didn't withdraw from the crowd to avoid contaminating others or to purify himself.

The law also stipulated that people could not work on the Sabbath. In fact, a person could be stoned to death for simply picking up sticks or lighting a candle in their home on that day of the week![27] But Jesus displayed a more relaxed attitude toward the Sabbath, even defending his disciples when they violated a law that prohibited harvesting food on the Sabbath (Mark 2:23–28). And when confronted by a woman who was guilty of adultery, Jesus subverted the OT law that demanded she be stoned.[28] Indeed, he subverted all the OT laws that

25. G. M. Burge, *John*, NIVAC (Grand Rapids: Zondervan, 2000), 60.
26. D. Flood, *Disarming Scripture: Cherry-Picking Liberals, Violence-Loving Conservatives, and Why We All Need to Learn to Read the Bible Like Jesus Did* (San Francisco: Metanoia, 2014), 24.
27. Num 15:32–36; Exod 35:2–3.
28. Deut 22:22; Lev 20:10.

require execution by making it clear that only a sinless person would be justified carrying out an execution (John 8:1–11).

Along similar lines, in Deuteronomy Yahweh is depicted as telling his people to make oaths in his name (Deut 6:13). By contrast, Jesus taught that we are not to make oaths in anyone's name or in the name of anything (Matt 5:34). In fact, Jesus went further and said that anything beyond a simple Yes or No "comes from the evil one" (v. 37).

Does this not imply that Jesus considered the inclination to *obey* Deuteronomy 6:13 to be a temptation of the devil, at least for his followers? And what does this say about the OT portrait of God giving this command?

Whatever it implies, it's clear that while Jesus regarded the entire OT to be God-breathed, as should all his followers, he also possessed the authority to cancel, and even reverse, its teachings.[29] Jesus viewed the OT as a divinely inspired authority that was *under*, not *alongside*, his own divine authority.

Rebuking Elijah

Another striking example of Jesus's superior authority takes place when James and John returned from a failed missionary endeavor to Samaria. Angered because certain Samaritan towns had rejected their message, they ask Jesus if they should call down fire from the sky to incinerate these people (Luke 9:54). They had a clear precedent for their request, for Elijah had used fire from heaven to incinerate a hundred people in this same region (2 Kgs 1:10–12).

Although Elijah is regarded as a hero of the faith, and although the fire that fell from the sky was clearly supernatural, Jesus rebuked his disciples for wanting to follow his example. Some early manuscripts even add that Jesus accused them of manifesting a different "spirit" from that of Jesus. Their request obviously contradicted Jesus's instruction to refrain from violence and to instead love, bless, and do good to enemies.[30]

Consider this: had Elijah carried out his destructive miracle at the time of Jesus, Jesus would have rebuked him and possibly would have credited his supernatural feat to a different "spirit." In fact, given that

29. If you're wondering about what Jesus meant when he said he had not come "to abolish the law" but "to fulfill it" (Matt 5:17), see Matt 22:34–39; Rom 13:8, 10. I discuss this at length in *CWG*, vol. 1, ch. 2.
30. Matt 5:39–45; Luke 6:27–36.

Jesus made refraining from violence and loving enemies the main criterion for being considered a "child of the Father" (Matt 5:45), we can only conclude that Jesus would not have considered this OT hero to be a child of God at all.

This isn't in any way to suggest that Jesus thought Elijah wasn't "saved," only that his destructive miracle didn't reflect the character of the Father. And the fact that Jesus could speak this way once again demonstrates that Jesus's authority trumps that of any prophet leading up to him.

No More "Eye for an Eye"

Yet the most astonishing example of Jesus repudiating a law of the OT is his rejection of the foundational law of just retaliation (known as the *lex talionis*). According to this law, which is found in three places in the OT, the severity of a person's punishment must correspond to the severity of their crime: an eye for eye and a tooth for a tooth.[31] Jesus audaciously instructed people to set that OT law aside.

Instead, Jesus instructed his followers not to resist an evil person, adding, "if anyone slaps you on the right cheek, turn to them the other cheek also" (Matt 5:38–39).[32] Jesus then went on to tell them to love and bless their enemies so "that you may be children of your Father in heaven" (Matt 5:44–45).

To grasp how significant this is, we need to understand that two versions of this law do not merely limit how much a person *could* retaliate, as some have tried to argue; they rather stipulate how much a person *must* retaliate. To follow Jesus and be considered a "child of the Father," one has to be willing to violate this law. Indeed, Jesus taught that to be considered a "child of the Father," a person has to commit to doing the *exact opposite* of what this law commands!

On top of this, if Jesus believed that any urge to obey the law to take oaths in God's name "comes from the evil one," how can we avoid the conclusion that he believed the same thing about the urge to obey the OT law of just retaliation?

And if you're curious how the urge to obey a divinely inspired law could be a demonic temptation, keep reading.

31. Exod 21:24; Lev 24:19–20; Deut 19:21.
32. When Jesus instructed disciples to "not resist an evil person," he wasn't telling them to do *nothing*. The Greek word for "not resist" (*antistemi*) has the connotation of not resisting an aggressor with a *corresponding aggressive force*, as when someone responds violently to violence.

***

I trust this chapter has made it perfectly clear that Jesus possessed a weightier authority than the OT, to the point that he felt free to replace some of its commands with instructions of his own that flatly contradicted them. And I trust it is clear that, while all Scripture is divinely inspired, our understanding of God's character must be based entirely on the person of Jesus Christ, and, for reasons we will now explore, especially on Christ crucified.

Only when we grasp why the cross is the centerpiece to everything Jesus was about will we be able to see *what else is going on* in the OT's violent portraits of God and discern how this *something else* points us to the cross.

3

A Cruciform Through-Line

Through-Line: a theme or idea that runs from the beginning to the end of a book, film, play, etc.

Cruciform: the shape of a cross; reflecting the self-sacrificial character of the Crucifixion.

"... but he loves me."

Once again Marla showed up with a swollen black eye at the small charismatic church where I served as an assistant pastor while going to graduate school many years ago. Marla was a petite woman in her early twenties, and she and her beautiful two-year-old daughter had been attending the church for about a year. Marla told me she had recently recommitted her life to Christ after walking away from him as a teenager.

This was the second time I noticed she had come to church with a black eye. Several other times I noticed other bruises. Once she came with a broken wrist. Another time a front tooth was missing.

I asked Marla if I could speak with her after the service. We sat in the back pew of the now empty church, and, as I had done twice before, I asked her how she had gotten injured. As before, she blamed it on an accident, but this time I wasn't buying it. I paused for a moment before informing Marla that I strongly suspected that her husband, Jim, was beating her.

Marla acted shocked at my accusation, but the tears in her eyes told the truth. I gently grabbed Marla's shoulders as I pleaded,

"I understand how hard this is for you, but you don't deserve this!" Marla again denied the accusation with a gesture of her head. I pressed on: "If you won't end this for your own sake, Marla, think about your daughter. Do you want her growing up believing this is the kind of treatment she can expect from men?"

I could tell Marla was imagining the possibility of confronting the abuse, even as she continued to deny it, because I saw the fear in her eyes. I assured her that we would get a restraining order to protect her and her daughter after they'd left Jim. And I told her that her separation from him did not need to be permanent if Jim agreed to get into counseling. But, I added with a sense of urgency, I believed she and her daughter needed to act immediately.

After trying to get Marla to admit the truth for a while longer, I ended the conversation by giving her my phone number and promising to help her when she was ready to make a change.

Ten days later, just after Shelley and I had tucked our daughters into bed, Marla called. Sobbing, she told me that Jim had just given her a bloody nose and swollen lip in a fit of rage. "You were right," she cried. "I gotta get outta here! Jim is getting worse!" Jim was out of the house, so Marla wanted to take advantage of the opportunity and leave right away.

Thirty minutes later, Marla and her daughter arrived at our apartment. Her face was a mess. She also had a large welt on her arm as well as red marks on her wrist where Jim had held her. After briefly processing what happened, I told Marla that we would help her find legal counsel in the morning, but I wanted to call the police immediately so they could witness for themselves the full extent of her injuries.

Marla suddenly became frantic. "No!" she exclaimed. "You can't do that, and I am never going to press charges!"

"But Marla," I replied, "you said you wanted to end this."

"I do!" she said. "But you don't understand. Jim has issues, for sure, but he really does love me, and he's the only one who ever has. I would never want to get him in trouble with the law."

"No Marla," I replied. "This isn't love! People don't beat up people they love!"

Crying, Marla yelled back: "If you knew the terrible things Jim has had to go through and the terrible things he is dealing with now, you'd understand that it's not his fault!" Although Shelley and I implored Marla to reconsider, she wouldn't budge.

Marla and her daughter stayed with us two more days as we explored her options. When I returned home from school on the third day, Marla and her daughter were gone. We later learned that she and Jim had spoken on the phone. He once again declared his profound love for her and promised to never hit her again, so Marla went back to him.

Marla never showed up at church again. I called her several times over the following months, but either Jim miraculously became nonabusive, or, much more likely, Marla was playing the denial game again. "Yes, Jim has issues," she admitted each time. "But he really loves me."

Each time, it broke my heart.

An Ambiguous Love

The most beautiful message in the Bible is that "God is love" (1 John 4:8). But while every Christian believes this, many are as confused as Marla about what *love* means. And it's been this way throughout most of church history.

Much of the problem goes back to St. Augustine (354–430 CE), arguably the most influential theologian in church history. Augustine certainly believed that "God is love," for this is a theme that runs through his many writings. Augustine even argued that we should interpret the Bible with a "rule of love," meaning that anything we find in the Bible that isn't consistent with love should be interpreted figuratively.[1]

So far, I'd say Augustine was heading in the right direction.

Unfortunately, Augustine defined love as an inner attitude that did not have any necessary implications for how we actually treat others.[2] He went so far as to argue that Christians could imprison, torture, and, if necessary, even execute heretics in the name of love, which makes me wonder: If it's sometimes loving for Christians to imprison, torture, and kill people with whom we disagree, what would it look like for us to treat such people in *un*loving ways?

missed the works part

1. Augustine, *On Christian Teaching*, trans. R. P. H. Green (Oxford: Oxford University Press, 1997), 75–80.
2. *Against Faustus*, 22.76; cited in O. O'Donovan and J. L. O'Donovan, eds., *From Irenaeus to Grotius: A Sourcebook in Christian Political Thought, 100-1625* (Grand Rapids: Eerdmans, 1999), 118. For a more extensive and in-depth discussion of Augustine's views on justified violence and their tragic impact on church history, see *CWG*, vol. 1, ch. 4.

This same ambiguity attaches to God's love in Augustine's writings. For example, Augustine was the first Christian to teach that, while God is perfect love, he nevertheless predestined every atrocity in history and even predestined the majority of humans to suffer forever in hell! Which again makes me wonder: If this is what a God of perfect love does, what would a *less* loving God do? *Not* predestine the majority to hell?

The example of Augustine demonstrates that without a clear and objective definition of *love*, the declaration that "God is love," and the teaching that followers of Jesus are supposed to love all others, can mean pretty much whatever anyone wants them to mean.

The Supreme Revelation

There is no such ambiguity about the meaning of love in the NT. And once we understand the NT's definition, we will see why the cross is the unsurpassable revelation of God's love and why this must be considered the through-line of Jesus's ministry.

The NT defines love not by giving us an abstract definition, but by pointing us to its supreme illustration. "*This* is how we know what love is," John writes, "Jesus Christ laid down his life for us." And from this John concludes, "we ought to lay down our lives for one another" (1 John 3:16, emphasis added). The love that characterizes God's eternal nature, and the love that his children are to extend to all others, *looks like the cross*. We might say that the cross is the definitive revelation of God's cross-like, or *cruciform*, character.

To see why the cross is the definitive revelation of God's cruciform character, consider Paul's teaching that on the cross, "God made him who had no sin *to be sin* for us" (2 Cor 5:21, emphasis added). This means that, on Calvary, the *all-holy* God fully identified with our sin.

Not only that, but Paul also teaches that on the cross, "Christ redeemed us from the curse of the law by *becoming a curse* for us" (Gal 3:13, emphasis added). One who is cursed is estranged from God, which is why Jesus cried out: "My God, my God, why have you forsaken me?" (Matt 27:46). As Jesus identified with our sin, he experienced the separation from God that we deserved. And this means that, on Calvary, God, whose very nature is the perfect, loving union of Father, Son, and Spirit, experienced our God-forsakenness.

There is no greater extremity to which the perfected united and all-holy God could have gone on our behalf than to become our sin and curse. Indeed, as beautifully mysterious as it is, Paul reveals that on Calvary, God went to the extreme of experiencing *his own antithesis*! And it's the unsurpassable extremity to which God was willing to go on our behalf that reveals the unsurpassable perfection of the love that God is, and the love God has for us.

This is why the cross is the supreme—indeed, the unsurpassable—revelation of God's loving nature. In all eternity, no event could ever reveal God's true self-sacrificial character more perfectly, for God could never go further for the sake of love than he went on Calvary.

Glorifying the Father

The supremacy of the revelation that took place on Calvary is confirmed throughout the NT.[3] To begin, in John we find Jesus wishing he could be spared the terrible fate that awaits him. But he quickly expresses his resolve to go forward by saying, "No, it was for this very reason that I have come to this hour" (John 12:27).

Then, with a view toward the crucifixion, Jesus exclaims, "Father, glorify your name!" at which point the voice of the Father thunders from the sky: "I have glorified it, and will glorify it again." Jesus then declares, "When I am lifted up from the earth, I will draw all people to myself." And just to make sure readers don't miss the point, John adds: "He said this to show the kind of death he was going to die" (12:28, 31–33).

This passage unambiguously identifies Jesus's crucifixion as the hour when he would glorify the Father's name. In ancient Jewish culture, to speak of a person's name was to speak about their character and reputation. So, Jesus and the Father are both indicating that the Father's character would most clearly shine forth—be "glorified"—when Jesus was crucified. While Jesus reflects the Father's cruciform character throughout his ministry, the Father is "most glorified through the . . . 'lifting-up' . . . of the Son."[4]

On top of this, Jesus tells us that it was "for this very reason" that he came into the world. As N. T. Wright puts it, the supreme

3. For a more comprehensive and in-depth treatment of the centrality of the cross in the NT and Christian tradition, see *CWG*, vol. 1, chs. 4–5.

4. A. Moody, "That All May Honour the Son: Holding Out for a Deeper Christocentrism," *Themelios* 36, no. 3 (2011): 403–14 (414n437). The original has "through" italicized.

glorification of the Father on the cross was "*the climax and purpose of his whole work*." For, as Wright goes on to note, "In being thus 'lifted up' . . . Jesus will draw all people to himself. How could it not be so, if indeed his cross is the true revelation of the true God, and if what we see in that revelation is the face of love?"[5]

Now, if the crucifixion is the "climax and purpose of Jesus's work," we should understand everything else Jesus taught and did from this vantage point. That is, if it was "for this very reason" that Jesus came into the world, then his Incarnation, miracles, exorcisms, and teachings, and even his resurrection must be understood in light of, and as part of, this reason.[6]

So, if Jesus is the center to which all Scripture points, then the cruciform character of God that was supremely revealed on the cross must be regarded as the epicenter of this center. And if all Scripture is about *Christ*, then all Scripture is more specifically about *Christ crucified*.

The Incarnation

Paul confirms the centrality of the cross in a remarkable passage in his letter to the Philippians. Paul sums up the humble, other-oriented lifestyle he is instructing this congregation to cultivate when he says, "In your relationships with one another, have the same mindset as Christ Jesus" (Phil 2:5).

Though Jesus was "in very nature God," he "did not consider equality with God something to be used to his own advantage." Instead, Christ "made himself nothing (*kenosis*) by taking on the very nature of a servant, being made in human likeness" (vv. 6–7). The Greek verb (*kenosis*) has the connotation of emptying oneself of something. So Paul is teaching that, rather than sitting back and enjoying the advantages of being equal with God, the Son of God emptied himself of these advantages to become one of us.

5. N. T. Wright, *Following Jesus: Biblical Reflections on Discipleship* (Grand Rapids: Eerdmans, 1994), 37.
6. The "Incarnation" refers to God becoming a full human being in Jesus. I should also clarify that the reason I claim the resurrection must be understood in light of the culminating revelation of God on Calvary is that its meaning is entirely derived from the cross. Only because Jesus rose from the dead do we know that the crucifixion of Jesus reveals God's true character and was God's way of defeating Satan, restoring creation, and saving humanity. Moreover, as we're about to see, only because of the resurrection do we know that the cross displays the kind of self-sacrificial character that God wants followers of Jesus to cultivate.

This demonstrates that the cruciform mindset most clearly reflected on the cross was already present in the Incarnation. But the cruciform through-line of the Incarnation and the cross becomes even more apparent when Paul continues:

> And being found in appearance as a man,
> he humbled himself
> by becoming obedient to death—
> even death on a cross! (v. 8)

As if it were not enough for the Son to humble himself to become a servant, he humbled himself even further by becoming "obedient to death." And not just any old death: the Son voluntarily submitted to the humiliating torture of being crucified! And it was ultimately for this reason that he became a human in the first place.

This passage thus demonstrates that the Incarnation anticipates the crucifixion, and the crucifixion culminates the Incarnation. The other-oriented, self-sacrificial love that is magnificently reflected in Christ's decision to set aside his advantages to become a human is even more magnificently reflected in his decision to set aside advantages to allow himself to be crucified—advantages like having twelve legions of angels fight in his defense (Matt 26:53).

From beginning to end, but most clearly on the cross, Jesus revealed his Father's cruciform character.

Jesus's Cruciform Ministry

The cruciform through-line of Jesus's ministry is reflected throughout the Gospels as well. In fact, it's reflected in the very fact that each of the Gospels is, from the start, oriented toward Jesus's crucifixion (which NT scholars refer to as the Gospels' "passion narratives"). Martin Kahler, who was one of the most renowned NT scholars at the turn of the twentieth century, described the Gospels as "passion narratives with extended introductions."[7] At every turn, the Gospels move in the direction of the cross.

Many particular episodes in Jesus's ministry reflect the humble, self-sacrificial character that was most dramatically and most clearly displayed on the cross. For example, in the temptation narratives, the

7. M. Kähler, *The So-Called Historical Jesus and the Historic Biblical Christ*, trans. C. E. Braaten (Philadelphia: Fortress Press, 1964 [1896]), 80n11.

devil tempts Jesus by offering him all the splendor and authority of the kingdoms of the world (Matt 4:8–10). Jesus had come to win back all these kingdoms, but he refused to acquire them by submitting to the devil's coercive way of ruling. He had instead come to win and rule these kingdoms through the noncoercive power of self-sacrificial love, which he perfectly displayed on the cross.

The same self-sacrificial conception of power is evident as well in the way Jesus confronted his disciples' traditional but misguided expectations about the messiah. Whereas they expected a triumphant warrior king, Jesus taught them that he had come "not to be served, but to serve, and to give his life as a ransom for many."[8]

Along the same lines, Jesus repeatedly told his disciples that he had to go to Jerusalem to "suffer many things" and be executed.[9] When Peter, who fully embraced the triumphant warrior conception of the messiah, tried to prevent Jesus from following through on his call to suffer, Jesus rebuked him and even called him "Satan" (Matt 16:23). This stern rebuke demonstrates that the cruciform conception of power that runs throughout Jesus's ministry and that is supremely expressed on the cross is "the antithesis of the self-oriented power that the devil offered the Son of God."[10]

A particularly poignant illustration of Jesus's cruciform conception of power is found in John just after Jesus and his disciples had celebrated Passover.

> Jesus knew that the Father had put all things under his power, and that he had come from God and was returning to God; so he got up from the meal, took off his outer clothing, and wrapped a towel around his waist. After that, he poured water into a basin and began to wash his disciples' feet, drying them with the towel that was wrapped around him. (John 13:3–5)

What do you do when you know that you have the power to do anything you want? If you're Jesus, you put a towel around your waste and start washing the dirty smelly feet of your disciples—the very disciples you know are going to soon abandon you in your hour of greatest need! This is the humble, other-oriented, cruciform character that Jesus displayed throughout his cross-centered ministry.

8. Matt 20:28; cf. Mark 10:45.
9. Matt 16:21; 17:23; 20:19; 26:2; Mark 10:32–34; Luke 17:25; cf. 24:7.
10. R. Feldmeier and H. Spieckermann, *God of the Living: A Biblical Theology*, trans. M. E. Biddle (Waco, TX: Baylor University Press, 2011), 189.

The Cruciform Kingdom

After washing their feet, Jesus told his disciples, "I have set you an example that you should do as I have done for you" (John 13:15). Jesus was talking more about the servant attitude he'd just displayed than about the particular way it was expressed. For everywhere we find him calling on disciples to adopt his cruciform mindset.

While the world associates greatness with power and privilege, in Jesus's kingdom greatness is associated with humility, innocence, and service to others.[11] To even be considered a disciple, one must be willing to "pick up their cross daily and follow me," Jesus said.[12] Yet, he assured them that all who were willing to lose their present self-centered life to serve others would thereby find their true life.[13]

On top of this, both the importance and the radical nature of the cruciform lifestyle to which Jesus calls his disciples is reflected in the way he reverses some of the OT's covenantal blessings (which, we should note, also further illustrates Jesus's superior authority to the OT). Throughout the OT, wealth, power, and security were considered signs of God's blessing.[14] According to Jesus, however, the "blessed" are those who are poor, hungry, weak, and vulnerable, and he pronounces woes over the rich, well fed, secure, and powerful.[15] And whereas the OT consistently presents people who are victorious in battle as being blessed by God, Jesus taught that it is the peacemakers who will be blessed (Matt 5:9).

The nonviolent and enemy-loving nature of the cross-centered kingdom that Jesus brought is clearly reflected in Jesus's call to set aside the OT's laws of just retaliation, discussed in the previous chapter.[16] Instead of retaliating, disciples are to swear off violence and to love enemies so that they "may be children of [their] Father in heaven." The nature of the Father's love is reflected in the fact that he "causes his sun to rise on the evil and the good, and sends rain on the righteous and the unrighteous." And as we've seen, this is why Jesus states that the telltale mark that someone is his child is that they also

11. Matt 16:11–14; 20:20–28; 23:11–12; Luke 18:15–17.
12. Luke 9:23; 14:27.
13. Matt 10:39; 16:25.
14. Deut 28:1–14; Lev 26:3–12.
15. Luke 6:20–26; cf. Matt 5:3–12. It may be worth mentioning that Jesus is warning, not condemning, people who are rich, well fed, secure, and powerful. And the warning is necessary precisely because people in this state generally find it more challenging to cultivate the cruciform lifestyle Jesus calls people to.
16. Matt 5:38–45; cf. Exod 21:24; Lev 24:19–20; Deut 19:21.

love the evil and the unrighteous as well as the good and the righteous. In short, children of the Father are to love others indiscriminately and unconditionally, for this alone reflects the character of the Father, as it is most perfectly revealed on the cross.

***

It's important to understand that for first-century Jews living in Palestine, to speak of enemies was first and foremost to speak about the Roman soldiers who oppressively, and often violently, ruled their land. Any individual or group that dared to defy Rome was punished in horrific ways that instilled terror and thus motivated fear-based compliance. And their favorite instrument of terror was crucifixion.[17]

I say this because many have tried to make exceptions to Jesus's command. People generally assume they have the right to kill enemies that threaten them, their loved ones, or their country. But if Romans weren't excluded from the sorts of enemies we are called to love and refuse to retaliate against, I submit there is no conceivable enemy that's excluded from this teaching.

If there's any remaining doubt, however, remember that it was these very Romans that Jesus decided not to defend himself against, choosing instead to be crucified by them, and out of love for them. And, according to the NT, Jesus did this not only *for* us, but also to set an *example that we are to follow*.[18]

But all this is almost beside the point, for the very fact that Jesus bases his command to love unconditionally on the indiscriminately loving character of the Father, not on the worthiness of those we are called to love, rules out any possible exception to this command.

Martin Hengel calls this Jesus's most revolutionary teaching, and it is so foundational to Jesus's vision of the kingdom that Hengel refers to it as his "Magna Carta."[19] I completely agree and would simply like us to notice that this Magna Carta was supremely modeled and expressed on Calvary.

***

17. On the horrific brutality of Roman crucifixion, see M. Hengel, *Crucifixion*, trans. J. Bowden (Philadelphia: Fortress Press, 1977).
18. Phil 2:5; Eph 5:1–2; 1 Pet 2:20–21; 3:14–18; 4:1.
19. M. Hengel, *Was Jesus a Revolutionist?*, trans. W. Klassen (Eugene, OR: Wipf & Stock, rpt., 1971), 27.

So, following Jesus requires us to cultivate a cruciform character that is willing to suffer for others and that rules out responding to violence with violence. It's important to note, however, that there's a world of difference between *choosing* out of love to suffer *for* another, and *being forced* to suffer *at the hands of* another. Following Jesus rules out resorting to violence against an abuser, but it also rules out enabling an abuser.

As I said to Marla, in these sorts of situations love requires that we do everything necessary to end the abuse, including distancing ourselves from the abuser.

***

As a final illustration of the cruciform kingdom that Jesus inaugurated, consider the humble, loving, and countercultural way Jesus interacted with people. The cruciform love that eventually led Jesus to enter into solidarity with sinners and to appear as a guilty criminal on Calvary was already leading him to enter into solidarity with sinners and to appear as one of them throughout his ministry.

Jesus scandalously fellowshipped with prostitutes, tax collectors, and others who were harshly judged by the religious establishment of his day.[20] He broke religious taboos by interacting with, and even touching, people who were viewed as unclean and whom the OT law prohibited touching.[21] And Jesus rebelled against the patriarchal social structure of his day by interacting with women—even women with shameful pasts—in respectful ways.[22]

Along similar lines, the love that eventually led Jesus to demolish "the dividing wall of hostility" between all ethnic groups on the cross (Eph 2:14–15) was already leading Jesus to tear down these walls throughout his ministry. The loving way Jesus interacted with, and spoke about, people whom most Jews despised—e.g., Samaritans, Gentiles, and Roman centurions—was scandalous, to say the least. Sometimes Jesus even held the faith and behavior of these people up as more exemplary than his fellow Israelites.[23]

In all these ways, Jesus was sacrificially resisting racial prejudices within his culture, and as is true of every other aspect of Jesus's min-

20. Matt 21:32; Luke 5:30–32; 7:34; 15:1–2.
21. Matt 8:1–3; 9:20–22; 10:8; 11:5; 26:6.
22. Matt 9:27–34; Luke 7:38–50; 18:35–42; 26:6–13; John 4:1–26.
23. Matt 8:5–13; 15:21–28; Luke 10:25–37.

istry, this aspect culminates on the cross. For the cross reveals God stooping an unsurpassable distance and paying an unsurpassable price to ascribe unsurpassable worth to every human from every tribe and nation throughout history.

Paul's Cruciform Gospel

The thematic centrality of the cross in Jesus's ministry is strongly confirmed throughout the writings of Paul. As Jürgen Moltmann notes, and as we will now see, whenever Paul speaks of "Christ," he has *Christ crucified* in mind. This is the case even when Paul speaks of Christ's resurrection, according to Moltmann, for the resurrection is the triumph of the self-sacrificial love that Jesus demonstrated on the cross.[24]

The centrality of the cross in Paul's thinking is also reflected in the fact that whenever Paul offers brief summaries of his understanding of the gospel, the cross holds center stage.[25] In fact, Paul actually equates the "gospel" with "the message of the cross," using the two phrases interchangeably.[26] This is why he speaks of people who oppose the spreading of *the gospel* as "enemies of *the cross* of Christ" (Phil 3:18, emphasis added).

This is also why Paul could tell the Corinthians that he "resolved to know nothing while I was with you except Jesus Christ and him crucified" (1 Cor 2:2). This statement reflects Paul's assumption that, if you understand the meaning of Jesus's crucifixion, you understand everything you need to know about God and about the gospel.

Paul reflects this conviction in many other ways as well. For Paul, the cross is the way God's love is displayed and the way the powers of evil are defeated.[27] It's also the way sin is atoned for, the way people are reconciled to God and to each other, and the way people are made righteous, healed, and empowered to live for God.[28]

Moreover, as I mentioned above, for Paul, the self-sacrificial love

24. J. Moltmann, *The Crucified God: The Cross and the Criterion and Criticism of Christian Theology* (Minneapolis: Fortress Press, 1993 [orig. German, 1973]), 73–75.

25. See M. J. Gorman, *Cruciformity: Paul's Narrative Spirituality of the Cross* (Grand Rapids: Eerdmans, 2001), 75–94; J. T. Carroll and J. Green, "Nothing but Christ and Him Crucified: Paul's Theology of the Cross," in *The Death of Jesus in Early Christianity* (Peabody, MA: Hendrickson, 1995), 123–32.

26. 1 Cor 1:17–18, 23.

27. Rom 5:8; 1 Cor 2:6–8; Col 2:14–15; Eph 5:1–2.

28. Rom 3:15; 5:9–10, 15–19; 6:6; 2 Cor 5:14–21; 13:4; Phil 3:10; Col 1:33; Eph 1:7; 2:14–16.

that was manifested on the cross is the model that disciples are to follow.[29] In fact, Paul defines a disciple as one who has been "crucified with Christ."[30] Jerome Murphy-O'Connor summarizes Paul's cross-centered understanding of discipleship by noting that for Paul, disciples are called to "exhibit the self-sacrificing, empowering love that Christ showed in his crucifixion." In short, "Crucifixion is what makes a Christian."[31]

Given Paul's cross-centered understanding of both the gospel and discipleship, we are not surprised to find him giving the same revolutionary Magna Carta that Jesus gave. Instead of resorting to violence, Paul instructs disciples to never repay evil with evil but to instead repay evil with good. Among other things, this means they are to feed their enemies if they are hungry and give them something to drink if they are thirsty (Rom 12:14–21).

The Cruciform Power of God

Yet, the most astounding reflection of how centrally important the cross was for Paul is that he proclaims that, as foolish and weak as it may look to nonbelievers, the cross must be seen by believers as both the power and the wisdom of God (1 Cor 1:18, 24). In direct opposition to the controlling power and wisdom that people have ascribed to God or the gods throughout history—including in much of the OT and, unfortunately, throughout most of church history—Paul allowed the humble self-sacrificial love expressed on the cross to completely reframe his understanding of God's power and wisdom.

This means that Paul didn't view the cross merely as God's means of achieving salvation. It was for him also the clearest expression of the power that God uses to rule the world and to defeat evil.[32] N. T. Wright sums up the central role the cross plays in Paul's view of God, his understanding of the gospel, and his view of discipleship, when he states that, for Paul, "the cross is . . . the sign of the center. . . . It is the middle of everywhere [and] . . . the axis of everything."[33]

29. Eph 5:1–2. Similarly, Paul holds up his own life as a model to be followed, for it was patterned after the cross (1 Cor 11:1; Phil 3:15–17; 2 Thess 3:7).
30. Gal 2:19–20; cf. 5:24, 6:14. A great book on the centrality of the cross in Paul's model of discipleship is Gorman, *Cruciformity*.
31. J. Murphy-O'Connor, "Crucifixion in the Pauline Letters," in Dreyer, *The Cross in Christian Tradition*, 21–50 (43).
32. This is also a central theme of the book of Revelation. See *CWG*, vol. 1, appendix IV.

This cross-centered understanding of God's weak-looking power and foolish-looking wisdom is so radical that even the majority of Christians throughout history have not been able to fully accept it. Despite the NT's emphasis on the centrality of the cross, most assume that God relies on coercive power to run the world and to punish sinners, not the meek-looking power of self-sacrificial love.

What All This Means

First, once we understand the NT's cross-based definition of love and appreciate how absolutely central it is to Jesus's revelation of God, it means that it is never loving for any person to abuse another. Nor is it ever loving to let another abuse you. If any part of Marla's story overlaps with your own, *please* take this to heart.

Second, it means that our mental picture of God should not merely be anchored in Christ; it should be anchored in *Christ crucified.* It means that it is not enough to merely say that "God is Christlike, and in him is no un-Christlikeness at all," though this is certainly true.[34] We must go further and say that God is *cruciform love*, and in him there is no noncruciform love at all. Which is to say, there is no aspect of God that is not characterized by the nonviolent, self-sacrificial, enemy-embracing love that is revealed on the cross.

Third, it means it's not enough to say that all Scripture is inspired for the ultimate purpose of bearing witness to Christ, though this also is true. We must go further and say that all Scripture is inspired for the ultimate purpose of bearing witness to the cruciform through-line that weaves together everything Jesus was about and that was supremely expressed on the cross.

***

Now, finally, we are in a position to fully appreciate the problem we are wrestling with in this book. *How do macabre portraits of God, such as the portrait of Yahweh commanding Israelites to mercilessly engage in*

33. N. T. Wright, *Paul and the Faithfulness of God*, book 2 (Minneapolis: Fortress Press, 2013), 910. For the convenience of my American audience, I have altered Wright's British spelling of "centre."
34. A. M. Ramsey, *God, Christ, and the World: A Study in Contemporary Theology* (London: SCM, 1969), 98.

genocide, reflect and point to the nonviolent, self-sacrificial, enemy-embracing love of God that is supremely revealed on the cross?

Putting the best possible spin on the OT's violent portraits of God isn't going to cut it. In fact, the very attempt to defend the violence ascribed to God in these portraits indicates that we still believe that God is capable of this sort of behavior, which in turn indicates that we do not yet fully trust that the crucified Christ is the *full* revelation of God's true character. And until we fully trust that God is as he's revealed to be on the cross and therefore stop trying to justify these violent divine portraits, the cross cannot function like Alice's looking-glass, reversing the violent meaning of these portraits to show how they bear witness to the cross.

Think of it like this. We saw in the previous chapter that the OT is a shadow of the reality we are given in Christ. The shadow will point you to the reality, but only if you remember that it's a mere shadow. If you instead mistake the shadow for the reality, the shadow can't point you anywhere. You're trapped in its darkness. So I encourage you to trust that the cross reveals *the reality* of what God is truly like. For when you do this—but only when you do this—you will discover how everything in the OT that on the surface conflicts with the revelation of God on the crucified Christ, including its violent depictions of God, is actually a shadow that points to the revelation of God in the crucified Christ.

If you're still skeptical about this, that's okay. I just ask that you keep an open mind as I demonstrate in the next chapter how the cross itself answers the question of how the OT's violent portraits of God lead to it.

4

Revolting Beauty

When the crucified Jesus is called "the image of the invisible God," the meaning is that THIS is God, and God is like THIS.
—Jürgen Moltmann[1]

Cookbooks and Detective Novels

Shelley occasionally enjoys cooking, and she relies on an old three-ring notebook of recipes that she's collected. This compiled cookbook is a complete mess. It's actually a stretch to call it a cook*book*. It's more like a cook*pile* or a cook*heap*. Whenever I attempt to open it, a bunch of recipes fall out because most of the holes in the envelopes that hold the recipes have been torn open.

The truth is, Shelley no longer even bothers to put her recipes into those tattered envelopes. And little care is taken to keep the recipes in order, beyond returning them to their correct general category (e.g., "Soups," "Desserts," "Salads"). But this is just fine, because it doesn't matter *where* a recipe is located in a cookbook. A recipe remains the same regardless of what comes before or after it. A recipe does not have a context.

Not so with detective novels. The meaning of an event within a detective novel is dependent on where it is in the story and how it relates to all that comes before and after it. Something that seems completely insignificant early on can turn out to be the telltale clue

1. Jürgen Moltmann, *The Crucified God: The Cross of Christ as the Foundation and Criticism of Christian Theology* (Minneapolis: Fortress Press, 1993), 295.

that solves the mystery. And sometimes an event toward the end of the novel can completely reframe the meaning of everything that preceded it.

The same holds true for certain movies, such as *The Sixth Sense*, *The Book of Eli*, or *The Usual Suspects*. (Spoiler alert: if you haven't yet seen these movies, but you think you may want to, stop reading right now and go watch them. I'll wait.)

***

Okay, as you now know, if you didn't before, the last shocking minute of each of these movies completely reframes everything that preceded it. When the movie ended, didn't you find yourself staring at the screen for a few puzzled moments thinking, "No way!"? After movies like that, I have to rethink (and sometimes even rewatch) the entire movie. Events that meant one thing at the time they occurred turn out to mean something totally different when understood from the perspective of the ending.

That just doesn't happen with a cookbook.

The Bible's Surprise Ending

A lot of Christians quote passages from the Bible the way Shelley grabs recipes from her cookbook: it doesn't matter much where the passage is located. "God said it, I believe it, and that settles it," as we used to say in the Pentecostal church where I first became a Christian. This slogan sounds pious, but among its many problems is the fact that the Bible is not a cookbook, it's a story. And, similar to the movies I just mentioned, it's a story with a surprise ending that reframes everything.

So, just because God "said it" does not "settle it." For the meaning of what God "said" may change depending on whether it's heard from the perspective of the people at the time it was said or from the perspective of the surprise ending that takes place with Jesus's crucifixion and resurrection.

What, you ask, is so surprising about Jesus's crucifixion and resurrection?

If you read the OT without knowing what happens next, you'd expect that a mighty warrior messiah is going to arrive on the scene, rise up in holy hatred against the Romans and smite them, thereby delivering Israel from their oppressive rule and restoring it to the power and prosperity that Israel enjoyed under King David. You'd also expect that this messiah was going to crack down on sinners and call the Jewish people back to their nationalistic, law-based covenant.

Sure, there are hints here and there in the OT that God was planning something radically different. But, as with the hints that are present in the movies I mentioned, the hints in the OT only become clear after Jesus arrives on the scene.

Jesus didn't fit these expectations. Far from rising up in holy hatred to smite the Romans, Jesus let himself get crucified by them, and he did so out of love for them. Nor did Jesus crack down on sinners and call people back to their nationalistic, law-based covenant. Rather, he repudiated aspects of the law, hung out with sinners, and cracked down on those legalistic religious leaders who were always cracking down on sinners. And far from calling people back to their nationalistic, law-based covenant with God, Jesus forged a new covenant that was transnational in character and that was based on God's grace and empowering Spirit.

This is why Jesus disappointed the masses of expectant Jews, so much so that many turned on him and called for his execution. But, lo and behold, Jesus rose from the dead, thereby confirming that he was indeed the Messiah and that the surprising direction he took the story of God and Israel was precisely the way God wanted it to go from the start.

This surprising culmination of the biblical narrative reframes everything. The entire inspired narrative leading up to the crucified Christ must now be interpreted with a view toward this culminating revelation. And this brings us back to the all-important question: How does the surprising culmination of the OT narrative in the crucified Christ reframe this story's disturbing portraits of God such that they bear witness to the surprising, nonviolent, self-sacrificial love of God revealed on the cross?

The key to unlocking this mystery is found in the cross itself—*if* we are willing to completely trust it to reveal what God is truly like. There are four steps to seeing how the cross functions as this key.

Step 1: How the Cross Reveals God

Several months after I quit trying to justify the violence that some OT authors ascribe to God, I found myself asking a question I've never heard anyone ask. Yet, the moment I asked it, it struck me as one of the most important theological questions we could ever ask.

The question is: *How does the crucified Christ become the supreme revelation of God for us?* This was the question that first set me down the path to discovering the looking-glass cross.

Consider this: when first-century Jews looked at the crucified Christ "from a worldly point of view," as Paul once did (2 Cor 5:16), all they saw was a guilty, God-cursed criminal, no different from the thousands of other criminals that were crucified by the Romans. This is all anyone can see with the natural eye. So what is it that allows believers to look at the cross and see *more* than this? What is it about the way believers view this particular crucified criminal that enables us to discern the supreme display of God's cruciform character?

The answer is that by faith we see *something else going on* behind the scenes of Jesus's crucifixion that sets him apart from all other crucified people. By faith, we look beyond surface appearances to behold God stooping an infinite distance out of love to bear our sin as this particular guilty-appearing, God-cursed criminal. And, as I noted in the previous chapter, it is the unsurpassable extremity to which God was willing to stoop that reveals the unsurpassably loving character of God. But we can only see this if we trust "the message of the cross" that tells us that in Christ, God was stooping to bear the sin of the world to reconcile the world to himself (1 Cor 1:18).

This is why the cross is both supremely ugly and supremely beautiful to those who view it with eyes of faith. The surface of the event is revoltingly ugly, for it reflects the ugly sin and the horrific God-forsaken curse that Jesus bore. But to those who by faith see beyond this surface appearance, the cross also reveals the supreme beauty of a God who, out of love, was willing to stoop an infinite distance to bear our sin, suffer our curse, and thereby take on this revoltingly ugly, sin-mirroring, surface appearance.

We might think of the cross along the lines of a two-way mirror in which you are able to look through your own reflection and see what is taking place on the other side of the mirror—but only if the other side of the mirror is lit up. Otherwise you only see your own reflection.

So too, the faith of believers lightens up what is going on behind the scenes of the crucifixion. It thus allows them to see through the ugly sin-mirroring surface of the cross to behold God stooping an infinite distance to enter into solidarity with our sin and to thereby take on an ugly appearance that mirrors this sin.

This is why the cross is for believers both the revelation of the revolting ugliness of our sin and the revelation of the supremely beautiful God who was willing to stoop to take on this revolting ugliness.

Step 2: Reading Scripture with a Cross-Informed Faith

If the cross reveals what God is *truly* like, it also reveals what God has *always* been like. It's not as if God first acquired a loving cruciform character when Jesus was crucified. No, the cross reveals what God is truly like because God has always had the character that the cross reveals. And we must always remember that the God who is revealed on the cross is the same God who inspired Scripture for the ultimate purpose of bearing witness to his self-revelation on the cross.

In this light, doesn't it make sense to read Scripture expecting to find God sometimes revealing himself the same way he reveals himself on the cross? I submit that we should read Scripture expecting to find God sometimes revealing his beautiful character by stooping to bear the ugly sin of his people, thereby taking on a surface appearance that mirrors that sin, just as he does on the cross. And to discern this beauty, we should expect that we will need to exercise faith to look through the sin-mirroring surface of these portraits to discern *something else going on* behind the scenes.

Along the same lines, we should expect that the *something else that is going on* behind the scenes of these sin-mirroring portraits is precisely what is going on behind the sin-mirroring cross: God, out of his love, is humbly stooping to bear the sin of his people, thereby taking on an ugly appearance that reflects this sin. This is how I propose we interpret all portraits of God in the Bible that on the surface reflect a character that is inconsistent with the cruciform character of God revealed on the cross, including especially the OT's violent depictions of God.[2]

Consider, for example, Jeremiah's macabre representation of Yahweh vowing not to let mercy or compassion stop him from

2. For a discussion of other ugly portraits of God, such as those that depict him in sexist and/or otherwise oppressive ways, see P. Trible, *Texts of Terror: Literary-Feminist Readings of Biblical Narratives* (Philadelphia: Fortress Press, 1984), and G. F. Ellwood, *Batter My Heart* (Wallingford, PA: Pendle Hill, 1988).

smashing families together (Jer 13:14). If we trust that the cross reveals what God is truly like, then we know that God would never vow to surpress his mercy and compassion in order to mercilessly smash families to death. So we must assess this ugly surface appearance of God to be a reflection of Jeremiah's own fallen, culturally conditioned, ugly conception of God.[3]

However, our faith in the God revealed on the cross also transforms this portrait into a two-way mirror. For when read in light of the cross we are able to look through this ugly sin-mirroring surface to behold the beautiful cruciform God stooping to bear Jeremiah's sinful conception of him, which is why God takes on this ugly appearance in Jeremiah's contribution to the biblical narrative. Interpreted through the looking-glass cross, violent divine portraits like Jeremiah's become both beautiful and revolting for all the same reasons the cross is both beautiful and revolting.

This, I submit, is precisely how the OT's warrior portraits of God point to the crucified God. We might say that violent divine portraits become literary crucifixes that bear witness to the historical crucifixion when interpreted through the looking-glass cross.

I want to once again stress this all-important foundational point: we will only see Scripture's violent divine portraits as literary crucifixes if we remain resolved in our faith that God has always been exactly as he's revealed himself to be on the cross. If you trust in the revelation of God's beautiful cruciform character on the cross as you interpret ugly divine portraits like Jeremiah's, you will find this same beautiful character in the depth of these portraits. But if you instead trust in the mercilessly violent character of God that is reflected on the surface of Jeremiah's ugly portrait, God's true cruciform character will remain as hidden from you as it was from Jeremiah.

So the most important question that we end up answering by the way we interpret the OT's violent depictions of God is, Who are we going to trust to reveal God's true character to us? Since all Scripture is supposed to point to the crucified Christ, I think the answer should be obvious.

***

3. In the following chapter we'll see that the culturally conditioned nature of the OT's violent depictions of God is confirmed by how closely these portraits resemble the violent depictions of warrior gods among Israel's ANE neighbors.

You might think of it like this: In chapter 2 we saw that Hebrews teaches us that people in the OT only caught glimpses of the true character of God. Now, if you're outside on a day when you can only catch glimpses of the sun, it means it's a mostly cloudy day. So, as we read the OT, we should remain aware that these authors had a rather cloudy vision of God. By contrast, Hebrews teaches that the Son is the very "radiance of God's glory" and "the exact representation of his being." He is the very brilliance of the sun shining forth on a cloudless day.

So why on earth would we ever place more trust in someone who had a cloudy vision of God's glory than we place in the one who is himself the very radiance of God's glory?

Step 3: A Cross-Centered Conception of God's "Breathing"

Insofar as the cross is beautiful, it reflects God *acting toward us*. It was God who planned this event, who voluntarily set aside his advantages to become a human, and who submitted to the humiliation and pain of the cross when he could have easily crushed his enemies. Most amazing of all, it was God who voluntarily entered into solidarity with the sin of the human race as well as with the God-forsaken curse that we deserved. All of this reveals the unsurpassable beauty of a humble, loving God *acting toward us.*

But insofar as the cross is ugly, it reflects God humbly allowing other agents to *act upon him*. Humans chose to unjustly arrest and condemn Jesus. Humans whipped, spat upon, mocked, and crucified Jesus. And they did this under the influence of Satan and other fallen powers that were also acting upon Jesus.[4]

Yet the most important way God allowed others to act upon him was by bearing the sin and the deserved curse of every human who has ever existed or who will ever exist. And this is precisely why the surface appearance of the cross is as ugly as its depth is beautiful.

Now, since all of God's wisdom is found in the crucified Christ, shouldn't we allow the way God breathed his supreme revelation on the cross to inform how we think about the way God breathes revelations of himself in Scripture? After all, we are in no position to claim to know ahead of time how God breathes revelations of himself

4. John 13:2, 27; 1 Cor 2:6–8.

through people. Indeed, if the cross reveals anything, it's that Jesus tends to turn our common assumptions about God on their head!

***

It seems to me that most Evangelicals assume that God's "breathing" is a *unilateral* and *unidirectional* activity, which implies that nothing conditions what results from God's breathing other than God's will. This is why so many assume that, since God is perfect, whatever results from his breathing must also be perfect. So, they conclude, the Bible must reflect God's own perfection.

This is nothing more than an unwarranted assumption, and it creates a number of problems, not least of which is that it sets Christians up for a fall when they discover that the Bible is actually filled with human imperfections. I am among a countless number of Christians or former Christians whose faith was temporarily or permanently shipwrecked when we discovered this. It may have been the Bible's unscientific cosmology, or its irreconcilable contradictions, or its conflict with historical evidence, or its less-than-edifying depictions of God. But whatever the cause, this shipwreck of faith was as tragic as it was unnecessary.

To be clear, I affirm the traditional view that the Bible is infallible. If we trust the Bible to do what God inspired it to do, and if we are interpreting it correctly, it will not fail us. But the all-important question is, *what did God inspire the Bible to infallibly accomplish*?

If you expect the Bible to conform to contemporary standards of scientific, historical, literary, or logical perfection, I'm afraid you're going to be greatly disappointed. God did not inspire the Bible to meet these standards. As we've seen, God inspired all Scripture to point us to Jesus, and more specifically, to the cross that culminates everything Jesus was about. If we faithfully trust that God is as the crucified Christ reveals him to be, Scripture will unfailingly keep bringing us back to him.

But precisely because the cross appears foolish and weak according to ordinary human standards of strength, wisdom and perfection, why would anyone think that the Bible that is divinely inspired to point to the cross would appear any less foolish and weak? To the contrary, since God always furthers his purposes through "the foolish," "weak," "lowly" and "despised" things of the world, as the cross supremely illustrates (1 Cor 1:27–28), shouldn't we expect that the Bible also will appear "foolish," "weak," "lowly," and "despised" according to the world's standards of wisdom, strength and perfection?

Along similar lines, if God breathed his supreme revelation by becoming a limited human being and then becoming the sin and curse of humanity, why would anyone assume that the Bible, which is inspired to bear witness to this supreme revelation, is devoid of material that reflects the limitations, sin and God-forsaken curse of humanity?

***

The reason the revelations that God breathes in Scripture don't share in God's perfection is that, as the cross reveals, God breathing isn't a unilateral or unidirectional activity. When God breathed his supreme revelation on the cross, he did it in a mutually impacting relational way. So what results from God's breathing reflects not only God acting toward us, but also God allowing us to act toward him.

This explains why Scripture contains a prescientific cosmology, historical inaccuracies, contradictions, and other sorts of human imperfections. While these fallible qualities are devastating if you're expecting Scripture to meet a presupposed human standard of perfection, they are to be expected if we instead assess our divinely inspired Scripture by the standard of the cross.[5]

Step 4: The Relational, Noncoercive God

This brings me to the last step in my proposal. Some readers may be wondering: Why would God allow fallen and culturally conditioned people to affect the results of his breathing in his written word?

5. Someone might at this point object that my cross-centered conception of inspiration has refuted itself, for if Scripture is full of human imperfections, we can't be confident the Gospel authors and Paul have accurately interpreted Jesus's life and death. Hence, it could be argued, the cross can't function as the standard by which we assess all Scripture. In response, there are compelling historical reasons supporting the conclusion that the way the Gospels and Paul interpret Jesus's cross-centered life and ministry is solidly anchored in history. See, for example, P. R. Eddy and G. Boyd, *The Jesus Legend: A Case for the Historical Reliability of the Synoptic Tradition* (Grand Rapids: Baker Academic, 2007); G. Boyd, *Cynic Sage or Son of God? Recovering the Real Jesus in an Age of Revisionist Replies* (Eugene, OR: Wipf & Stock, 2010); C. Blomberg, *The Historical Reliability of John's Gospel: Issues and Commentary* (Downers Grove, IL: InterVarsity, 2001); C. S. Keener, *The Gospel of John: A Commentary*, 2 vols. (Peabody, MA: Hendrickson, 2003); L. McGrew, *Hidden in Plain View: Undesigned Coincidences in the Gospel and Acts* (Chillicothe, OH: DeWard, 2017).

Well, ask yourself: Why did God allow this on the cross?

God could have created us without the capacity to choose to sin, thereby sparing himself the need to suffer on our behalf. Instead, God created us as free, decision-making persons, for only decision- making persons have the capacity to choose to enter into loving relationships with him and with one another. In fact, that is God's ultimate goal for his creation, at least as far as we are told. More specifically, God's goal is to have a people who eternally participate in and mirror his triune love in their relationship with him, with each other, and with the rest of creation.

Given this goal, God has always dealt with people as free, decision-making persons. He does not coercively control us to ensure that we will comply with his will. Nor does God lobotomize sinners to make us saints. God rather respects our personhood by giving us the choice to follow him or not. And this is why we often find in Scripture that God is grieved, frustrated, and disappointed when people choose to reject him and instead go down their own self-destructive paths.[6] Because God sovereignly chose to create a world in which true freedom exists, he refuses to override the personhood of people by controlling us.

This is what we should expect, given that we know that the kind of power God relies on is revealed on the cross. And since God will not lobotomize people to get them where he wishes they were, he must be willing to humbly stoop to relate to us *as we are*. And this, in turn, means God must patiently bear our sin as he continues to influence us in the direction he wants for us.

This is why God allowed the sin of humanity to *act upon him* and to condition the way he appeared when he breathed his supreme revelation on the cross. And this is also why God has always been willing to allow the sin of his people—including their sinful conceptions of him—to condition how he appears whenever he breathes revelations of himself. His breathing always reflects the reciprocal give-and-take of a noncoercive, authentic relationship.

Moreover, because God created a world in which agents have the capacity to freely enter into authentic relationships, God must always act by means of *influence* rather than *coercion*. As the early church uniformly confessed, "coercion is no attribute of God."[7] And for this

6. On free will in Scripture and how it affects God when it is misused, see G. Boyd, *Is God to Blame? Beyond Pat Answers to the Problem of Suffering* (Downers Grove, IL: InterVarsity, 2003), 61–77.

reason, the loving, relational God has always *acted toward* people to reveal his true self *as much as possible*. But he also has always been willing to humbly allow his people to *act upon him* as he bears their sin *as much as necessary*.

To the degree that any portrait reflects the cruciform character of God, we can consider it a reflection of God *acting toward* people. It is a literary testament to the Spirit of the crucified Christ breaking through the sin and cultural conditioning of his people. I label these *direct* revelations, for they directly reflect the cruciform character of God that is supremely revealed on the cross.

Conversely, to the degree that the surface appearance of a biblical portrait fails to reflect the cruciform character of God, we can consider it to be a literary testament to God's willingness to humbly stoop to allow the sin and cultural conditioning of his people to *act upon him* as he bears the sin of his people. I label these *indirect* revelations, for to see how these portraits reflect the cruciform character of God we must exercise our cross-informed faith to see through their sin-mirroring surface to discern "what else is going on" behind the scenes.

***

This is the cornerstone of my proposal for how to interpret the OT's violent portraits of God such that they bear witness to the cross. It was by reflecting on what it means to see the cross as the supreme revelation of God while trying to understand the OT's violent portraits of God through this lens that I began to discover how the OT's portraits of God as a violent warrior actually reveal the self-sacrificial love of the crucified God.

But the truth is, we're just getting warmed up. There are many questions yet to be addressed, such as: Does the Bible itself provide evidence that God didn't engage in the violence that biblical authors ascribe to him? Does Scripture support the notion that the OT's violent divine portraits of God reflect the fallen and culturally conditioned state of their authors? If so, how do we make sense of the Flood that Noah and his family survived on the Ark? How do we explain instances of God's prophets using their power in destructive ways?

7. *Epistle to Diognetus*, 7.4, in *The Apostolic Fathers: Greek Texts and English Translations of Their Writings*, ed. and trans. J. B. Lightfoot and J. R. Harner, rev. ed. Michael W. Holmes (Grand Rapids: Baker, 1992), 545.

And if God doesn't actually engage in violence, will unrepentant sinners never be judged for their sin?

Before tackling these questions, however, I need to address a legitimate concern that I am sure many readers are pondering: If the cross-centered interpretation of the OT's violent depictions of God is the way God intends us to interpret them, why has no one in church history proposed this before? This is undoubtedly the biggest hurdle that people will need to clear if they are to accept the looking-glass cross interpretation.

But as we'll see in the following chapter, this hurdle is not nearly as high as you might think.

5

Building on Tradition

The cross alone is our theology.
—Martin Luther[1]

I see nothing in Scripture except Christ crucified.
—Martin Luther[2]

"If It's New, It Can't Be True"

The topic of the day was the atonement, the doctrine of how Jesus's death on the cross reconciles us to God. I was teaching a university theology class, and I had just given an overview of a novel and recent theory. I asked the students to share their thoughts about this theory, and as was usually (and most often, unfortunately) the case, the first student to speak up was Eugene. "That modern theory is false!" he blurted out.

I responded, "You sure about that?"

"Absolutely!" he quipped back with the aggravating know-it-all grin I'd come to expect from him.

I stared at Eugene with a baffled look for a moment or two before asking him if he cared to elaborate as to why he believed this modern theory was false. "It's like my pastor always says," he responded. "If it's new, it can't be true, and if it's old, it's already been told."

1. WA 5.176, 32–33, cited in Alister E. McGrath, *Luther's Theology of the Cross: Martin Luther's Theological Breakthrough* (New York: Blackwell, 1985), 169.
2. WA 4:153, quoted in A. Skevington Wood, *Captive to the Word: Martin Luther, Doctor of Sacred Scripture* (Exeter, UK: Paternoster, 1969), 171.

"How clever," I said with a smile and slightly sarcastic tone of voice. I then decided to try to turn Eugene's response into a teaching moment.

"So you must be Catholic?" I asked. My question was sarcastic, since everyone in the classroom knew from previous conversations that Eugene was vehemently opposed to Catholicism. As I expected, Eugene angrily replied, "Of course not!"

"Interesting," I said. "So what denomination *do* you belong to?"

"Denominations are of the devil!" he replied. "My church is part of the Independent Baptist *Fellowship*."

Not wanting to split hairs over the distinction between a "fellowship" and a "denomination," I asked Eugene, "Would you happen to know when it was that Baptists first arrived on the scene in church history?"

"The Baptist teaching didn't 'arrive on the scene,'" he said, using his fingers to form mocking quotes. "Our teaching goes back to the Bible."

I, and I suspect others in the classroom, found Eugene's arrogant tone of voice to be irritating.

"Of course you *believe* that," I said with a forced smile. "And you may very well be right. But it's kind of significant, isn't it, that no one had practiced adult baptism by immersion for centuries before the first Baptists began practicing it in the sixteenth century? They were viewed by everyone else as heretics and were often persecuted. And that's because their understanding of baptism was new to everyone at that time." Then I added: "And they were persecuted as heretics because most people at the time assumed: 'If it's new, it can't be true.'"

"But their teaching *wasn't* new!" Eugene blurted out. "It's as old as the New Testament."

"Let's assume you're right," I said. "It's nevertheless true that it needed to be newly discovered. And if your Baptist pioneers had believed that anything new can't possibly be true, they would have remained Catholic, which means you would be a Catholic now."

Eugene just stared at me with a look of angry bewilderment.

"In fact," I added, "every particular belief that distinguishes each branch of the Protestant Reformation was 'new' when it was first proposed. So, had everyone stuck to your pastor's motto, Eugene, Protestantism wouldn't even exist."

"Well," Eugene replied, "the church shouldn't have dropped the ball by leaving the Baptist faith in the first place!"

We talked in frustrating circles for another minute or so, at which point I despaired of making progress and hollered out, "Anyone *else* care to share their thoughts about this 'new' theory of the atonement?"

***

The thing is, because Protestants hold that Scripture is our final authority in matters of faith, there's a sense in which we have always espoused something like the motto of Eugene's pastor: if a theological teaching is new—that is, if it's not grounded in Scripture—then it can't be true. At the same time, as heirs of a tradition that was initially resisted on the grounds that it was innovating, we have also always agreed that the Spirit sometimes opens people's eyes to new insights into Scripture.

In fact, one of the hallmarks of the Reformation is the Latin slogan: *Ecclesia reformata, semper reformanda,* which means, "The church is reformed and always being reformed."

All major branches of the historic-orthodox church have assumed that the church tradition should carry some degree of authority over believers. Consequently, whenever a belief or interpretation of Scripture has been proposed that seems novel, the burden of proof has been on the person or group that is putting it forth. While the cross-centered interpretation of the OT's violent divine portraits that I'm proposing in this book has clear precedents in the early church, I nevertheless concede that it runs counter to the way the church has interpreted these portraits for the last 1500 years.[3] My proposal is thus new to people today, which is why I must accept that the burden of proof is on me to demonstrate the validity of this interpretation.

Only time will tell the extent to which the Christian community as a whole will embrace or reject my proposal. In the meantime, I simply encourage you to consider it with an open mind. Because once in a while, what is new to you *can* be true, and what is old has *not* yet been told, at least not for a long while.

As a matter of fact, my proposal is not nearly as novel as it may initially appear. There are four ways in which it intersects with, builds on, and critiques the church tradition.[4]

3. On the precedent of my interpretation in the early church, see *CWG,* vol. 1, ch. 10.
4. For a more comprehensive and in-depth discussion of the material covered in this chapter, see *CWG,* vol. 1, chs. 4–6, and 12.

The Tradition of Finding the Crucified Christ in Scripture

While the emphasis on the cross certainly waxed and waned in different periods of church history and among various theologians, the church has always seen it as the centerpiece of our salvation, of our understanding of God, and of our interpretation of Scripture. But the theologian who most emphasized the centrality of the cross was Martin Luther (1483–1546). In fact, he's often referred to as the "theologian of the cross."[5]

The general consensus among scholars is that Luther's theology of the cross is the major theme underlying all of his theology.[6] Luther went so far as to remark, "The cross alone is our theology."[7] This statement constitutes "the foundation point upon which Luther based his theology."[8]

In keeping with this foundation, Luther defined all true theology as the "wisdom of the cross," meaning that all true theology should be, from beginning to end, anchored in the cross.[9] For Luther, the cross was nothing less than "the standard by which all genuine theological knowledge is measured, whether of the reality of God, of his grace, of his salvation, of the Christian life, or of the church of Christ."[10]

But it is Luther's method of interpreting the Bible—his *hermeneutics*—that most closely anticipates my proposal. For Luther, the cross is "the key hermeneutical principle in understanding Scripture."[11] In a sermon preached in November 1515, Luther proclaimed,

> He who would read the Bible must simply take heed that he does not err, for the Scripture may permit itself to be stretched and led, but let no

5. For several excellent studies on Luther's theology of the cross, see McGrath, *Luther's Theology*; D. K. P. Ngien, *The Suffering of God According to Martin Luther's "Theologia Crucis"* (New York: Peter Lang, 1995); W. von Loewenich, *Luther's Theology of the Cross*, trans. H. J. A. Bouman (Minneapolis: Augsburg, 1967).
6. V.-M. Kärkkäinen, "'Evil, Love and the Left Hand of God': The Contribution of Luther's Theology of the Cross to an Evangelical Theology of Evil," *Evangel Quarterly* 74, no. 3 (2002): 215–34 (216).
7. McGrath, *Luther's Theology*, 169, citing *Luthers Werke, kritische Gesamtausgabe*, ed. J. F. K Knaake et al. (Weimar, 1883–), vol. 5, 176; cf. 32–33.
8. McGrath, *Luther's Theology*, 169.
9. Luther, *Luther's Works*, ed. J. Pelikan, vols. 1–30 and H. Lehmann, vols. 31–55 (Philadelphia/St. Louis: Fortress Press/Concordia, 1955–), vol. 14, 305, 309; vol. 35, 396.
10. Paul Althaus, *The Theology of Martin Luther*, trans. Robert, C. Schultz (Philadelphia: Fortress Press, 1966), 30.
11. G. Tomlin, *The Power of the Cross: Theology and the Death of Christ in Paul, Luther and Pascal* (Carlisle, UK: Paternoster, 1999), 173.

> one lead it according to his own inclinations but let him lead it to the source that is the cross of Christ. Then he will surely strike the center.[12]

In this statement Luther shows an awareness that people can make Scripture say whatever they want by the way they stretch and lead it. Consequently, Luther argues that we should intentionally read all Scripture in a way that leads to the cross. As Luther frequently said, the cross is the center around which everything else in Scripture revolves, and the center around which all of our theology should revolve.[13] Luther even went so far as to apply Paul's resolve to know "nothing except Jesus Christ and him crucified" (1 Cor 2:2) to his reading of Scripture. He thus claimed to "see nothing in Scripture except Christ crucified."[14]

***

Unfortunately, Luther was far from consistent in the way he applied his cross-centered hermeneutic. For example, despite his claim to see nothing in Scripture except Christ crucified, Luther held that everything any evil agent does, including everything that Satan does, was directly caused by God. He even refers to Satan and other evil agents as "masks" of God![15] How this belief is related to Luther's claim to derive his whole theology from the cross is not clear to me.

Related to this, Luther never demonstrated how he saw "nothing except Jesus Christ and him crucified" in portraits of Yahweh commanding Israelites to mercilessly slaughter women, children and infants.

The proposal I'm presently putting forth is simply my attempt to apply Luther's cross-centered hermeneutic consistently. Since I agree with Luther that all true theology is the "wisdom of the cross," I am trying to find this cruciform wisdom in divinely inspired grissly portraits of God like the one I just mentioned.

12. A. S. Wood, *Captive to the Word: Martin Luther, Doctor of Sacred Scripture* (Carlisle, UK: Paternoster, 1969), 172–73, citing *Luthers Werke*, vol. 1, 52.
13. Wood, *Captive to the Word*, 171.
14. Ibid. citing *Luthers Werkes*, vol. 4, 153. On the significance of 1 Cor 2:2 in Luther's theology, see Tomlin, *Power of the Cross*, 176–78.
15. See H.-M. Barth, *The Theology of Martin Luther: A Critical Assessment* (Minneapolis: Fortress Press, 2013), 108–11; D. Steinmetz, *Luther in Context*, 2nd ed. (Grand Rapids: Baker Academic, 2002), 24–27. For an in-depth treatment of this aspect of Luther's thought, see *CWG*, vol. 2, ch. 13.

Looking Beyond the Surface Meaning

The second way my proposal builds upon church tradition centers on my conviction that *we should interpret the OT through the lens of the cross instead of restricting ourselves to the authors' originally intended meaning.* To many readers this will sound new, for it conflicts with the widespread conservative assumption that the only meaning a text should have for us today is the meaning that it had for the original audience.

Interestingly enough, the authors of the NT didn't share this assumption. They read the OT in the light of Christ and found meanings in passages that the original authors could not have dreamed of. For example, Matthew said that Joseph and Mary fled to Egypt to fulfill "what the Lord had said through the prophet: 'Out of Egypt I called my son'" (Matt 2:15). This is just one of the many ways Jesus "fulfilled" the OT according to the Gospels.

If you read Hosea 11:1, which Matthew is quoting, you'll see that Hosea wasn't predicting anything about the future; he wasn't even speaking about an individual person. He was referring to Israel's exodus out of Egypt.

If we insist that the only meaning a passage can have is the meaning it had for the original audience, then Matthew was grossly misinterpreting Hosea. But if we accept that God can intend passages to have meanings for later audiences that the original audience couldn't have understood, then Matthew's quote is not at all problematic. Interpreted in the light of Christ, Hosea's statement can be seen as anticipating, and thereby pointing to, Jesus's exodus from Egypt. And Matthew is making this point because his Gospel is focused on portraying Jesus as the fulfillment of all of God's plans for Israel. Something similar could be argued for the vast majority of passages that the Gospel authors claim Jesus "fulfilled."

***

Not only this, but the church always assumed that passages of Scripture can have meanings that go well beyond their plain sense. The belief that we must restrict ourselves to the original intended meaning of a passage only arose in the post-Enlightenment period (sixteenth to eighteenth centuries) when humanistic scholars began to deny that the Bible was a unique, divinely inspired book and thus began to insist that it should be interpreted the same way we interpret other ancient books.

This soon was viewed as the only academically respectable way of reading the Bible and it unfortunately became widespread throughout the church, despite the fact that the church on the whole continued to affirm that Scripture was a unique, divinely inspired book.

An increasing number of Bible scholars and theologians today contend that it was a grave mistake for the church to embrace this secular way of reading Scripture. In their view, we need to go back to reading the Bible like the unique, God-breathed book that it is, which means we need to recover the ability to discern God-intended meanings that go beyond the authors' original meaning.[16]

***

This doesn't mean the original meaning is unimportant. To the contrary, I agree with those scholars who argue that the original intended meaning of a passage should only be departed from when there are good reasons to do so.[17] While there's no clear consensus among scholars about what these "good reasons" are, I submit that if anything should justify departing from the original intended meaning of a passage, it should be when portraits of God conflict with the supreme revelation of God on the cross.

I am thus dedicated to what I call the Conservative Hermeneutical Principle, which stipulates that I must stick as close as possible to the original meaning of passages. My commitment to this principle has significant implications for my cross-centered interpretation of the OT's violent portraits of God. Among other things, while I believe the cross requires me to reject the violence that OT authors ascribed to God when he brought judgments on people, this principle nevertheless compels me to affirm every other aspect of the narratives containing these judgments.

For example, I will later argue that the supreme revelation of God in the crucified Christ requires us to conclude that the author of the biblical Flood account (Genesis 6–8) was reflecting his fallen and culturally conditioned view of God when he portrayed God as the

16. The movement of scholars arguing this is known as "The Theological Interpretation of Scripture" (TIS). For a good introduction, see D. Treier, *Introducing Theological Interpretation of Scripture: Recovering a Christian Practice* (Grand Rapids: Baker, 2008).

17. See, e.g., N. Wolterstorff, *Divine Discourse: Philosophical Reflections on the Claim That God Speaks* (Cambridge: Cambridge University Press, 1995), 130–70.

agent who caused this flood. Yet, my commitment to the Conservative Hermeneutical Principle nevertheless compels me to affirm this author's claim that a flood occurred and that it was indeed a judgment of God. I must therefore give an account of how the Flood could be a judgment of God while denying that God was the agent who brought it about. That's one of the places that you can put my thesis to the test.

***

In my view, the Conservative Hermeneutical Principle would apply to a biblical story even if historical evidence persuaded me that this particular story was not solidly anchored in actual history.[18] My belief that the OT is divinely inspired is based on the authority of Jesus Christ who endorses it, not on the manner in which any of its narratives are related to someone's version of actual history. Or, to put it another way, it is *the text* of Scripture that Jesus endorses as divinely inspired, not the relationship between the text and actual history.

For this reason, my confidence that the Bible is divinely inspired would not be adversely affected even if historical evidence convinced me that a particular story in the Bible was not historically accurate.[19] And for the same reason, I am compelled to apply the Conservative Hermeneutical Principle to all biblical narratives, regardless of the degree to which they conform, or fail to conform, to some scholar's determination of what actually took place.

***

One of the reasons this point is important is that a number of scholars believe the only way to resolve the challenge posed by the OT's violent portraits of God is by arguing that the violent judgments that are ascribed to God never happened. For example, Eric Seibert argues that, "Acknowledging that there are some things in the Bible that did

18. It is important to remember that, since no one has direct access to what happened in the past, what we call "actual history" is always a scholar's imaginative reconstruction of what they believed happened in the past. For a much fuller discussion of this perspective, see *CWG*, vol. 1, ch. 8.
19. However, my faith in Jesus, and therefore my faith in Scripture as God's word, would be completely undermined if I ever concluded that historical evidence indicates that the way *the Gospels* present Jesus was not substantially anchored in "actual history." For defenses, see footnote #5 in the previous chapter.

not happen effectively exonerates God from certain kinds of morally questionable behavior."[20]

One could certainly dispute the interpretation of the archeological evidence that Seibert cites when he argues these divine judgments aren't historical. But the more important point, in my view, is that the challenge posed by violent portraits of God remains *even if one grants Seibert's skeptical arguments*. For as I've said, Scripture derives its divine authority from Jesus, not from the degree to which it corresponds to someone's opinion about what happened in the past.

***

Along similar lines, because I consider the text to be divinely inspired, regardless of how it relates to someone's view of what actually happened, readers should know that when I refer to biblical characters and events, I am speaking of them from within the world of the inspired biblical narrative. There are numerous scholarly debates surrounding the historicity of almost all of the characters and events within the biblical narrative. But while there is certainly a place for scholars to debate these matters, I consider them irrelevant when our purpose is to study the Bible as the authoritative word of God, which is what I'm doing in this book.

The Conservative Hermeneutical Principle thus compels me to treat all biblical characters and events as *real*, for this is how they are portrayed within the world of the biblical narrative. But by treating them as such, I am not thereby attempting to weigh in on whatever historical-critical debates may surround these characters and events.

On a side note, I think it worth mentioning that this uncritical way of reading Scripture reflects the traditional way of reading Scripture prior to the earlier mentioned humanistic approach to Scripture in the post-Enlightment period.

The Relational Nature of God's Breathing

A third way my proposal builds on the church tradition concerns my cross-centered, relational conception of God's breathing. Though they haven't always thought about it consistently, theologians throughout church history have almost always assumed that God's

20. Eric A. Seibert, *Disturbing Divine Behavior: Troubling Images of God* (Minneapolis: Fortress Press, 2009), 112.

breathing of Scripture is conditioned by the medium he breathes through. Everyone acknowledged that God didn't override the distinct personalities, styles, cultural perspectives, or intellectual capabilities of the authors of Scripture that he breathed through. And the reason is because the biblical writings obviously reflect the distinctive traits of their human authors.

This alone is enough to prove that God's breathing is not a unilateral activity. He allowed these distinctive traits to condition the results of his breathing.

Most theologians have also acknowledged that, when God inspired biblical authors, he had to accommodate their cognitive limitations and cultural perspectives.[21] Here again the point is rather obvious.

For example, Paul at one point says to the Corinthians, "I thank God that I did not baptize any of you except Crispus and Gaius, so no one can say that you were baptized in my name." But he then immediately adds, "Yes, I also baptized the household of Stephanas; beyond that, I don't remember if I baptized anyone else" (1 Cor 1:15–16).

Paul admits that when he initially claimed that he hadn't baptized anyone, he forgot that he actually had baptized a number of people. Since this passage is divinely inspired, it demonstrates that God allowed Paul's cognitive limitations to condition what was written as a result of God breathing through him.

***

The relational model of God's breathing relates to the church tradition in another important way, though this also brings us to one way in which my cross-centered approach to Scripture differs sharply from the church tradition.

Throughout church history theologians have agreed that many of the portraits of God in Scripture reflect divine accommodations. And they've agreed that to the degree that any portrait is an accommodation, it reflects not the way God *actually is*, but merely the way God *appears to us*, given our limitations.

The thing is, we are only able to discern that a portrait of God is an accommodation if we know what God is like apart from any accommodation, and it is at this point that I part company with the dominant (or "classical") theological tradition. Theologians within

21. S. Brenin, *The Footprints of God: Divine Accommodation in Jewish and Christian Thought* (Albany: State University of New York Press, 1993).

the classical tradition assume that God is "above" time, "above" experiencing any kind of change, "above" being affected by anything outside himself, and "above" experiencing strong emotions or any kind of pain.[22] They thus interpret all biblical portraits of God moving with humans in time, changing his mind, being affected by what others do, or experiencing any sort of surprise, disappointment, frustration, sorrow or grief, to be accommodations.

By contrast, I believe that, from beginning to end, all of our thinking about God should be anchored in the cross. And if we anchored all our thinking in the Word who became flesh and suffered for us on Calvary, I don't believe it would ever occur to us to suspect for a moment that God is "above" time or "above" experiencing any kind of change. The Word *became* flesh! Nor would we ever suspect that God is "above" being affected by anything outside himself, or "above" experiencing strong emotions or any kind of pain. Jesus was tortured and crucified by wicked people operating under the influence of principalities and powers!

I thus see no need to interpret all biblical portraits of God moving with humans from the past into the future, changing his mind, being affected by what others do, or experiencing surprise, disappointment, frustration, sorrow or grief, to be accommodations.[23] And this, I contend, is a distinct advantage, since it's hard to find a biblical portrait of God that doesn't include one or more of these features!

***

Here is another difference. The classical tradition was mostly concerned with protecting what are called the "metaphysical" attributes of God (for example, his being "above" time and change, impervious to suffering, etc.). But if we focus our thinking about God on the crucified Christ, our concern is much more with protecting the moral

22. I place cautionary quotes around "above" to register my disagreement that the attributes classical theologians ascribed to God are actually superior to the attributes they thought God was "above." For a sampling of primary sources defending the classical view of God, going back to pre-Christian Greek philosophers (which, I contend, is where it first originated), see C. Hartshorne and W. L. Reese, *Philosophers Speak of God* (Chicago: University of Chicago Press, rpt. 1976 [1953]), 76–164. For my critique of this conception of God, see *CWG*, vol. 2, ch. 13.
23. Several defenses of this position are J. Sanders, *The God Who Risks: A Theology of Divine Providence*, 2nd ed. (Downers Grove, IL: IVP Academic, 2007); C. Pinnock, *Most Moved Mover: A Theology of God's Openness* (Grand Rapids: Baker Academic, 2001); and G. Boyd, *God of the Possible: A Biblical Introduction to the Open View of God* (Grand Rapids: Baker, 2000).

character of God, for the revelation of God on the cross is primarily a revelation of God's loving character.

This was a driving concern in the early church. For example, a third-century theologian named Novatian (c. 200–258) explained the "mediocre" way God sometimes appears in the OT by arguing that God's revelation had to be "fitted to [the Israelites'] state of belief."[24] The result was that the Israelites viewed God "not as God was, but as the people were able to understand." And from this, Novatian concluded: "God, therefore, is not mediocre, but the people's understanding is mediocre; God is not limited, but the intellectual capacity of the people's mind is limited."[25]

In this light, I trust it is clear that my claim that God allows the spiritual and intellectual condition of those he breathes through to condition the results of his breathing is not at all novel. The only novel aspect of my proposal is that I am applying this understanding to the OT's violent portraits of God as a means of protecting the moral character of God as it is revealed on the cross and to disclose how these violent portraits bear witness to the cross.

Yet, even this is not novel, since it was widespread in the early church prior to the fourth and fifth centuries.

Progressive Revelation

A fourth way my proposal builds on church tradition concerns a widely shared conviction that there is a discernible progress in God's self-revelation throughout the biblical narrative. Early on, the thinking goes, God had to relate to his people as spiritual infants. Gradually, if unevenly, God's people developed a capacity to receive clearer revelations of him, and the process finally culminated with God's fullest and clearest revelation in Christ.

To give one illustration, a fourth-century theologian, Gregory of Nazianzus (c. 329–390), argued that God needed to allow aspects of his people's fallen culture to get mixed in with his self-revelation, for otherwise they would not have been capable of receiving it. God was acting like a wise physician who needs to blend flavorful juice with

24. I should acknowledge that Novatian unfortunately got caught up in a political church schism that led to his excommunication. However, this excommunication had nothing to do with his interpretation of Scripture, which was uniformly acknowledged as sound, learned, and insightful.

25. Novatian, *De Trinitate*, 6, cited in R. Swinburne, *Revelation: From Metaphor to Analogy* (New York: Oxford University Press, 2007), 263.

his nasty-tasting medicine, otherwise his patient would not be able to stomach it.[26] As his people acclimated to the revelation they received, however, God was able to peel away more and more remnants of their fallen, culturally conditioned beliefs and practices to reveal more and more truth about himself.

Gregory argues that God first "cut off the idol" from his people, but he "left the sacrifices."[27] Although we later learn that God doesn't actually approve of animal sacrifices, God saw that his people at this time were too spiritually immature to abandon this barbaric practice. So, for a period of time, God graciously stooped to take on the appearance of a deity who enjoys, and even demands, the ritualistic killing of animals. While Yahweh was able to influence the Israelites away from the ANE assumption that gods actually eat these sacrifices, he nevertheless accommodated their culturally conditioned belief that he enjoyed their "pleasing aroma."[28]

However, when the Israelites had grown more mature, Gregory argues, God "destroyed sacrifices," but he "did not forbid circumcision" (though this too was also eventually removed). By taking incremental steps, God grew his people to the point where at least some of them were ready to be freed completely from their past paganism. Gregory sums up the process by saying God "beguiled his people into the Gospel by gradual changes."[29]

***

At its heart, my proposal is nothing more than this. As I argued in the previous chapter, I hold that God has always revealed his true character and will *as much as possible* while stooping to accommodate the fallen and culturally conditioned state of his people *as much as necessary*. In his love, God was willing to allow his people to think of him along the lines of an ANE warrior deity, to the degree this was necessary, in order to progressively influence them to the point where they

26. Gregory of Nazianzus, "Fifth Oration: On the Holy Spirit," in *Nicene and Post Nicene Fathers*, vol. 7, trans. P. Schaff and H. Wace (Grand Rapids: Eerdmans, n.d.), 326.
27. Ibid.
28. For example, Gen 8:21; Exod 29:18, 25; Lev 1:9, 13; 2:9; 4:31.
29. Nazianzus, "Fifth Oration," 326. I would argue the maturation process continues throughout the NT. For though it contains Christ-based principles that work against slavery and the subordination of women to men (Gal 3:26–29; Col 3:11), it nevertheless accommodates these fallen aspects of its surrounding culture.

eventually would be capable of receiving the truth that he is actually radically unlike these violent ANE deities.

In this sense, I could agree with Gregory and say that, by making gradual changes, God beguiled his people into the gospel, wherein it was revealed that God would rather be killed by enemies than kill them.

***

While my conception of progressive revelation is perfectly consistent with that of Gregory of Nazianzus and much of the broader church tradition, it differs from the way most Evangelicals conceive it today. To protect a particular understanding of biblical inerrancy, many Evangelicals argue that, while God's revelation progressed over time, God never needed to accommodate error.

For example, while the 1978 "Chicago Statement on Biblical Inerrancy" affirms that "God's revelation within the Holy Scriptures was progressive," it denies that later revelation "ever corrects or contradicts" earlier revelation.[30] Similarly, F. F. Bruce argues, "Divine revelation is . . . progressive, but the progression is not from the less true to the more true, from the less worthy to the more worthy, or from the less mature to the more mature."[31]

If you ask me, these folks are trying to have their cake and eat it too. If later conceptions of God in Scripture aren't "more true," "more worthy," and "more mature" than earlier ones, in what sense do the later ones progress over the earlier ones? These Evangelical scholars want to acknowledge that God's ancient people lacked clarity about God's true character but were nevertheless perfectly clear—indeed, inerrant—when it came to identifying false beliefs about God.

The trouble is, we are only able to identify false conceptions of God *as false* to the degree that we can identify true conceptions of God *as true*. So to assert that the ancient Israelites were unclear about the latter *is* to assert that they were also unclear about the former.

In this light, it's significant that the OT repeatedly emphasizes how much ancient Israelites lacked any knowledge of God's true character and will, which, again, entails that they were filled with misconceptions of God's character and will.[32] If we fully trust the

30. Article V. See http://defendinginerrancy.com/chicago-statements/ (accessed 7/21/2015).
31. F. F. Bruce, *The Epistle to the Hebrews* (Grand Rapids: Eerdmans, 1964), 2.
32. Isa 1:3; Jer 4:22; 5:4–5; 9:3–6; Hos 4:1, 6.

revelation of God in the crucified Christ, the ignorant ways ancient Israelites sometimes conceived of God become obvious, for (among other things) they ascribe violent actions and attitudes to God that blatantly contradict this revelation.

***

Even apart from this, however, consider the implications if someone insists that ancient Israelites were accurately reflecting the one true God when they ascribed violence to him. To accept this, we must believe that, while God needed to progressively reveal himself to his people in a multitude of other ways, when it came to understanding God's character vis-à-vis violence, no progress has ever been necessary! On this one point, we're supposed to believe that ancient Israelites got it absolutely right from the start!

Not only this, but since OT authors closely parallel their ANE neighbors whenever they depict Yahweh as a violent warrior, as we'll see in the following chapter, we must accept that, on the topic of God's attitude toward violence, ANE people generally had about as mature and clear an understanding as we who know God as he's revealed on the cross!

Even apart from all the reasons that were given in chapters 2 and 3 for placing our complete trust in the revelation of God in the crucified Christ, I submit that these implications are completely implausible. If any aspect of God has needed to be progressively revealed to people over time, it concerns God's nonviolent, self-sacrificial, loving character. For it is on precisely this point that the true God revealed in the crucified Christ most thoroughly *contrasts* with the way fallen humans have always tended to conceive of God and the gods, including, unfortunately, with the way most Christians have conceived God throughout history!

A Reflection on Church History

Christian theologians have always applied the concepts of divine accommodation and progressive revelation to explain a number of puzzling things in the Bible. Since the fifth century, however, these concepts have never been applied to the OT's violent portraits of God.

Which raises this interesting question: How is it that theologians since the fifth century were willing to go to extreme lengths to reinterpret major portions of Scripture as divine accommodations to protect their classical understanding of God's metaphysical attributes, but did not even consider the possibility of interpreting the violence that OT authors ascribe to God to be a divine accommodation in order to protect the cruciform character of God revealed on the cross? The answer has to do with a profound transformation that took place within the church in the fourth and fifth centuries.

Prior to this time Christians took very seriously Jesus's call to refrain from violence and to love and serve enemies.[33] But in the early fourth century, a Roman emperor named Constantine allegedly had a vision just before a major battle. This vision convinced him that he and his army would defeat their foes if he fought under the banner of Christ. This was the first (but unfortunately not the last) time the name of Jesus Christ was associated with violence.

Well, Constantine ended up enjoying a rather spectacular victory, and since pagans have always assumed that military victories go to the army with the stronger god, Constantine decided to pledge his allegiance to Christ—but Christ envisioned more along the lines of a triumphant pagan warrior deity than as a nonviolent, self-sacrificial, loving Savior.

Constantine legalized Christianity in 313 and began to shower the church with wealth and political power. In the span of less than a century, the church went from being a despised and persecuted minority to the official religion of the Roman Empire, making it illegal for everyone except Jews not to be a Christian. And since the religion of Rome had always played an important role in the running of the state, the church began to play this role.

***

The thing is, if you're going to help run an empire, you've got to be willing to use the sword. How else can you preserve law and order and protect the empire from threatening foes? So, not surprisingly, in the fourth and fifth centuries, Christian theologians like Augustine began to look for clever ways to justify the use of violence, despite Jesus and Paul's clear teachings to the contrary.

Whereas the persecuted church of the first three centuries believed

33. For discussions of this point, see *CWG*, vol. 1, ch. 1.

it was called to refrain from violence and serve the world by carrying the cross, the politically empowered church of the fourth and fifth centuries believed it was called to conquer the world for Christ, wielding the sword whenever necessary. The persecuted church became the persecuting "Church Triumphant," since it now had the political authority to persecute heretics and unbelievers. The Roman Empire was retitled the "*Holy* Roman Empire," and Christ was its triumphant emperor. Christendom was born, and while this religion has (thankfully) been dying for the last several hundred years, it has been the dominant face of Christianity for the last fifteen centuries.

Not coincidentally, as the church of Christendom arose, the reinterpretation approach to the OT's violent portraits of God quickly faded away. And the reason is obvious. As Christians acclimated to the use of violence, the OT's violent depictions of God became less problematic.

In fact, these portraits went from being problematic to being positively *advantageous*, for now Christendom's leaders could appeal to them whenever they needed to motivate Christians to engage in violence on behalf of the empire.

Tragically, this is the primary role these violent portraits have played ever since.

***

If my proposal to reinterpret Scripture's violent portraits of God strikes you as radical and novel, this is why. These portraits have been taken at face value for the last fifteen hundred years![34] But in light of the material we reviewed in chapters 2 and 3, I believe it's time to recover the long-abandoned approach of many early church leaders. And in this chapter I've tried to show that to do this, we need only apply elements that have been present in the church's theological tradition all along in a more consistent way while anchoring all of our thinking about God and the interpretation of Scripture in the cross.

***

34. There were some exceptions, the most prominent being the sixteenth-century Anabaptists. This group embraced an intensely Christocentric and cross-centered theology that led some of them to recover the early church project of exploring alternative, nonliteral, ways of interpreting violent portraits of God. Unfortunately, by the end of the sixteenth century, most Anabaptist theologians and church leaders had been martyred (by other Christians!). For more on this, see *CWG*, vol. 1, ch. 3.

Let's return for a moment to the story of my wife's encounter with a panhandler. After witnessing my wife's bizarre behavior, I have a choice to make. I can trust that my thirty-seven years of marriage tell the whole story of Shelley's kind and generous character. In this case, I must conclude that my wife's apparently cruel behavior does not tell the whole story and that *something else is going on.*

Alternatively, I can assume that nothing else is going on when Shelley appears to act cruelly, which means I am trusting that her apparent cruel behavior is telling the whole story. And in this case, I am no longer trusting that my thirty-seven years of marriage tell the whole story of Shelley's character.

We have a similar choice to make when we encounter the OT's violent portraits of God. We can trust the crucified Christ to tell the whole story of God's cruciform character, in which case we are forced to believe that *something else is going on* when God appears to act in un-Christlike ways in the OT. Alternatively, we can assume that nothing else is going on when God appears to act in un-Christlike ways, in which case we're trusting the OT's violent portraits to tell the whole story. And in this case, we are no longer trusting the cross to tell us the whole story of God's cruciform character.

This is where the church of the fourth and fifth centuries went wrong. Once it embraced the political power Constantine offered, it stopped trusting that the cross told the whole story of God's character and instead began trusting that the OT's violent portraits of God were telling the whole story. And this is why it stopped suspecting that *something else is going on* when God is depicted in these violent ways.

At its heart, this entire book could be summed up as a plea for Christians to once again place their complete trust in the cross. Dare to believe that God really is, to the core of his being, as beautiful as the cross reveals him to be. For if our faith in the crucified Christ remains resolved, we will necessarily believe that *something else is going on* when we encounter sub-Christlike portraits of God in Scripture. And we will by faith discern that this *something else* is the same thing that was going on when God breathed his full revelation on Calvary.

In both cases, God is stooping as low as necessary to bear the sin of people, thereby taking on an ugly appearance that mirrors that sin.

And interestingly enough, when we assume this cross-centered interpretation of the OT's violent divine portraits, we begin to discover a wealth of evidence that confirms its correctness, as we will see in the following chapter.

PART II

Biblical, Historical, and Ancient Cultural Support

6

The Heavenly Missionary

I once saw God, as through a window I peered;
He was just as I suspected,
just as I feared.
So selfish and cruel He appeared to be;
So very ugly,
so unlike me.
Then I looked deeper, still deeper with time;
T'was a mirror all along,
and the image was mine.
—Ty Gibson[1]

. . . you thought I was just like you.
—Yahweh (Ps 50:21)

A number of years ago an acquaintance told me about an American missionary couple he knew who, in the early 1980s, felt called to evangelize an isolated tribe in central Africa. This tribe practiced female genital mutilation (once known as "female circumcision"). In this horrific ritual, the genitalia of young women are cut and partly removed in a misguided effort to preserve their virginity and purity. In the case of this tribe, girls were typically subjected to this excruciating ordeal around the age of five.

Although this missionary couple knew ahead of time that the tribe engaged in this barbaric rite, it was emotionally devastating for them to allow young girls with whom they had bonded to be subject to it.

1. Used by permission from the author.

But they also knew they had no other choice. This ritual had been deeply imbedded in the tribe's culture for hundreds of years. The couple knew that, as new guests, they were in no position to demand that it be stopped.

So initially, they did whatever they could to make the best of a terrible situation. Among other things, they acquired anesthesia and pain medication for the girls and better surgical knives for those who performed the cutting. Beyond this, however, this couple had to remain silent as young girls suffered, and they did so for three emotionally wrenching years! Only by remaining silent as they taught and ministered to this tribe could they hope to eventually help them understand for themselves why girls should never be subjected to such cruelty.

***

In Psalms, the Lord told the Israelites that when he remained silent as they engaged in wicked behavior, "You thought I was exactly like you" (Ps 50:21). Is this not similar to the way this tribe would have interpreted the silence of these missionaries? As we saw Gregory of Nazianzus argue about the Lord's strategy in dealing with the ancient Israelites, out of their love for this tribe, this couple had to beguile the tribe by accommodating their barbaric practice. In other words, the missionaries had to be willing to appear guilty of condoning, and even assisting in, a sinful practice they actually despised if they hoped to eventually free these people from this practice.

The correct interpretation of this couple's silence and assistance became clear only after the tribe embraced the gospel and were eventually able to see for themselves that their ancient practice was contrary to God's will. Only then could they understand that this couple had been heroically accommodating their sinful practice out of love, and only then could they appreciate the depth of grief the missionaries had quietly endured for these three years.

We can think of God as a heavenly missionary to our fallen and all-too-barbaric planet. And we can think of the biblical narrative as the inspired written witness to God's missionary activity. Like the missionaries to that African tribe, God couldn't simply barge in and force people to stop practices he found offensive. Given that God created people free and thus with the potential for love, he must work by means of a loving influence rather than coercion. God has therefore always worked to reveal as much of his true character and will *as was possible* while accommodating the fallen state of his people *as much as was necessary*—though, like the missionaries in the above story, it certainly grieved God deeply to do so.

Now that we know the true character and will of God in the crucified Christ, we can look back in the inspired record of his missionary activity and discern the many ways God had to stoop to accommodate the fallen and culturally conditioned beliefs and practices of his people. So too, we can now discern the many ways in which God's ancient people mistakenly assumed he was like them. We can also understand that, every time the heavenly missionary allowed his people to view him in fallen and culturally conditioned ways, he was in a sense beguiling them.

Most importantly, since God's nonviolent, self-sacrificial, enemy-embracing love is the central theme of Jesus's cross-centered ministry, we can discern this beguiling accommodating love behind all the depictions of the heavenly missionary as a rather typical ANE warrior deity.

We will now see that when we read the God-breathed, written record of God's missionary activity in light of God's full revelation on the cross, we can find a number of things that confirm that God has always been willing to stoop as low as necessary, and to appear as pagan as necessary, to continue to develop his people and to further his missionary purposes through them. In what follows, I will review four confirming accommodations.[2]

Accommodations to God's Marriage Ideal

The first accommodation concerns God's ideal for marriage, which, from the start, was for a man and woman to become "one flesh" for life (Gen 2:22–25). Yet, according to the Genesis narrative, it wasn't long after Adam and Eve's rebellion that polygamy shows up and becomes the norm.[3] Curiously, God never once speaks out against this practice, even when leaders like Samuel, David, and Solomon acquire multiple wives (e.g., 1 Sam 1:2; 27:3).

In fact, in the course of chastising King David for his affair with Bathsheba and for murdering her husband, Yahweh tells David, "I

2. For a more extensive and in-depth exploration of passages reflecting divine accommodation, see *CWG*, vol. 2, ch. 14.

3. For example, Gen 4:23; 28:9; 30:26; 31:17, 50.

gave your master's house to you, and your master's wives into your arms. And if all this had been too little, I would have given you even more" (2 Sam 12:8). If we didn't know better, this passage would lead us to believe that Yahweh was perfectly happy with David's multiple wives. After all, Yahweh not only gave David these wives, he says he would have given him even more if David had remained obedient!

Our heavenly missionary here appears guilty of condoning the sin of polygamy, just as the missionaries in my opening story looked guilty of condoning the ritualistic mutilation of young girls. But, of course, we who read this account after the coming of Christ know how deeply God values monogamy, and this knowledge should enable us to see *what else is going on* in this passage. Behind Yahweh's guilty appearance, we should discern our heavenly missionary humbly stooping out of love to bear the sin of his people, despite the grief this certainly caused him.

Even more remarkable is that God was willing to stoop to allow men to acquire concubines, which were women who bore men's children but who were not officially married to them.[4] In the ANE, women and children who were not under the protection of men were extremely vulnerable. It thus seems that God saw that it would do more harm than good to try to enforce his ideal of restricting sex to the marriage covenant.[5]

Even with these accommodations, however, men were still divorcing their wives, leaving them in vulnerable situations. So, because the people's "hearts were hard," as Jesus said (Matt 19:8), the heavenly missionary stooped still further to allow for divorce and remarriage while putting some humane rules in place for the sake of the vulnerable women. To appreciate what a huge concession this was—and is still—we must remember that Jesus taught that remarriage technically involves adultery (Matt 5:32). So, by permitting remarriage, Yahweh was actually permitting people to break the prohibition on adultery, which is one of the Ten Commandments![6]

4. For example, 1 Sam 15:16; 20:3; 1 Kgs 11:3.
5. For two insightful discussions on the rationale behind God's concession to allow polygamy and concubines, see R. M. Davidson, *Flame of Yahweh: Sexuality in the Old Testament* (Peabody, MA: Hendrickson, 2007), 177–212, and D. Daube, "Concessions to Sinfulness in Jewish Law," *Journal of Jewish Studies* 10 (1959): 1–13.
6. J. Meier, *A Marginal Jew: Rethinking the Historical Jesus*, vol. 4, *Law and Love* (New Haven: Yale University Press, 2009), 113. It's worth noting that Jesus says that whoever divorces his wife "*makes her a victim of adultery*" (Matt 5:32, emphasis added). Jesus thus assumes that the woman will remarry, which means that he was not revoking God's accommodation of divorce and remarriage in the OT.

***

God clearly is not an inflexible legalist! If people's fallen state makes his ideal Plan A unattainable, God bends his ideal and mercifully offers them a Plan B. And if his Plan B also proves unattainable, God bends his ideal further and offers them a Plan C, and then a Plan D, and so on. And he does this despite the fact that every plan after God's Plan A "misses the mark" of his ideal, which is the biblical definition of "sin." Out of his love and compassion, our heavenly missionary has never been afraid of coming down to our level and getting his hands dirty, so to speak, by continuing to work with people in their sinful circumstances.

It's also interesting that once God decides to accommodate non-ideal circumstances, he doesn't keep reminding his people that he's doing so. To the contrary, once Yahweh decides he must stoop to accommodate polygamy, he allows his people to believe he is a rather typical ANE deity who approves of polygamy, which is why God sometimes appears this way in the inspired witness to his missionary activity. Only when we remember how important God's ideal plan for marriage is to him can we see that these polygamy-approving portraits of God actually reflect remarkable divine accommodations.

This accommodating behavior is precisely what the revelation of God's self-sacrificial, sin-bearing love on the cross would lead us to expect. As such, accommodations such as this one support interpreting the OT's violent depictions of God the same way.

Accommodating a Human King

God originally wanted to be the only king humans submitted to, and he had hoped his chosen people would model this ideal to the other nations by getting by without a human king. Unfortunately, there came a time when the Israelites grew fearful of threatening nations around them and began to clamor for the security they thought a human king would provide.

They cried out to the prophet Samuel, "We want a king . . . to be like all the other nations, with a king to lead us and to go out before us and fight our battles" (1 Sam 8:19). Yahweh told Samuel, "It is not you they have rejected, but they have rejected me as their king" (v. 7). Yahweh then had Samuel warn the Israelites about the numerous negative consequences that would happen once they embraced the institution of monarchy (vv. 10–18). But the people persisted, so Yahweh acquiesced (v. 21).

Once Yahweh decided to yield to his people's demand, the biblical narrative consistently depicts Yahweh as approving, working through and blessing Israel's kings, despite the fact that he acquiesced to this demand in anger (e.g., Hos 13:11). Even when kings screwed up badly and people regretted that they had demanded a king (1 Kgs 12:4, 12), Yahweh never said, "I told you so!" He rather kept working through the institution of kingship, almost giving the impression that it was his idea all along.

***

To appreciate the significance of this accommodation, you need to know that kings were a big deal throughout the ANE. The monarchy, which was always passed on to the king's eldest son, was at the center of the religion in all the nations surrounding Israel. Moreover, everyone believed that their nation's god elected and worked through their king. And they all believed that the fate of their nation rested with their king. If the king obeyed the wishes of their god, their national deity would bless them and help the king win battles. But if their king was disobedient, their god would punish the nation and he would lose battles.

Once God accommodates Israel's need for a human king, this is precisely what we find in the OT.[7] And in this light, it's apparent that when the Israelites demanded a king, they were at the same time asking Yahweh to function like the gods of all those other nations. So when Yahweh acquiesced to the one, he was acquiescing to the other—or at least he allowed his people to view him that way.

If God was willing to accommodate portraits of him as a rather typical ANE deity who operates through a rather typical monarchial religion and government, why should we not say the same about the OT's violent divine portraits, especially when we realize that the main role of the national deity throughout the ANE was to fight on the side of the king and to bless him and his nation with military victories if he was obedient?[8]

7. For a comprehensive discussion of the relationship between God/gods and kings in the ANE and OT, see *CWG*, vol. 2, ch. 18.
8. Pss 18:50; 20:6, 9; 144:10.

***

Does the accommodating nature of the portrait of God as Israel's warrior mean that we should simply dismiss the many biblical narratives where Yahweh fights on behalf of the king and/or of Israel? In light of my commitment to the Conservative Hermeneutical Principle, my answer to this question is *absolutely not.* I fully accept the events recounted in these narratives. The only thing that must be questioned in light of the cross is the author's violent *interpretation* of *how* God gave the king and/or Israel the victory that is credited him.

When we interpret these episodes through the looking-glass cross, we can see that *something else is going on* in the accounts of Israel's military victories (and defeats), something that the original authors could not clearly see given their cloudy understanding of God's true character and will. And this *something else* makes it clear that God never needed to engage in violence when he fought for Israel.

I'll have more to say about that later on. For now I'd simply like us to understand that the OT's many portraits of Yahweh as a king-approving deity are accommodations, and this supports interpreting the portraits of Yahweh as a violent divine warrior who fights with, and for, the king the same way.

Accommodating Animal Sacrifices

The third accommodation I'd like to discuss concerns the OT's many commands to sacrifice animals. I will admit that, as a person who has a compassionate heart toward animals, I have always been disturbed by these often detailed, gory, and cruel commands.

For instance, when a dove or young pigeon was being offered up to God in ancient Israel, the priest first had to bring it to the altar and "wring off the head and burn it on the altar." The poor bird had its head manually ripped from its body! Then its blood had to be "drained out on the side of the altar." The priest would then "remove the crop and the feathers and throw them down east of the altar where the ashes are." Following this, the priest was to "tear it open by the wings, not dividing it completely" and then "burn it on the wood" as "a burnt offering, a food offering, an aroma pleasing to the Lord" (Lev 1:14–17).

I could never do such a thing! I'd have made a lousy OT priest!

Until several years ago, I didn't know what to make of these bizarre instructions. And I especially had no clue what to make of the claim that the smell of these burning sacrifices was an "aroma pleasing to the Lord." We find this phrase all over the place in the earliest sections of the OT. But are we to believe that the God who is fully revealed in Jesus actually sanctioned this animal cruelty and enjoyed the smell of burning animal carcasses? Surely *something else is going on.*

***

The Israelites weren't the first or only people who thought God, or the gods, enjoyed the smell of animal sacrifices. It was actually a widespread view throughout the ANE. For example, in an ancient writing called *The Epic of Gilgamesh*, a guy named Utnapishtim offers a sacrifice to the gods. The text says that the "gods smelled the sweet savor" and then "crowded like flies about the sacrifice."[9] People in the ANE believed their sacrifices were feeding the gods, and it was the sweet aroma of these burning carcasses that told them it was suppertime.[10]

Thankfully, biblical authors never depict Yahweh devouring sacrifices—though the fact that Yahweh is sometimes depicted as referring to sacrifices as "my food" (Num 28:2) while sacrifices could be spoken of as "the food of your God" (Lev 21:8) may reflect a lingering echo of the standard ANE view.[11] This improvement reflects the influence of the Holy Spirit gradually weaning God's people off a deeply engrained, culturally conditioned misconception.

At the same time, it's also clear that the ancient Israelites were not ready to let go of the belief that Yahweh enjoyed their burning aroma.[12] And since God will not coerce people into having true conceptions of him, the heavenly missionary accommodated this misconception, which is why it frequently shows up in the inspired record of God's missionary activity.

Now, the very fact that everybody in the ANE sacrificed animals

9. "The Epic of Gilgamesh," in J. B. Prichard, *The Ancient Near East*, vol. 1, *An Anthology of Texts and Pictures* (Princeton: Princeton University Press, 1958), 70.
10. This belief is reflected in Deuteronomy, which mentions "the gods ate the fat of their sacrifices and drank the wine of their drink offerings" (32:38). On sacrifices as meals for the gods, see M. Smith, "Myth and Mythmaking in Canaan and Ancient Israel," in *Civilizations of the Ancient Near East*, vol. 3, ed. J. Sasson (New York: Scribner's, 1995), 2031–41.
11. See also Lev 21:6, 17, 21, 22.
12. For example, Exod 29:25, 41; Lev 1:9, 13, 17. While OT authors believed that Yahweh literally enjoyed this aroma, the phrase would eventually become a metaphor for living in a way that pleases the Lord (2 Cor 2:14–16; Eph 5:1–2).

long before the Hebrews came along proves that this practice did not originate with Yahweh. In fact, Yahweh at one point told the Israelites they were to "no longer sacrifice their sacrifices to goat demons" but were instead to sacrifice animals to him alone (Lev 17:7).[13] This suggests that the Israelites had already adopted the ANE practice of sacrificing animals to goat demons from their ANE neigbhors, so the heavenly missionary decided that having the Israelites sacrifice animals to him rather than to demons was the lesser of two evils. As we saw Gregory of Nazianzus taught in the previous chapter, God "cut off the idol, but left the sacrifices."

Yahweh thus decided to accommodate this ancient barbaric ritual as a means of increasing the Israelites' loyalty to him and to teach them some important truths. Among other things, God used these sacrifices to graphically illustrate the need for repentance and the death-consequences of breaking covenant with him. And he used this practice to prepare the way for the time when he himself would become the sacrifice that was offered up on behalf of Israel and of the whole world.

***

But the strongest confirmation of the accommodating nature of these sacrifices is that later authors make it perfectly clear that Yahweh actually despised them! "You have neither desired nor taken pleasure in sacrifices and offerings and burnt offerings and sin offerings," the author of Hebrews states (Heb 10:8). So too, in a passage that Jesus would later quote, Hosea says that Yahweh "desires mercy, and not sacrifice" (Hos 6:6).[14] And in Isaiah we read,

> I have more than enough of burnt offerings,
> of rams and the fat of fattened animals;
> I have no pleasure
> in the blood of bulls and lambs and goats. (Isa 1:11)

13. "Goat demons" were a particular class of demonic agents that many ANE people believed in and sought to appease by feeding them sacrifices.
14. See also Matt 9:13.

And a few verses later he adds,

> Stop bringing meaningless offerings!
> They have become a burden to me;
> I am weary of bearing them. (Isa 1:13)[15]

Later authors understood certain things about our heavenly missionary that earlier authors had not, one of them being that Yahweh actually is not at all pleased with the aroma of burning animal carcasses. This is the progressive nature of revelation.

This doesn't mean that the earlier mistaken depictions of Yahweh commanding animal sacrifices and enjoying their aroma were not God-breathed. It simply means that in breathing these depictions, God had to stoop to accommodate the fallen and culturally conditioned views and practices of his people at the time. These depictions thus stand within the inspired record of God's missionary activity as literary testaments to the fact that God has always been a noncoercive God who is willing to stoop to embrace his people as they are and to therefore bear their sin.

***

In the above cited passage from Isaiah, Yahweh confesses that he is "weary of bearing" these "meaningless offerings." A number of other passages also reflect the grief and pain Yahweh endured as he bore the sin of his people.[16] Isaiah even likens it to the pain of a woman giving birth (Isa 42:14).

To appreciate the depth of God's pain in accommodating this barbaric practice, it's important to know that throughout the Bible God demonstrates a profound love and concern for animals.[17] God even includes animals in his covenants (e.g., Hos 2:18). Yet, because God refuses to lobotomize people, he had to be willing to suffer and let his people go on believing that he demanded and enjoyed the butchery of animals, just as other ANE deities did.

***

15. See also Mic 6:6–8.
16. On God's willingness to bear sins in the OT, see Isa 43:24; Jer 15:6; Ezek 24:12; Mal 2:17. On the pain of God's sin-bearing, see T. Fretheim, *The Suffering of God: An Old Testament Perspective* (Philadelphia: Fortress Press, 1984), 14.
17. See S. Webb, *On God and Dogs: A Christian Theology of Compassion for Animals* (Oxford: Oxford University Press, 2002).

The sacrificial system, together with its sacrifice-demanding portrait of God, represents a significant portion of the OT. So the fact that the whole thing is a clear accommodation on God's part gives us some indication of how important and pervasive God's accommodating activity was in the OT. And this, I contend, lends further weight to the claim that the violent depictions of God in the OT should also be interpreted as divine accommodations.

Not only this, but if we have reason to conclude that the commands to slaughter animals as an act of worship were accommodations, how much more reason do we have to conclude that the commands to slaughter humans as an act of worship were divine accommodations? And if God experienced pain bearing the sin of animals being sacrificed to him, how much unimaginably greater must the pain have been that God experienced as humans were sacrificed to him? For just as later prophets made it unmistakably clear that Yahweh never actually wanted animals killed, Jesus made it unmistakably clear that Yahweh never actually wanted humans killed.

Indeed, as we've seen, the call to reflect the Father's character by refusing to strike back and by loving enemies is Jesus's precondition for being considered a child of the Father (Matt 5:44–45)!

Accommodating the Law

Finally, it's not just the laws regarding animal sacrifices that reflect a divine accommodation. We have compelling reasons to interpret the entire Mosaic law, together with the law-oriented portrait of God it presupposes, to be an accommodation. First, the very fact that, with the exception of the Ten Commandments, all these laws were only given in response to the Israelites' unfaithfulness while Moses was away on top of Mt. Sinai indicates that they are divine accommodations.[18]

Even the Ten Commandments reflect highly accommodating elements, however. For example, they reflect the common ANE assumption that women are the property of men. Men are told not to covet a neighbor's wife, nor his house or male or female servant, nor his ox or donkey, or anything that belongs to their neighbor (Exod 20:17). In other words, men can't covet their neighbor's wives

18. J. Sailhammer, *The Pentateuch as Narrative: A Biblical-Theological Commentary* (Grand Rapids: Zondervan, 1992), 44–67.

because they are *his neighbor's property*, which is why there's no similar prohibition on wives coveting husbands.

While God obviously is opposed to all forms of coveting, the patriarchal manner in which this opposition is expressed clearly reflects a high degree of cultural conditioning that our noncoercive heavenly missionary had to stoop to accommodate.

Second, the author of Hebrews tells us that God did not desire, and was not pleased with, the animal sacrifices in the OT "though they were offered *in accordance with the law*" (10:8, emphasis added). This one sentence is enough to prove that there were aspects of the law that didn't please God but rather reflect him adjusting his will to the fallen state of his people. As we saw above, Jesus says this about the law that permitted divorce and remarriage (Matt 19:8–9), and the same can be said of a multitude of other laws. They "reflect God's accommodation to the 'hardness' of human hearts, rather than God's actual desire for how his people would live in the world."[19]

***

But the most important indication that the law was an accommodation on God's part comes from the apostle Paul. Yahweh had promised Abraham that his offspring would be blessed (Gen 12:7) and Paul interpreted this to refer to "one person, who is Christ" (Gal 3:16). In recording this promise, Paul says, "Scripture foresaw that God would justify the Gentiles by faith" (Gal 3:8). For everyone who has faith as Abraham did, whether they are Jew or Gentile, is placed in Christ and is thereby made a spiritual descendant of Abraham. That is, they are incorporated into Abraham's "seed."[20] This is why Paul refers to all Christians, whether Jew or Gentile, as the true descendants of Abraham and the true "Israel of God" (Gal 6:16).

Now, if Scripture foresaw that people would be rightly related to God on the basis of faith, apart from the law, why then was the law given? Paul says that a primary reason was that God's people first needed to be "kept in custody" and "locked up" under the law before we would be ready to receive "the faith that was later to be revealed" (Gal 3:23). In this sense the law functioned as a "guardian" to "lead us to Christ" so that "we might be justified by faith" (v. 24, NASB).

19. J. Goldingay, *Theological Diversity and the Authority of the Old Testament* (Grand Rapids: Eerdmans, 1987), 155–56.

20. Gal 3:29; Eph 3:6.

Paul also stresses that no one can be made righteous before God—which means to be rightly related to God—on the basis of the law.[21] In fact, while the law is "good" in-and-of itself, Paul says that our fallen nature is such that the law only serves to increase our sin and condemn us![22] Paul is thus teaching that the spiritual state of God's people in the OT was such that God first needed to demonstrate how people *cannot* be rightly related to him—namely, by perfectly complying with the law—before he could reveal the only way people *can* be rightly related to him, which is by faith in Christ.

***

The provisional nature of the law is further reflected by Paul as well as the author of Hebrews when they teach that the law was a mere "shadow of the things that were to come," for "the reality . . . is found in Christ."[23] In the progress of revelation, people apparently needed to first be introduced to the "shadow" before they could be ready to experience "the reality." Now that "the reality" of Christ has come, however, we can see that there was something "wrong with the first covenant" (Heb 8:7) and that it must now be considered "obsolete" (v. 13).

If we had only the OT to go on, I seriously doubt anyone would get the impression that Yahweh gave the law for the purpose of proving it couldn't work. If anything, the hundreds of passages in which God commands compliance with the law as well as the dozens of passages, especially in the Psalms, that celebrate the law give the *opposite* impression. People were supposed to place their hope in Yahweh's laws (Ps 119:43).[24]

Yes, there are *hints* here and there that *something else is going on*, as when Ezekiel and Jeremiah express an awareness that a better covenant is coming.[25] But the general impression is that complying with the law is the means by which people can be rightly related to Yahweh. Yet, with the coming of Christ, Paul could look back and discern that *something else was going on*: the law was a provisional accommodation that served to put us in custody and lead us to Christ.

21. Gal 2:16; 3:11; 5:4.
22. Rom 5:20; 7:5, 8–9; 1 Cor 15:56.
23. Col 2:16; Heb 10:1.
24. See also Pss 1:2; 19:7; 119:1, 43, 70, 77, 92, 174.
25. Jeremiah 32; Ezekiel 36.

***

We can take this line of thinking a step further by noticing that the depictions of the law as the means to be rightly related to God are inextricably bound up with the portrait of God as a deity who promises to save or destroy people based on whether or not they comply with the law. So, if there was something wrong with the law-centered covenant, it follows that there was something wrong with the law-oriented portrait of God that this covenant presupposes.

So too, if the law was given to ultimately demonstrate that people can't be rightly related to God on this basis, doesn't it follow that the portrait of God as a law-oriented deity was also adopted to ultimately demonstrate the futility of trying to be rightly related to such a deity? And if the law was a mere "shadow" that is rendered "obsolete" once "the reality" of Christ appears, doesn't it follow that the law-oriented portrait of God was a mere "shadow" that was rendered "obsolete" once the real character of God was fully revealed in Christ?

It thus seems that Paul's teaching on the law demonstrates that the law-oriented portrait of God, which constitutes a foundational aspect of the OT, is a divine accommodation. And God stooped to allow his people to view him like this, and to try to relate to him on this basis, only as a loving means of eventually demonstrating to Israel, and therefore to the world, that *no one can ever be rightly related to this sort of deity*.

Moreover, God needed to demonstrate the futility of this false conception so that, "at just the right time" (Rom 5:6), he could reveal the only kind of God that anyone *can* ever be rightly related to. And this, of course, is the unfathomably gracious God who gave his life on Calvary to reconcile all sinners back to himself and who now motivates people to live according to his will by giving his Spirit to all who simply trust him, the way Abraham did.

No wonder John contrasted the "law" that "was given through Moses" with the "grace and *truth*" that "came through Jesus Christ" (John 1:17, emphasis added).

At the same time, if we interpret the law-oriented depictions of God through the looking-glass cross, we will find in their depths the same grace and truth that was revealed in the crucified Christ. For these sub-Christlike portraits bear witness to the glorious truth that God has always been stooping to bear the sin of his people and to thereby take on ugly appearances that reflect the ugliness of this sin.

Which is precisely what God does on Calvary.

***

The fact that something as foundational to the OT as the law-oriented portrait of God was an accommodation reinforces our conviction that accommodating sin was a foundational aspect of the heavenly missionary's strategy in the OT. And this provides further support for my claim that this is what God was up to when he allowed himself to be depicted as a violent ANE warrior deity in the written witness to his missionary activity.

If further confirmation is needed, consider the fact that a number of the law-oriented portraits of God are themselves violent portraits of God! For example, in chapter 1 we reviewed laws, presumably given by God, requiring the execution of various sorts of criminals, including fornicators, homosexuals, and children who were stubborn, lazy, gluttonous, or who struck their parents.[26]

Then there's that strange law, presumably given by God, that stipulates that if a wife grabs another man's genitals in the process of defending her husband against him, people are to "show her no pity" and "cut off her hand," regardless of whether she did so intentionally or accidentally (Deut 25:11–12)! Can you imagine Jesus uttering such an atrocious command?

If violent and otherwise dubious laws such as these are provisional accommodations, it follows that the portraits of God giving these laws are provisional accommodations as well.

Assessing These Accommodations

Let me at this point address a possible objection. Some have argued that the four accommodations discussed in this chapter do not merely reflect God accommodating his people's fallen and culturally conditioned views of him. They rather reflect accommodating behaviors that God actually engaged in.[27] In this view, for example, God didn't merely stoop to accommodate his people's culturally conditioned

26. Deut 21:18–21; Exod 21:15, 17; Lev 20:9.

27. P. Copan, *Is God a Moral Monster?: Making Sense of the Old Testament God* (Grand Rapids: Baker, 2011); D. Lamb, *God Behaving Badly: Is the God of the Old Testament Angry, Sexist and Racist?* (Downers Grove, IL: InterVarsity, 2011); A. Thompson, *Who's Afraid of the Old Testament God?*, 4th rev. ed. (Gonzalez, FL: Pacesetters Bible School, 2003).

view of him as capable of giving remarkably violent laws. God actually stooped to giving these violent laws.

I can agree with this perspective up to the point that the accommodating activity ascribed to God does not conflict with the self-sacrificial, nonviolent, enemy-embracing love of God revealed in the crucified Christ. But insofar as any divine portrait is not consistent with this revelation, fidelity to Christ compels me to see it not as an accurate depiction of something God actually did, but as a reflection of something God's people at the time assumed God did.

To this degree, it doesn't reflect God acting toward people; it rather reflects God humbly stooping to allow the fallen and culturally conditioned state of his people to *act upon him*. To the extent that any portrait conflicts with the crucified Christ, in other words, I must assess it as an *indirect*, rather than a *direct*, revelation.

To be more specific, I do not in principle have a problem accepting that God actually stooped to play the roles that are ascribed to him surrounding the accommodations of polygamy, concubines, divorce and remarriage, as well as the institution of monarchy.[28] However, when it comes to assessing the 613 laws that pertain to the first covenant, including commands to perform animal sacrifices and to execute certain types of people, things get more complex and ambiguous. We would actually need to assess each law individually, which obviously is beyond the scope of this book.

So let us settle on this guiding principle: Insofar as any law reflects an improvement over the prevailing laws of the ANE, I submit that it reflects God *acting toward* his people. As barbaric as many of the OT laws are, most reflect an improvement, and sometimes a significant improvement, over the laws of Israel's neighbors, and this surely is the result of the influential work of God's Spirit. But insofar as any law falls short of the character of God revealed in Jesus's cross-centered ministry, it reflects the point at which the fallen and cultur-

28. I say "in principle" because some of the particular things ascribed to God in the narratives that reflect these accommodations must be assessed as *indirect* revelations. For example, when the author of 2 Samuel depicts Yahweh as giving Saul's wives to David and then telling David he was going to take his wives and give them to another man who would rape them "in broad daylight" (2 Sam 12:8, 11), fidelity to Christ requires me to conclude that this reflects the author's own fallen *interpretation* of how Yahweh was involved in this judgment. If we see Jesus, we see the Father (John 14:7–9), and I can't imagine Jesus giving a group of wives to someone to be raped in front of others as a means of punishing their husband! But with this qualification, I *in principle* see nothing inherently un-Christlike about God bending his ideals to meet people where they are, especially when insisting on his ideal for marriage would harm vulnerable people, as we saw was the case with his ideal for marriage.

ally conditioned state of his people resisted the Spirit and, therefore, the point at which God stooped to allow his people to *act upon him*. In my view, all portraits of God in the Bible should be assessed by this criterion.

While there is ambiguity and complexity surrounding the particulars, what is most important for our purposes is perfectly clear: insofar as any law or any activity that is ascribed to God involves violence against humans or animals, it must to this degree be considered an accommodating, sin-mirroring portrait that indirectly bears witness to the sin-bearing God revealed on Calvary. It may yet reflect God's positive influence inasmuch as it improves over similar but even more violent laws found among Israel's neighbors. But insofar as it is sub-Christlike, it must be assessed to be a divine accommodation.

***

In this chapter I've reviewed the prevalence of our heavenly missionary's sin-bearing activity throughout the OT in regard to his divine accommodations for marriage, Israel's monarchy, animal sacrifices, and the OT law. I've argued that these accommodations lend credibility to the claim that we ought to interpret the OT's violent divine portraits as reflecting the same sin-bearing activity of our heavenly missionary. But these four examples are actually just the tip of an iceberg of evidence supporting the looking-glass interpretation of the OT's violent divine portraits. In the following chapter, for example, we'll explore the biblical teaching that the way people experience God often says more about them than it does about God.

7

Rorschach God

God created man in his own image,
And man, being a gentleman, returned the favor.
—Author Unknown

I pulled my battered twelve-year-old Toyota Corolla into the parking lot of the university where I was scheduled to deliver a speech. I had bought this vehicle two years earlier for $1850, and while I admit it wasn't much to look at, it was reliable, which is the only thing I care about when it comes to cars.

I had pulled into the first available space and only then noticed that I had parked just to the right of an unusual, low-to-the-ground, expensive-looking bright yellow sports car. I had no idea what kind of sports car it was because, as I just indicated, I have never been the least bit interested in anything having to do with cars. But as ignorant as I am about such matters, even I could tell that this was a posh vehicle!

In a moment, I would learn that it was a Lamborghini, which I had never heard of before. I have since learned it is a *very* expensive vehicle.

As I unbuckled my seatbelt I noticed a rather petite gray-haired man sitting behind the steering wheel of this vehicle. Then I noticed that he was staring at me with an intense frown. For a moment I wondered if I had done something wrong. Nothing came to mind, so I pretended not to notice his frown and greeted him with an awkward smile and a quick, sheepish wave.

As I cracked my door open, I noticed there wasn't much space between our cars—which probably explains the drivers irritated look. I was therefore very careful as I opened my door and slowly squeezed my body out of my car. But just as I was shutting the door behind me, this guy bolted out of his car and started screaming at me from the driver's side of his car. "I knew it, I knew it, I *knew it*!," he yelled in a high-pitched voice.

I stared at him in stunned silence.

"As soon as you pulled up next to me in that shit-mobile of yours," he yelled, "I said to myself, 'He's going to nick my car, he's *going to nick my car*!' And you did! *You did*! I f**king knew it!"

"Sir," I said, "I am certain I did *not* nick your car."

"Liar!" the fellow exploded. "F**king liar!"

I tried to reply, but this guy continued screaming as he began making his way over to me. "I heard your door hit mine. I *heard it*, you f**king liar!" he repeated. He planted himself a foot away from me and pointed his finger up to my nose as he shouted, "And you did this *on purpose*!"

The accusation left me dumbfounded. I could not fathom how anyone could suspect that someone would nick another person's expensive car on purpose. But this irate guy quickly answered my question.

"Admit it," he yelled in his squeaky voice. "You're a f**king loser who has to drive around in that pathetic piece of shit, and pulling up next to a Lamborghini is just too much for you to handle, isn't it?"

"What is a lamber genie?" I asked. My question was sincere. I honestly wasn't even sure he was referring to the model of a car. It sounded to me like he was referencing an Italian pasta dish or something. But this poor fellow clearly thought my question was meant to mock him, and he was furious.

It probably didn't help that the idea that this guy suspected me of intentionally nicking his car out of jealousy was starting to make me giggle. He crossed his arms in disbelief, and his face was so red and intense it looked like it was going to pop.

A simple solution to our dispute suddenly occurred to me. I slowly opened my car door to the point where it would have made contact with his car. "Sir," I said as I pointed to this spot, "as you can see, there is no scratch."

The man quickly adjusted his oversized glasses, bent down to within two inches of his car and studied the area in question. After a moment, and to my great surprise, he began to enthusiastically nod his head up and down as as he exclaimed, "Yep, Yep. There it is! I knew it! There it is!" In utter disbelief I bent down as close to his car as he had been and studied the same area. I'm telling you, there was absolutely no trace of a scratch or dent or anything!

I honestly didn't mean to be offensive, but the surrealistic turn this encounter had just taken made suppressing laughter impossible. "Please, show me the scratch," I said between laughs.

"You think this is funny," he erupted. "You lying f**king a**hole!" I tried to apologize for laughing, but he was far too disturbed to notice. "Let's see how much you laugh when I sue your ass in court!" He then abruptly turned around and briskly walked back to the driver's side of his car. Then, just as he was about to lower himself into his vehicular treasure, he took a deep breath, pointed his finger at me one last time, and with a tone that reminded me of an angry first-grader, he said: "It's not worth my time to go after the likes of you—a loser who couldn't possibly pay for these damages anyway."

With that closing statement he revved his motor loudly, quickly pulled out of his parking space and screeched his tires as he bolted away. I laughed again as it occurred to me that this display of power was probably intended to further intensify my alleged car envy.

***

This bizarre encounter is a textbook illustration of what psychiatrists call *projection*. It happens when people project their desires, fears, motives, and expectations onto other people and/or their circumstances. This man "heard" the nick he fearfully expected to hear and he "saw" the nick he expected to see. Not only that, but his tirade made it clear that *he* would feel like a "loser" and would enviously want to damage expensive cars out of jealousy if he had to drive an old and battered car like mine. So, he naturally assumed the same was true of me.

His accusations revealed a whole lot more about him than they did me. I honestly wouldn't drive a car like that even if I could afford it. Among other things, I might start worrying that someone might scratch or dent it, and I would never want my brain to be occupied with something so trivial! Much better to drive around carefree in an already-battered twelve-year-old Corolla!

Which brings me to Hermann Rorschach, who in 1921 established a brilliant way to evaluate people's mental health. He had people stare at ambiguously shaped inkblots and report what they saw. These "Rorschach tests" are premised on the established truth that, to one degree or another, everyone projects their desires, fears, motives, and expectations onto others. We all tend to interpret what we see and hear through a grid of what we want or expect to see and hear. And as was the case with the irate Lamborghini driver I encountered, often what a person thinks they see and hear says a lot more about them than it does about what they actually saw and heard.

If this is true of our relationship with other people, it is even truer of our relationship with God.

Seeing What Our Heart Allows Us to See

As we have several times noted, Jesus taught that all Scripture is about him and that he is the life of Scripture (John 5:39–40). Curiously enough, Jesus immediately went on to tell the Pharisees that they were incapable of accepting this truth, despite the fact that they studied Scripture diligently. And the reason, Jesus said, is because they did "not have the love of God in [their] hearts" (John 5:42).

Clearly, discerning how all Scripture points to Jesus requires more than diligent study. Jesus is the perfect revelation of God's love, and only those who have a heart to embrace and trust this love will be able to discern how it is reflected in all Scripture.

Along similar lines, because the Pharisees were constantly confused by Jesus, he at one point asked them, "Why is my language not clear to you?" He immediately answered his own question, saying, "Because you are unable to hear (*akouein*) what I say" (John 8:43).

Now, Jesus obviously wasn't saying that the Pharisees were deaf. Rather, Jesus was pointing out that these religious leaders were "unable to grasp his outward speech."[1] As Jesus elsewhere taught, when "people's hearts become calloused . . . they hardly hear with their ears, and they have closed eyes" (Matt 13:15).

***

Jesus's own disciples illustrate the truth of this teaching. At one point Jesus said, "Destroy this temple, and I will raise it again in three days." John tells us that the people thought he was talking about the tem-

1. See D. Carson, *The Gospel According to John*, PNTC (Grand Rapids: Eerdmans, 1991), 353.

ple in Jerusalem, but he was actually referring to his own body. Then John adds, "After he was raised from the dead, his disciples recalled what he had said. Then they believed the scripture and the words that Jesus had spoken" (John 2:19–22).

Only *after* Jesus's resurrection did the disciples believe that he fulfilled all Scripture or the words he had spoken. See, like most Jews of the time, Jesus's disciples expected a victorious military messiah. So when Jesus started talking about his need to go to Jerusalem to be arrested, beaten, and killed, it went in one ear and out the other.

Peter once objected to this sort of talk, but even he clearly forgot about it (Matt 16: 21–22). For when Jesus was arrested, beaten, and killed, just as he had said, they were totally shocked! And when Jesus rose from the dead, just as he had said, they were initially even more shocked! Only when the dust had settled and their eyes had been opened could they recall that Jesus had been telling them this all along.

What people see and hear is strongly conditioned by what they expect to see and hear.

Along the same lines, people are only able to receive the truth about God to the degree that their innermost hearts are aligned with his character. The good news is that John proclaims that when Christ appears, "we shall be like him, for *we shall see him as he is*," which is why "all who have this hope in him purify themselves, just as he is pure" (1 John 3:2, emphasis added). While all who are in Christ have had the veil over our minds "taken away" and can therefore "contemplate the Lord's glory" (2 Cor 3:14, 18), we still "see only a reflection as in a mirror" (1 Cor 13:12). But when the process of our transformation into Christlikeness is completed, we will finally have the capacity to grasp Christ in all his beauty. And it is only because "we shall be like him," that we will finally be able to "see him as he is."

***

In this light, it is significant that the Bible repeatedly stresses that the Israelites were a stiff-necked people who continually resisted the Spirit and broke God's heart.[2] This goes a long way toward explaining why they could only grasp glimpses of God's true character and

2. Exod 32:9; 33:3, 5; Deut 9:6; 31:27; Isa 5:1–5; Isa 46:12; 48:4; 66:4; Jer 3:17; 5:23; 7:23; 9:14; 19:15; Pss 78:8; 81:10–11; Neh 9:17, 29; Amos 4:6–11; Zech 7:11; Acts 7:51; Rom 10:21; Heb 3:8.

will. In fact, some prophets went so far as to declare that the Israelites lacked all knowledge of God and that even their leaders didn't know God![3]

Keep these verses in mind as you reflect on the significance of the following curious passage from a song of David to the Lord.

> To the faithful you show yourself faithful,
> to the blameless you show yourself blameless,
> to the pure you show yourself pure,
> but to the devious you show yourself shrewd.[4]

The Hebrew word for devious is *iqqesh*, and it is sometimes translated as "crooked" or "perverted." The Hebrew word for shrewd is *pathal*, and it is sometimes translated as "torturous" or "deceptive." Most importantly, both words have the connotation of something being *twisted*. This author is thus teaching that God appears faithful, blameless, and pure insofar as people's hearts and minds are faithful, blameless, and pure. But God appears in twisted ways insofar as people's hearts and minds are twisted.

We might say that, as is true of Rorschach tests, the way God appears to people says at least as much about *them* as it does about *God*. Insofar as God's noncoercive Spirit can break through the hearts and minds of people—insofar as these hearts are inclined in the direction of faithfulness, blamelessness, and purity—God can reveal himself as he truly is. But insofar as people have twisted hearts and minds that suppress God's Spirit, they inevitably understand and experience God in ways that reflect their own twisted hearts and minds.

Making God in Our Own Image

It's been said that "God created man in his own image, and man, being a gentleman, returned the favor." Whoever was the original author of this slogan, it's absolutely true! People have always tended to assume that God/the gods were just like them.

For example, throughout history men have craved power to rule over others, or to at least keep others from ruling over them. And since men have almost always controlled religious matters, it's no

3. Hos 4:1, 6; Isa 3:12; 5:12–13; Jer 2:8.
4. 2 Sam 22:26–27; cf. Ps 8:25–26.

coincidence that people have tended to assume that the power to rule over others was a defining attribute of God/gods.

When Paul instead defines the power of God as the self-sacrificial love revealed on the weak-looking cross (1 Cor 1:18, 30), you know this message had to be from God because it's not the kind of thing humans would ever make up on their own! In fact, it flatly contradicts the kind of coercive power people have typically ascribed to God/gods throughout history—including, unfortunately, throughout most of church history.

Now, since we know that God's people in OT times were generally stubborn, had no real knowledge of God, and tended to make God in their own twisted image, should we be surprised to find God sometimes being depicted in twisted ways in the God-breathed record of his missionary activity? To the contrary, I think we should be surprised that we find so many depictions that aren't twisted, as assessed by the criterion of the crucified Christ. Each one reflects the Spirit of Christ breaking through the Israelites' fallen and culturally conditioned hearts to reveal God's true, cruciform character!

***

To appreciate just how twisted the ancient Israelites' mental image of God could be, consider a passage I had not noticed until I began reading Scripture through the looking-glass cross. In the course of trying to get Pharaoh to let the Israelites go, Aaron makes this curious offhanded remark: "The God of the Hebrews has met with us. Now let us take a three-day journey into the wilderness to offer sacrifices to the Lord our God, *or he may strike us with plagues or with the sword*" (Exod 5:3, emphasis added).

There is no record of Yahweh threatening Moses and Aaron in this bizarre way. Nor is it clear why Moses and Aaron requested only a three-day furlough into the desert to worship Yahweh when Yahweh had told them he wanted his people out of Egypt permanently. Just as unclear is the reason Moses and Aaron thought they had to take the people into the desert to make sacrifices to Yahweh.

What is clear, however, is that these two believed that Yahweh had placed the burden of convincing Pharaoh *on them*. They believed that if they failed to convince Pharaoh, Yahweh would strike them (and perhaps all Israelites) down with "plagues or with the sword."

Talk about putting pressure on your sales reps!

Somewhere in the communication lines between Yahweh, on the one hand, and Moses and Aaron, on the other, something got a little twisted.

Honestly ask yourself: Who bears a closer resemblance to this portrait of God: Jesus Christ, or Al Capone?! The answer is obvious. Significantly enough, we don't have to look far to see where Moses and Aaron got this Al Capone version of Yahweh, for throughout the ANE we find people ascribing Al Capone-like threats to various gods.

But we can be thankful that this twisted and culturally conditioned portrait of God is retained in the written record of our heavenly missionary's activities, for it testifies to just how low God had to be willing to stoop to continue to further his purposes for history through this people. *This* is how God's stiff-necked and spiritually twisted people were inclined to view him! And since God refuses to lobotomize people into possessing accurate mental images of him, he had to be willing to leave these twisted images in place when he stooped to breathe the biblical narrative through them.

Which is to say, God had to be willing to bear the sin of these twisted conceptions of him and to therefore take on a twisted appearance in the inspired written witness to his missionary activity.

Adjustments from God's Side

So far we've seen that the way people experience and understand God is affected by their spiritual condition. But the way people experience and understand God can also be affected from God's side. Scripture indicates that, out of love for his people, God doesn't reveal more of himself than his people can handle.

The most famous example of this takes place when Moses asked the Lord to show him his glory (Exod 33:18). The Lord replied that he would "cause all [his] goodness to pass in front of [Moses]," telling him that he would "proclaim [his] name" in his presence. But, the Lord added, "You cannot see my face, for no one may see me and live" (vv. 19–20). And then, most interestingly, the Lord tells Moses: "When my glory passes by, I will put you in a cleft in the rock and cover you with my hand until I have passed by. Then I will remove my hand and you will see my back; but my face must not be seen" (vv. 21–23).

For the sake of Moses, God adjusted how much of his glory he revealed. Despite the fact that Moses is said to have had a face-to-face relationship with Yahweh (Exod 33:11), even he needed to be shielded in the cleft of a rock, and even he was only able to see God's back, not his full glory.[5]

We don't know how Yahweh appeared when he met with Moses face-to-face, but it clearly was an appearance that concealed some of his glory, for otherwise Moses wouldn't have survived the encounter. Only when God's glory became fully embodied in the person of Jesus Christ, who is the very "radiance of God's glory," could humans behold God's glory and live.[6] And, as we have seen, this glory turned out to be nothing other than the radiance of God's self-sacrificial love that was most perfectly displayed on the cross (John 12:27–33).

***

God's willingness to adjust his revelation to the low spiritual condition of people is reflected in a number of other ways in Scripture as well. For example, Jesus told his disciples that, while he had more to say to them, it would have to wait because they already had "more than [they] can now bear" (John 16:12). When they were ready, Jesus said, the Holy Spirit would come and "guide [them] into all truth" (v. 16).

Also, Jesus spoke in parables to the masses, only giving them "as much as they could understand." But when he was alone with his disciples who had a greater capacity to receive it, "he explained everything" (Mark 4:33–34). Reflecting this same point, Paul as well as the author of Hebrews distinguished between easily digestible teachings ("milk") that were appropriate for spiritual babes, and harder-to-digest teachings ("meat") that were appropriate only for those who were spiritually more mature (1 Cor 3:1–2; Heb 5:11–14).

So the way people experience and understand God is conditioned both by the spiritual condition of their heart and by how much God withholds for their own good. And in light of what we know about

5. According to many scholars, this passage, along with a number of others like it, suggests that ancient Israelites shared the common ANE assumption that God/gods possessed a sort of body that could be made visible to people. If this is correct, we must consider this aspect of the narrative to reflect an accommodation on God's part since Jesus taught that "God is Spirit" (John 4:24). True, God often *made himself* visible *in* a human form, but this is quite different from the ANE conception of gods *having* a body that they could make visible. On the ANE and (in some passages) biblical view, see B. Sommer, *The Bodies of God in the World of Ancient Israel* (New York: Cambridge University Press, 2009).

6. John 1:14, 18; Heb 1:3.

the sad spiritual condition of the ancient Israelites, this goes a long way in explaining why many portraits of God in the OT tell us more about them than they do about the true character of God.

Reflections of the Anti-Violent God

The material we've covered thus far supports the looking-glass interpretation of violent divine portraits by bearing witness to God's willingness to accommodate the fallen and culturally conditioned state of his people as much as necessary. But there is also an abundance of material in the OT that bears witness to the Spirit of Christ breaking through and revealing the same nonviolent character and will of God that we find in Jesus's cross-oriented ministry.

One of the grandest expressions of God's true, peace-loving character comes through in Isaiah 11. Here we find God dreaming of a time when his creation will be entirely free of violence. "The wolf will live with the lamb," Isaiah prophesies, and "the leopard will lie down with the goat." So it will be with "the calf . . . the lion and the yearling," and he adds that "a little child will lead them" (v. 6). In that day, he continues, predators and their prey will eat and sleep alongside one another, for there will no longer be any carnivores. Even "the lion will eat straw like the ox" (v. 7). In the end, there will be no fear between humans and animals, not even between young children and cobras (v. 8). For neither humans nor animals will be violent when God's dream for creation is realized, for "the earth will be filled with the knowledge of the Lord as the waters cover the sea" (v. 9).

This magnificent vision of the future reflects God's original vision for creation, according to the Genesis 1 account. God told the first couple that he had given them "every seed-bearing plant on the face of the whole earth and every tree that has fruit with seed in it . . . for food" (Gen 1:29). And he adds: "And to all the beasts of the earth and all the birds in the sky and all the creatures that move along the ground—*everything* that has the breath of life in it—I give *every green plant for food*" (Gen 1:29–30, emphasis added). In other words, in God's original ideal for creation, no animal was to be food for another animal or for humans.

This passage makes it clear that God's original plan was for the whole creation to be free of violence. This means that all violence among humans and within the animal kingdom is the result of something gone wrong.[7] And, as the passage from Isaiah makes clear, what is currently wrong is that our world is no longer "filled with the knowledge of the Lord" (Isa 11:9).

This means that, *whenever* there is violence in God's creation, it is an indication that the true knowledge of the Lord is absent. *That* surely is significant as we consider Scripture's violent portraits of God.

***

We can see the Spirit of Christ breaking through to reveal God's true nonviolent character in many other passages as well. For example, through Micah, the Lord expresses his dream that someday people "will beat their swords into plowshares and their spears into pruning hooks. Nation will not take up sword against nation, nor will they train for war anymore."[8]

When humanity is once again "filled with the knowledge of the Lord," instruments of death will be transformed into instruments that support life, and people will no longer even be worried about the possibility of war.

We find the Spirit breaking through as well when the Psalmist declares that God

> . . . makes wars cease
> to the ends of the earth.
> He breaks the bow and shatters the spear;
> he burns the shields with fire. (Ps 46:9)

Though some Psalms reflect twisted and culturally conditioned violent conceptions of God, we here see the Spirit of Christ breaking through to turn the warrior image of God on its head. God is indeed a heavenly warrior, but he is a warrior who "fights for peace."[9] God is

7. Since we know that violence has permeated the animal kingdom since the Early Cambrian explosion some 540 million years ago, we obviously can't appeal to the rebellion of Adam and Eve (however literally or figuratively they are understood) to explain what went wrong. I have elsewhere defended the uniform view of the early church that violence in nature and within the animal kingdom is the result of the corrupting influence of Satan and other fallen principalities and powers (which we will discuss in chapter 12). See G. Boyd, "Evolution as Cosmic Warfare," in *Creation Made Free: Open Theology Engaging Science*, ed. T. J. Oord (Eugene, OR: Pickwick 2009), 125–45.
8. Mic 4:3; cf. Isa 2:4.
9. J. C. McCann Jr., "The Book of Psalms," in *The New Interpreter's Bible*, vol. 4, ed. L. E. Keck (Nashville: Abingdon, 1996), 641–1280 (866). See also Hos 2:18; Mic 5:10.

not only nonviolent, he's passionately *anti*-violence. No wonder Jesus refused to call legions of angels to his defense.

***

We can also see our heavenly missionary at work to free his people from their sinful reliance on violence in the many passages in which Yahweh admonishes them to place their trust in him rather than the sword. For example, as Judah was facing an ominous threat from the brutally violent nation of Assyria, the Lord told Hosea that they would be saved, "not by bow, sword or battle, or by horses and horsemen, but by the Lord their God" (Hos 1:7).

So too, through the Psalmist the Lord encourages his people by saying:

> Do not put your trust in princes,
> in human beings, who cannot save. . . .
> Blessed are those whose help is the God of Jacob,
> whose hope is in the Lord their God. (Ps 146:3, 5)

Over and over, and in a variety of different ways, we are told that while "some trust in chariots and some in horses," Israelites were to "trust in the name of the Lord our God" (Ps 20:7), for "no king is saved by the size of his army" and "no warrior escapes by his great strength." Yet, "the eyes of the Lord are on those who fear him" and whose "hope is in his unfailing love" to "deliver them from death" (Ps 33:16–19). And while Yahweh frequently promised the Israelites they would be blessed if they placed their complete trust in him, he just as frequently warned them that there would be terrible consequences if they placed their trust in anything or anyone else.[10]

Passages such as these suggest that, had the Israelites been able and willing to trust Yahweh to fight their battles, they never would have needed to lift a sword. And this alone is enough to prove that "wars are the outworking of the unwillingness of Israel . . . to trust Jahweh," as John Yoder notes.[11] In the words of James, violence is always the outgrowth "of the desires that battle within [us]" (Jas 4:1, cf. v. 2). It never originates in the heart of God.

10. Isa 31:1; Ezek 33:26; Hos 10:13.

11. J. H. Yoder, *The Politics of Jesus: Vicit Agnus Noster*, 2nd ed. (Grand Rapids: Eerdmans, 1992 [1972]), 83.

***

Unfortunately, while the Israelites had no problem trusting Yahweh to help them use their swords to conquer enemies, they had great trouble trusting Yahweh *instead of* their swords. The one thing the ancient Israelites seemed incapable of understanding was that "MAN IS NOT THE ENEMY" (see Eph 6:12).[12] And this shouldn't be too hard for us to understand, for while everybody in the ANE trusted their god to *help them fight*, no one ever dreamed that their god *didn't want them to fight*!

We catch a glimpse of the kind of battle Yahweh would have liked his people to fight in the remarkable story of Elisha's victory over the Arameans in 2 Kings 6. Elisha's prophetic gift had enabled him to help the Israelites avoid being ambushed by the Arameans several times. Frustrated by this, the king of Aram sent his army to capture Elisha (vv. 13–14). At Elisha's beckoning, the Lord temporarily blinded the Aramean army, at which point Elisha volunteered to lead them to the man they were looking for (vv. 18–19). When the Lord restored their sight, this army found itself in the court of the Israelite king, who suggested that the Israelites take advantage of this fortunate opportunity and slaughter the Arameans.

To everyone's surprise, Elisha instead instructed the king to throw them a banquet and send them back home (v. 22).

Now *that* looks like the way Jesus would fight!

It also looks completely unlike the way any other ANE people ever fought, which confirms that we are here witnessing the Spirit of Jesus breaking through. And although Aram and Israel had been engaged in a long and all-too-typical cycle of violence, Elisha's decision not to repay evil with evil but to instead "overcome evil with good" (Rom 12:17, 21) inspired Aram to bring their military campaign against Israel to a permanent halt (2 Kgs 6:23).

That is the kind of warfare Yahweh always wanted his people to engage in—*if only they could have trusted him*! So every time the Israelites wielded the sword, we should see this as evidence that they were not placing their complete trust in Yahweh and were not filled with the true knowledge of the Lord.

And note, this implies that the same holds true every time the

12. V. Eller, *War and Peace from Genesis to Revelation* (Eugene, OR: Wipf & Stock, 2003 [1981]), 59 (capitalization is Eller's).

ancient Israelites conceived of Yahweh as a violent ANE warrior deity who engages in violence and/or commands them to engage in violence.

An Abandoned Nonviolent Plan

I'd like us to consider two passages that I had never noticed before I began reading the Bible through the looking-glass cross but that I now find remarkably significant because they strongly confirm God's opposition to violence. What makes these passages particularly important is that they are part of the conquest narrative that depicts Yahweh commanding the Israelites to slaughter every man, woman, child, infant, and animal in certain regions of Canaan as an act of devotion to him.

The first is Exodus 23:28–30. A long while before the Israelites violently invaded the land that Yahweh wanted them to live in, he promised them that he would "send the hornet ahead of you to drive the Hivites, Canaanites, and Hittites out of your way." But, he added, he would "not drive them out in a single year, because the land would become desolate and the wild animals too numerous for you." Rather, he says, he would "drive them out . . . [l]ittle by little."

That's rather interesting. Getting the indigenous population of Canaan to slowly migrate off the land on their own by making it unpleasantly pesky strikes me as a much more Christlike way of acquiring real-estate than having your people engage in full-scale genocide. What ever happened to this nonviolent plan?

In the second passage, Yahweh told his people that the land he was going to give his people had become defiled by the Canaanites. So, as punishment for their sin, Yahweh was going to have the land vomit them out (Lev 18:24–25). Throughout the Bible the welfare of land is directly connected to the spiritual state of the people who occupy it.[13] It thus seems that the Lord decided he would allow the defilement of the Canaanites to render their land temporarily unfruitful so they would naturally migrate to greener pastures. No babies would need to be bludgeoned in the process.

Now, you may be wondering why God's land-vomiting relocation strategy in this passage is different from the previous pesky-

13. Jer 4:24–25; 9:9–10; 23:10; Isaiah 24; Joel 1:8–10. For a great book on this and related themes, see T. Fretheim, *God and World in the Old Testament* (Nashville: Abingdon, 2005).

insect strategy. Frankly, I have no idea. Perhaps God was considering several possible nonviolent strategies around the same time. But who cares? Both strategies look a whole lot more Christlike than the massacre-them-all strategy!

On top of this, there are a number of other passages in which Yahweh says he was going to drive out the indigenous population without specifying how he planned on doing it.[14] All these passages suggest that "the original intent of the conquest implied the dissipation of the Canaanite population, who had the possibility of emigrating outside the Promised Land."[15]

So I again ask, what happened to these nonviolent relocation strategies? And how are we to explain the mind-boggling leap from these gradual and entirely nonviolent plans to the plan to massacre every living thing as an act of worship?! Did God suddenly experience a psychotic mood change?

***

If I remain confident that God is as beautiful as the cross reveals him to be, I cannot believe it was God who changed. A far more plausible answer becomes apparent once we accept the cross-centered understanding that God's breathing involves both God influencing people as much as possible while allowing the fallen and culturally conditioned state of people to influence the result of his breathing as much as necessary.

With the cross as our criterion, we can assess the two nonviolent plans as reflecting the Spirit of Christ breaking through to reveal the way God actually hoped his people would inherit this land. This is

14. Exod 33:2; 34:11, 24; Lev 18:24; 20:23; Num 32:21; Deut 4:38; 7:1, 22. Readers should be advised that some of these nonviolent traditions are spliced together with traditions in which Yahweh commands the complete destruction of people groups, which is why many passages contain inconsistencies. For example, immediately after depicting Yahweh as telling Moses to have the Israelites mercilessly slaughter every man, woman, and child of certain populations, Yahweh is depicted as adding: "Do not intermarry with them" (Deut 7:2–3), which is a perfectly superfluous command if the indigineous population has all been slaughtered. Even this command is later contradicted, however, for God is portrayed as telling Israelite soldiers that they could marry Canaanite women who have been captured if they are attracted to them (Deut 21:10–14). Some attempt to explain inconsistencies like this by arguing that the command to slaughter everyone was hyperbolic, but as I have shown elsewhere, this view is untenable (*CWG*, vol, 2, , 945–60). In my view, the inconsistency and immoral nature of these commands confirm that we are dealing with fallible human ideas that Yahweh had to stoop to accommodate, not with commands that Yahweh actually gave.

15. B. Magyarosi, *Holy War and Cosmic Conflict in the Old Testament: From the Exodus to the Exile* (Berrien Springs, MI: Lithotech, 2010), 122.

confirmed by the fact that the portrait of God planning to acquire this land without the use of violence has no parallel in the ANE. To the contrary, throughout the ANE it was assumed that acquiring land from another nation meant that you had to conquer, if not exterminate, the people of that nation. And it was uniformly assumed that the job of your national deity was to help you do this.

The radically countercultural nature of these nonviolent plans not only supports seeing them as reflections of the Spirit breaking through, it also goes a long way in explaining why these plans were never carried out. Given the prevailing ANE assumption that acquiring land requires massive violence, it's not hard to understand why the ancient Israelites would have found it difficult to truly hear these plans. Similar to the way Jesus's countercultural teachings about the need for the Messiah to suffer fell on the deaf ears of his culturally conditioned disciples, it seems these nonviolent plans of Yahweh were simply too foreign to the Israelites' culturally conditioned ears to be heard.

Not only this, but we've already seen how hard it was for the stiff-necked Israelites to trust Yahweh instead of their swords, and in the next chapter we'll see how hard it was for them to accept that Yahweh's character was radically different than all the violent warrior gods that were worshiped by the surrounding nations. I am therefore in agreement with Yoder when he writes, "If only the Israelites had been able to place their complete trust in Yahweh, [the Canaanites] would have withdrawn without violence."[16]

If only. Unfortunately, this was precisely what the fallen and culturally conditioned hearts and minds of the Israelites prevented them from doing. And since the kind of world God created requires him to refrain from lobotomizing people, this meant that he would need to bear the sin of his people's inability to rise above their cultural conditioning and trust him. Though it certainly grieved him terribly to do so, God's plan to locate his people in the Promised Land would now have to proceed by means of the sword rather than by means of unpleasant insects or unfruitful land.

***

16. Yoder, *Politics*, 81n5. For an insightful discussion of how the Israelites' lack of faith transformed Yahweh's original plan of a nonviolent entry into the land into a genocidal assault, see Eller, *War & Peace*, 39–62.

For a variety of reasons I cannot presently get into, canceling the plan to acquire Canaan was simply not an option for God. Among other things, his long-term plans for the entire human race revolved around his people occupying this strategic parcel of land. But in light of the material we've covered, it seems that when Yahweh *said*, "I want my people to dwell in the land of Canaan," what Moses's fallen and culturally conditioned ears *heard* was, "I want you to slaughter the Canaanites so my people can dwell in the land of Canaan." For again, in Moses's ANE worldview, acquiring someone else's land and slaughtering the inhabitants of the land were two sides of the same coin.

Hence, when Moses reports that he "heard" Yahweh instruct him to have the Israelites mercilessly slaughter people to acquire this land, this tells us more about the character of Moses and the culture he was embedded in than it tells us about the true character and will of God.

Nevertheless, this is what Moses sincerely "heard," so this is what he instructed Joshua to do. And since this is exactly what any ANE person would have expected their god to command, Joshua and the people of God readily believed and obeyed Moses.

Should We Trust Moses?

Here is another seemingly insignificant fact that became significant to me when I began to reflect on it in light of the crucified Christ: Did you ever notice that the only person who claims to have heard Yahweh give the command to slaughter the Canaanites was Moses? Whenever Joshua later repeated this command, it was on the basis of what "God had commanded *his servant Moses*."[17]

Now, given their ANE context, we can understand why Joshua and the Israelites sincerely believed Moses. But the important question is, *should we*?

If we remain resolved that the cross is the full revelation of God's true character, I frankly do not see how we can. Can you imagine Jesus, who made refraining from violence and blessing enemies the

17. Emphasis added. See for example Josh 9:24; 10:40; 11:12, 15, 20; 14:2; 17:4; 21:2, 8. Much later, Samuel also "heard" Yahweh tell him to slaughter every man, woman, child, and infant from among the Amalekites (1 Sam 15:1–3). The accommodating nature of this particular portrait of God is confirmed in the fact that Samuel claimed that Yahweh wanted the Amalekites annihilated as punishment for attacking the Israelites *several hundreds of years earlier*! What makes this punishment even less fair is that the Amalekites were simply trying to defend their borders against the Israelites, who were the aggressors.

condition for being considered a child of the Father in heaven, telling Moses, or anyone else, to exterminate entire populations? Would it not be unfaithful for us to suspect that the one who taught and demonstrated the Father's indiscriminate love and mercy was capable of commanding indiscriminate killing?

***

In case you are not yet convinced, consider this. Paul at one point said, "Even if we or an angel from heaven should preach a gospel other than the one we preached to you, let them be under God's curse" (Gal 1:8). Paul's gospel was "the message of the cross" (1 Cor 1:18), and if there is any message that has ever conflicted with this message, it's got to be the message that claimed Yahweh wanted his people to mercilessly slaughter "anything that breathes" in various regions of Canaan, and to do this as an act of worship to him!

If we believe Paul, it seems we should not only *not* believe Moses, we should regard his command to exterminate people as an act of worship to be "under a curse." Indeed, we should draw this conclusion even if this command was given by *Paul himself* or *an angel from heaven*! And if it's hard for you to understand how God could possibly "breathe" through something that is cursed, remember that this is precisely what God did when he breathed his supreme revelation on Calvary (Gal 3:13)!

***

In light of all the material we've covered in this chapter, I don't think the conclusion that Moses's command was "under a curse" should surprise us. This is the conclusion we should expect since we've already seen that the Israelites only engaged in violence because they had an insufficient trust in Yahweh. This also is the conclusion we should expect since violence always indicates that people lack "the knowledge of the Lord" and since we are explicitly told that God's persistently stiff-necked people had little to no knowledge of God.

Moreover, the conclusion that Moses's command was "under a curse" is precisely what we should expect since we know the Israelites were always tempted to assume that God was "just like [them]" (Ps 50:21)—and a lot like the warrior gods of their neighbors, at least when it came to God's capacity for violence. And, most importantly, this is the conclusion we should expect since we know God's true, nonviolent, cruciform character in the crucified Christ, and it is the antithesis of the merciless character of God contained in Moses's genocidal message.

On top of this, the passages that reflect God's original non-violent plan to get his people into the Promised Land bear witness against Moses's claim to have received the genocidal command from Yahweh. They thus provide further confirmation that the violent portrait of God giving this command, along with all other violent depictions of God, are accommodations. Their ugliness tells us much more about the heart of the people God was striving to work through than they tell us about God.

At the same time, however, these horrific violent divine portraits also tell us something beautiful about God, if we interpret them through the looking-glass cross. For we can now see them as permanent testaments to just how low the heavenly missionary was willing to stoop to remain in relationship with, and to continue to further his purposes through, his fallen and culturally conditioned people. Interpreted through this lens, these grotesque portraits become literary crucifixes that reflect, and point to, the historical crucifixion of the humble, sin-bearing, heavenly missionary.

***

We've completed our review of confirming evidence within the Bible regarding the accommodating nature of the OT's violent divine portraits. But in the next chapter we're going to explore something else that strongly confirms that these portraits reflect the cultural conditioning of the people God breathed through: namely, the clear parallels that exist between the OT's warrior depictions of Yahweh and the warrior depictions of other gods in ANE literature.

8

Echoes of a Pagan Warrior

> If those things that are dimly sketched through Moses
> concerning the tabernacle or the sacrifices . . .
> are said to be a "type and shadow of heavenly things" (Heb 8:5),
> doubtless the wars that are waged through [Joshua]
> and the slaughter of kings and enemies
> must also be said to be "a shadow and type
> of heavenly things . . ."
> —Origen[1]

This last Christmas I heard a sweet Christmas tune by Don Moen titled "Some Children See Him." It tenderly celebrates how children see "the baby Jesus's face" appear "like theirs, but bright with Heavenly grace." While some see Jesus "lily white," others see him "dark" or "bronzed and brown."

I must confess that my more cynical side wants to ruin the sweetness of this tender tune by pointing out that, while the NT provides next to no descriptions of what Jesus looked like, forensic science has provided us with an accurate general picture of what a first-century Palestinian Jewish male like Jesus would have looked like.[2] A hint: he wasn't lily white! And if I were to give in to my more cynical side, I'd point out the harm that has been done when lily-white Americans and Europeans colonized nonwhite groups while evangelizing them with a lily-white Jesus in the process!

1. Origen, *Homilies on Joshua*, trans. B. Bruce, ed. C. White, Fathers of the Church 105 (Washington, DC: Catholic University of America Press, 2002) 12.1.
2. See http://www.popularmechanics.com/science/health/a234/1282186/ (accessed 4/11/2016).

But there is no need to be cynical. For our present purposes it will suffice to point out that this tune illustrates the fact that the way people view Jesus or God is inevitably influenced by their race, culture, and life circumstances. This inevitable influence may be completely harmless. But insofar as any such influences are contrary to the truth that is revealed in Jesus's cross-centered ministry, or insofar as these influences affect people in ways that are not consistent with the loving character of his ministry, they must be considered harmful and must be challenged.

Because God always works with people by means of influence, not coercion, we need to investigate the ways biblical authors were influenced by their surrounding culture, especially in terms of how they viewed God. The result may surprise you.

Yahweh's Battle with Cosmic Enemies

As is true of most people up until modern times, people in the ANE world, including the ancient Hebrews, believed that there were menacing cosmic forces that perpetually threatened the well-being of their nation and of the world. And, as strange as it may sound to us today, they conceived of these cosmic forces as a threatening personified sea that they believed encompassed the earth.[3] Moreover, they believed that this menacing sea (sometimes referred to as "the waters" or "the deep") had to be vanquished and held at bay by their nation's chief deity to keep it from swallowing up their nation and the world. Scholars refer to the many accounts we find in ANE literature of various deities defeating this sea as its *chaoskampf* ("conflict-with-chaos") motif.

This conflict-with-chaos motif permeates the OT. Indeed, the way OT authors speak about Yahweh's conflict with menacing cosmic forces closely parallels other ANE sources. And since most of the nonbiblical ANE sources predate the writing of the OT, there is little doubt among scholars that these parallels suggest that OT authors were influenced by these nonbiblical sources rather than the other way around. As a matter of fact, sometimes OT authors simply adopted the conflict-with-chaos material from an older ANE source,

3. While I will in certain contexts refer to "spiritual" agents, I prefer to refer to them as "cosmic forces" or "cosmic agents." For, as we will see in a moment, ANE people didn't divide reality into "earthly" and "spiritual" dimensions the way modern western people tend to do.

almost word for word, and simply substituted the victorious deity of the older source with Yahweh.[4]

For example, in several Psalms that have clear Canaanite parallels, the biblical authors proclaim that it was Yahweh (not *Baal*, the chief Canaanite god) who rebuked the waters or the depths and caused them to flee.[5] So too, OT authors utilize preexisting material when they proclaim that it was Yahweh, not some other deity, who assigned a place for these rebel waters to go and who set boundaries they could not trespass.[6]

The people of the ANE, including the ancient Israelites, also conceived of these threatening cosmic forces as cosmic monsters—most often as sea monsters. And, as is true of other ANE literature, OT authors refer to these monsters with names such as "Leviathan," "Rahab," and "Behemoth."[7] Some have tried to argue that the beasts that the OT refers to were just large animals. But, while there are a few passages where this interpretation may be possible (e.g., Ps 104:26), the cosmic-level roles these monsters typically play in the OT and in other ANE literature renders this impossible.

Not only this, but the way these monsters are sometimes described rules out their being natural animals. For example, the Psalmist describes Leviathan as having many heads (Ps 74:13), and in Job, Leviathan is said to do things like blow smoke and lightning bolts from its nostrils and breathe fire out of its mouth (Job 41:18–21). This description doesn't fit any natural creature. But, not coincidentally, it echoes the mythical way ANE people envisioned the cosmic forces of destruction that threatened their nation and/or world.

In keeping with the common theology of the ANE, some passages depict Yahweh battling a cosmic monster to create the present world.[8] Others depict him battling Leviathan or some similar creature

4. On the ANE background of the OT's conflict-with-chaos material, see J. Day, *God's Conflict with the Dragon and the Sea: Echoes of a Canaanite Myth in the Old Testament* (Cambridge: Cambridge University Press, 1985); J. Day, *Yahweh and the Gods and Goddesses of Canaan* (Sheffield: Sheffield Academic Press, 2000); and B. Batto, *Slaying the Dragon: Mythmaking in the Biblical Tradition* (Louisville: Westminster John Knox, 1992).
5. Pss 29:3; 77:16; 93:3–4; 104:7.
6. Pss 33:7; 104:8–11, 16; Prov 8:29; Job 38:8–11.
7. Job 3:8; 9:13; 26:12; 40:15–24; 41:1–34; Pss 74:14; 89:10; Isa 27:1; 30:7; 51:9.
8. Job 38:8–11; Ps 74:13–17. I say "the *present* world" to distinguish the world that is engulfed in cosmic conflict, which we now live in, from God's original creation of "the heavens and the earth" from nothing (Gen 1:1; Prov 3:19; Rom 4:17; Col 1:16; Acts 4:24; Heb 11:3). On the "common theology of the ANE," which refers to widespread concepts and images of deities and opposing cosmic forces in the ANE that are shared by the authors of the OT, see M. Smith,

in the present or defeating him in the future. In a passage that has very close parallels in Ugaritic mythology, Isaiah looks forward to a time when "the Lord will punish with his sword . . . Leviathan the gliding serpent, Leviathan the coiling serpent; he will slay the monster of the sea" (Isa 27:1). In passages like this, the ANE conflict-with-chaos motif "has been projected onto the onset of the future era."[9] And this implies that Leviathan continues to wreak havoc on creation at the present time.[10]

The close parallels between the OT's conflict-with-chaos motif and other ANE literature give us some indication of the degree to which OT authors were influenced by their surrounding culture. But while this cultural conditioning is mythological, it is harmless since it does not conflict with anything we learn about God or the spiritual realm from the crucified Christ. Instead, Jesus and the entire NT affirm the reality of the sinister cosmic forces that are mythically expressed by OT authors. It's just that, instead of talking about hostile waters or cosmic monsters, Jesus and the NT authors talk about Satan and principalities and powers.

Yahweh and Human Enemies

There is, however, another dimension of the ANE conflict-with-chaos motif that's not so harmless. For the people of the ANE, including the ancient Israelites, there was "no dichotomy between sacred and secular, or even between natural and supernatural."[11] They therefore didn't clearly distinguish between earthly and spiritual battles. To the contrary, everybody in the ANE, including biblical authors, assumed that earthly battles are always wrapped up with spiritual battles.

For example, the author of 2 Samuel tells us that Yahweh instructed David to wait until he could "hear the sound of marching in the tops of the poplar trees" before he attacked the Philistines (2 Sam 5:24). The assumption is that as David and his troops marched into battle on the ground, Yahweh and his heavenly hosts marched into

"The Common Theology of the Ancient Near East," *Journal of Biblical Literature* 71, no. 3 (1952): 135–47.

9. J. Levenson, *Creation and the Persistence of Evil: The Jewish Drama of Divine Omnipotence* (San Francisco: Harper & Row, 1988), 27.

10. Ibid., 48.

11. J. H. Walton, *Ancient Near Eastern Thought and the Old Testament: Introducing the Conceptual World of the Hebrew Bible* (Grand Rapids: Baker Academic, 2006), 87.

battle with them just above the trees. So too, as David and his troops fought earthly foes, Yahweh and his heavenly hosts fought on their side against spiritual warriors who fought on behalf of the Philistines.

In Judges we find a man named Jephthah, a captain of the Israelite army, settling a territorial dispute with the king of the Ammonites. He said: "Will you not take what your god Chemosh gives you? Likewise, whatever the Lord our God has given us, we will possess" (Judg 11:24). The assumption behind Jephthah's statement is that, whenever the Ammonites go into battle, Chemosh, their national deity, fights on their behalf. And if they win, they have a right to keep what Chemosh won for them. But by the same token, whenever the Israelites go into battle, Yahweh and his heavenly hosts fight on their behalf. Jephthah is thus arguing that the Israelites have the right to keep the land that Yahweh won for them when they conquered the original inhabitants of the land.

So closely did ANE people associate earthly and spiritual realities that they sometimes simply identified their earthly enemies with destructive cosmic forces. And, not surprisingly, this is what we frequently find in the OT. For example, when Isaiah declared that "the Lord . . . will slay the monster of the sea" (Isa 27:1), he was identifying "the monster of the sea" with the nation of Egypt. Isaiah later identifies Egypt and Babylon with the cosmic monster Rahab (Isa 30:7; 51:9–11), as did Jeremiah (51:34) as well as the Psalmist (87:4). Similarly, the Psalmist frequently identified personal or national enemies with the "waters," "the sea," or "the deep."[12]

***

If we assess the OT's conflict-with-chaos motif through the looking-glass cross, we must conclude that the Israelites were right insofar as they believed that cosmic foes threatened them, and that God battles the forces of destruction to protect people and to preserve the order of creation.[13] But if we use the looking-glass cross to assess the culturally conditioned assumption of OT authors that human foes are part of God's conflict-with-chaos and that it is appropriate for God's people to fight them as such, we must conclude that they were very mistaken. On this matter, their cultural conditioning clouded their

12. Pss 18:16; 69:1–2, 14–15; 124:4; 144:7.
13. The manner in which the cross establishes the reality of Satan and other fallen powers will be addressed in chapter 12.

vision of God's true character and will as it is revealed in the crucified Christ and developed in the NT.

For example, according to Paul, "our struggle is not against flesh and blood, but against the rulers, against the authorities, against the powers of this dark world and against the spiritual forces of evil in the heavenly realms" (Eph 6:12). We are to battle cosmic foes, not human foes. And one of the primary ways we battle cosmic foes is by refusing to battle human foes, choosing instead to love and bless them.

In this light, we have no choice but to consider the OT's application of the conflict-with-chaos to "flesh and blood" humans to be misguided.

***

The OT's adaptation of the ANE conflict-with-chaos motif illustrates the degree to which OT authors were influenced by their surrounding culture. But it also demonstrates that not all cultural conditioning is bad. Because God is at work everywhere, truth can be found anywhere (e.g., Acts 17:26–28). And this is why God sometimes appropriated truths that were already expressed in other ANE sources and incorporated them into the written witness to his missionary activity.

At the same time, the OT's adaptation of the ANE conflict-with-chaos motif also illustrates that the cultural conditioning of OT authors sometimes twisted their understanding of God's character, will, and way of operating in the world. And this is one of the reasons why we need a reliable criterion to distinguish between what OT authors got right and what they got wrong. On theological and ethical matters, this criterion is the cross.

But remember, to determine that certain biblical material is twisted does not mean it is any less a God-breathed revelation than any other biblical material. As I argued in chapter 4, it simply means that it reveals God in *a different way*. While material that conforms to the supreme revelation of God on the cross reveals God *directly*, material that falls short of this revelation reveals God *indirectly*.

So when we interpret this twisted material through the looking-glass cross, we are able to see through its surface meaning and discern *what else is going on*. In this way, we can see how this culturally conditioned material bears witness to the truth that God has always been willing to stoop as low as necessary to remain in solidarity with his people, just as he did in a supreme way on the cross.

Yahweh as a Warring Mountain and Storm Deity

As I mentioned earlier, nowhere is the cultural conditioning of the OT authors more evident than when they represent Yahweh as a violent divine warrior who battles Israel's earthly enemies.[14]

For starters, it is common knowledge among OT scholars that, insofar as Israel viewed Yahweh as a "man of war" (Exod 15:1, ASV) who helped them win battles, it "was taking the same perspective as other nations did."[15] Every nation in the ANE believed this about their chief god and their military campaigns. In fact, as unfortunate as it is, this assumption has been the common denominator of most nations and religions throughout history!

But let's examine the details.

All ANE people believed their chief warrior god lived on top of a sacred mountain, and we find this belief reflected throughout the OT. For example, the Psalmist declares that, when he calls "out to the Lord . . . he answers me from his holy mountain" (Ps 3:4). And the Psalmist professes his belief that only "one who has clean hands and a pure heart" can "ascend the mountain of the Lord" and "stand in his holy place" (Ps 24:3–4).[16]

Yet another Psalm celebrates God's "holy mountain" by declaring that it is "beautiful in its loftiness . . . like the heights of Zaphon" (Ps 48:1–3). Curiously enough, Zaphon happens to be the mountain that was considered most sacred among the Canaanites. And, just as we find in Canaanite literature, it is from his holy mountain that this Psalmist imagines Yahweh descending when he goes into battle or when he comes to meet his people (vv. 4–8).[17]

Related to this, Zechariah depicts Yahweh as a warrior standing "on the mount of Olives" as he is about to "go out and fight against [the] nations." As he prepares to descend into battle, his holy mountain splits in two "from east to west, forming a great valley, with half of the mountain moving north and half moving south" (Zech 14:3–4). Zechariah's imagery suggests that Yahweh has a foot on each mountain and grows in stature as these mountains move further and further apart. Not coincidentally, this strange depiction echoes

14. For a more comprehensive and in-depth discussion of these parallels that interacts with academic issues surrounding them, see *CWG*, vol. 2, ch. 15.

15. J. Goldingay, *Theological Diversity and the Authority of the Old Testament* (Grand Rapids: Eerdmans, 1987), 162–63.

16. See also Pss 15:1; 24:3; 43:4; Isa 27:13; 31:4; Joel 3:17.

17. See also Deut 33:2; Judg 5:4–5; Pss 68:7–8, 17; 144:5–6.

"depictions of the Hittite and Syrian storm-gods standing with each foot on a mountain."[18]

***

One of the most common images of warrior deities in the ANE depicts them descending into battle from their holy mountains while riding on storm clouds and throwing lightning bolts as arrows.[19] We find this same imagery throughout the OT.[20]

One passage that is particularly full of standard ANE warrior god imagery is Psalm 18. The Psalmist says he "cried to my God for help," and "from his temple," which was located on a mountaintop above the clouds (v. 9), "he heard my voice" (v. 6). Then, when the heavenly warrior responded to this prayer,

> . . . the foundations of the mountains shook;
> they trembled because he was angry.
> Smoke rose from his nostrils;
> consuming fire came from his mouth,
> He parted the heavens and came down;
> dark clouds were under his feet.
> He mounted the cherubim and flew;
> he soared on the wings of the wind.
> He made darkness his covering, his canopy around him—
> the dark rain clouds of the sky.
> Out of the brightness of his presence clouds advanced,
> with hailstones and bolts of lightning.
> The Lord thundered from heaven;
> the voice of the Most High resounded.
> He shot his arrows and scattered the enemy,
> with great bolts of lightning he routed them.
> The valleys of the sea were exposed
> and the foundations of the earth laid bare
> at your rebuke, Lord,
> at the blast of breath from your nostrils. (vv. 7–19)

18. M. Smith, "Myth and Mythmaking in Canaan and Ancient Israel," in *Civilizations of the Ancient Near East*, vol. 3, ed. J. Sasson (New York: Scribner's, 1995), 2031–41 (2036).
19. See R. J. Clifford, *The Cosmic Mountain in Canaan and the Old Testament* (Cambridge, MA: Harvard University Press, 1972); M. S. Smith, *The Early History of God: Yahweh and the Other Deities in Ancient Israel* (San Francisco: Harper & Row, 1990); M. Smith, "Common Theology," 35–47.
20. Deut 32:23; Pss 7:13; 18:14; 64:7; 77:17; 144:6; Hab 3:9, 11.

Every aspect of this depiction of Yahweh as a fire-breathing, smoke-snorting, cloud-riding, lightning-bolt-throwing, violent warrior deity has clear parallels with other ANE violent warrior deities.

***

Now, I think I can safely assume that no reader thinks God actually breathes fire, snorts out smoke, rides on clouds, or throws lightning bolts as arrows. These are obviously divine accommodations on the part of the heavenly missionary to the fallen and culturally conditioned hearts and minds of his people at the time. But if we grant that this imagery is a culturally conditioned accommodation, *why should we not conclude the same about the violence that is associated with this imagery?*

Indeed, since God's revelation on the cross is the ultimate criterion by which we are to assess such matters, how can we avoid concluding that the violence associated with this imagery is at least as much a culturally conditioned accommodation as is the imagery itself?

Yahweh and Anat

We could discuss a variety of similar warrior images that biblical authors borrow from their ANE neighbors, but I think it will be more helpful, and less redundant, to bring this chapter to a close by focusing in even more detail on the way various depictions of Yahweh echo one particularly interesting, and particularly violent, ANE deity.

It's not uncommon to find in ANE literature depictions of deities gloating over the grisly way they butchered masses of people. Not surprisingly, OT authors sometimes do the same thing. We can see this in the way in which the "savage battling" attributed to Yahweh parallels the "savage battling" that had been earlier ascribed to a Ugaritic goddess named Anat.[21]

Both Yahweh and Anat are described as leaving a bloodsoaked land with heaps of rotting corpses and piles of skulls in the wake of their ferocious warfare.[22] And both are portrayed as crushing enemies like grapes in a winepress and joyously wading or dancing with their soldiers in their blood.[23] Yet, the most grisly activity Anat was

21. Smith, "Myth and Mythmaking," 2037.
22. Ibid. See Ps 110:5–6; Isa 34:3, 7; Jer 33:5.
23. Pss 58:10; 68:23; 110:5–6; Lam 1:15; Isa 63:3.

known for was eating the flesh and drinking the blood of her enemies.[24]

This imagery is based on the ancient barbaric practice of military cannibalism. Victorious armies would sometimes celebrate their victory and humiliate their foes by eating some of the flesh and drinking some of the blood of their defeated enemies. Since ascribing macabre violence to their deities was the primary way ANE people exalted them, it's not too surprising that the Ugaritic people exalted the ferociousness of Anat in this macabre fashion.

***

What may shock some readers, however, is that biblical authors exalt the ferociousness of Yahweh along similar lines. Several authors arguably tap into this cannabilistic imagery when they speak of the Lord swallowing up foes.[25] So too, the author of Deuteronomy depicts Yahweh proclaiming:

> I will make arrows drunk with blood,
> while my sword devours flesh:
> the blood of the slain and the captives,
> the heads of the enemy leaders. (32:42)

This passage is an example of Hebraic parallelism, which means the last two lines are restatements of the first two. This passage is thus depicting Yahweh as declaring that his arrows will drink so much of his enemies' blood that they will become intoxicated, while his sword will eat his enemies' heads! As gruesome as this imagery is, however, we can nevertheless detect the Spirit at work. For this passage represents a slight improvement over the older Anat imagery inasmuch as the blood drinking and flesh eating are attributed to Yahweh's arrows and sword rather than to Yahweh himself.

Other authors also reflect a slightly more refined use of divine cannibalistic imagery. For example, Jeremiah declares, "the sword of the Lord will devour from one end of the land to the other" (Jer 12:12), and he later announces that this sword "will devour till it is satisfied, till it has quenched its thirst with blood" (46:10). Similarly, Isaiah paints a picture of Yahweh declaring, "My sword has drunk its fill

24. M. Smith, "Myth and Mythmaking," 2037.
25. Ps 21:9, Lam 2:2, 5. See also Exod 33:5, which depicts Yahweh threatening to "consume" (*kalah*) the Israelites (ESV, NKJV, RSV, YLT, DBY, WEB, HNV).

in the heavens" from "the people I have totally destroyed," which is why he concludes, "The sword of the Lord is bathed in blood" (Isa 34:5–6).

Insofar as these authors retain the barbaric Anat imagery of Yahweh as a cannibalistic warrior, our cross-centered perspective leads us to interpret these passages as literary crucifixes. They reflect and point to the cross, where God stooped to bear the horrifically ugly sin and curse of the world and to thereby take on a horrifically ugly appearance that mirrored that sin and curse. Inasmuch as these passages stop short of representing Yahweh as drinking the blood and eating the flesh of his enemies, however, we can detect the influence of the Spirit pushing back on the negative cultural conditioning of these authors.

We can see the Spirit breaking through even further when Isaiah depicts Yahweh telling the Israelites, "I will make your oppressors *eat their own flesh*" (Isa 49:26, emphasis added). While still macabre, this depiction is a significant improvement over all the previous uses of Anat imagery, for this depiction completely separates Yahweh from Anat's warrior cannibalism.

Indeed, by depicting Yahweh as somehow causing Israel's oppressors to devour one another, Isaiah is capturing the self-destructive nature of sin and evil, which we will later see is a profound aspect of God's revelation on the cross.

***

Nowhere does the OT contrast with its surrounding ANE culture more than when it depicts God in Christlike ways. Conversely, nowhere does the OT conform to its surrounding ANE culture more than when it depicts Yahweh as a violent warrior God. And this fact, together with the material covered in the previous two chapters, strongly confirms the cross-centered interpretation of the OT's violent divine portraits. If accepted, these often grisly divine portraits bear witness to the truth that the humble heavenly missionary has always been willing to bear the ugly sin of his people and to thereby take on a semblance that mirrors that ugly sin.

But this brings us to a very important question. If the violence that biblical authors ascribe to God reflects their cultural conditioning, does this mean that God never actually judged people? If so, does this imply that we must interpret every story of God bringing judgments on people to be nothing but a reflection of the fallen and culturally conditioned imaginations of biblical authors? In short, have I erased God's judgment with my interpretation?

While there are some Bible scholars who accept this conclusion, I cannot. Not only would this violate my commitment to the Conservative Hermeneutical Principle, but Jesus explicitly referred to a number of violent divine judgments in the OT.[26] In fact, Jesus frequently warned people of impending divine judgments, such as the judgment that was coming on Jerusalem at the hands of Roman soldiers that took place in 70 CE (Luke 19:41–44). On Jesus's authority, therefore, I have to assume that there is no incompatibility between Jesus's cross-centered ministry, on the one hand, and the belief that God sometimes judges people, on the other.

In fact, far from being incompatible, the revelation of God on the cross was *itself a divine judgment*! As such, the cross should serve as the lens through which we interpret all other divine judgments. And, as we will begin to demonstrate in the following chapter, when we interpret accounts of divine judgment through the looking-glass cross, we can see how it is possible to affirm that God justly judges sin while denying that God ever *acts violently* in the process.

26. For example, Jesus refers to the Flood (Matt 24:37–38) as well as to the destruction of Sodom and Gomorrah (Matt 10:34; 11:23–24). Related to this, the NT cites the conquest narrative several times. For example, Paul cites God's assistance in giving the land of Canaan over to the Israelites (Acts 13:19), as does Stephen (7:45), while the author of Hebrews as well as James hold up the prostitute Rahab as a hero of faith, thus endorsing the story of Jericho's overthrow (Heb 11:30–32; Jas 2:25).

PART III

The True Nature of God's Judgment

9

Divine Aikido

Aikido: a Japanese art of self-defense that
utilizes the principle of nonresistance
to cause an opponent's own momentum to work against him.

You will do evil, but it will come back on you. . . .
Yield to evil, and evil will yield to you.
—Leo Tolstoy ("A Candle")

Over the last three chapters we've discussed the first and most fundamental aspect of the revelation of God on the cross, which is the revelation that God has always been willing to humbly bear the sin of his people and to take on ugly appearances that mirror that sin. In this and the following two chapters I will flesh out a second aspect of God's revelation on the cross that allows us to see another piece of *what else is going on* when God is depicted as violent in the OT. It concerns the true nature of God's judgment on sin and the actual way that God overcomes evil.

When Love Must Leave

By the time Charlie was twenty-two, his drinking had already cost him two jobs. Angela told me that she knew this when she married him, but she chalked up his excessive and irresponsible drinking to youthful immaturity and was quite sure he would outgrow it once he became a husband and father. Besides, in all other respects Charlie was a wonderful person.

Seven years, two children, three jobs, and two rehab clinics later, Charlie hadn't outgrown his drinking problem—and it would have been five jobs had not Charlie's father, a well-respected police chief, intervened on his behalf.

Over these seven years Angela, with the help of Charlie's co-dependent parents, mopped up the messes Charlie made with his persistent drunkenness. Angela picked him up at the bar when the bartender wouldn't let him drive home. She picked him up at the police station after each of his three DWIs. She cleaned up his vomit and got him off the bathroom floor whenever he passed out. And, as badly as she wanted to be a stay-at-home mom, she got a job as a waitress so the family would have a steady income, however meager.

But over time, and with the help of a friend who introduced her to Al-Anon, Angela began to realize she wasn't doing Charlie or anyone else any favors by enabling his drinking. Over the last two years of their marriage Angela had given Charlie increasingly forceful warnings that she and the kids were going to leave him if his drinking didn't stop. That motivated Charlie to commit himself to rehab clinics twice, but in both cases it was only weeks before he relapsed.

After the second relapse Angela told Charlie that although she still loved him deeply, and although it broke her heart to do so, she and the children had to leave. Even though Angela was sharing her story almost two years after the fact, she choked up as she told me that this was the hardest and most painful thing she'd ever done. She really did love Charlie, despite his self-destructive behavior.

Angela really had no other choice. She simply could not in good conscience continue to be an accomplice to behavior that was slowly killing her husband, putting others at risk, setting a terrible example for their children, and driving the family toward financial ruin. On top of this, Angela hoped that her leaving would cause Charlie to finally hit rock bottom and come to his senses. In fact, as far as she could see, this was the only remaining hope Charlie had.

So after Charlie's second relapse, Angela and the kids moved in with her mother, who lived in a different state. But Angela assured Charlie that if he ever demonstrated that he had turned his life around by remaining sober for six continuous months, she would move back and try to rebuild their family.

Sadly, it never happened.

We'll return to Angela's story in chapter 11. For now, I simply want it to illustrate the truth that sometimes love leaves us with no other choice but to let go of a loved one and allow them to suffer the consequences of their own self-destructive decisions. And what we're going to see in this chapter is that this is as true of God as it is of us.

An Unwarranted Assumption

Even though the cross reveals a God whose character, power, and wisdom are radically different from what humans have always tended to ascribe to God/gods, when it comes to understanding how God judges sin and evil, Christians have almost always assumed that God must do it the way humans have always done it and (not coincidentally) the way we've believed other gods do it: God must resort to violence.

So deeply is this assumption ingrained in people's minds that when they hear someone like me deny that God engages in violence, they generally assume that we're denying that God judges sin and evil. Even many pacifist theologians argue that while it's wrong for people to ever engage in violence, God *must* engage in it, for otherwise "evil will not be punished or judged."[1]

This is a classic example of people unwittingly making God in their own image. Since the God revealed on the cross has a way of turning our most fundamental assumptions about God on their head, I'd like to suggest that a better strategy would be to set aside everything we think we already know about the nature of God's judgment or God's wrath and resolve to "know nothing . . . except Jesus Christ, and him crucified." And as I will now show, if we keep our eyes firmly fixed on the cross, we will see that, as a matter of fact, God never needs to resort to violence to punish sin or to overcome evil.

We humans rely on brute force to stop evil only because we lack the character and wisdom to see alternative ways of arriving at peace (Luke 19:42). But the cross reveals a God whose loving character and unlimited wisdom is such that he never needs to resort to brute force. Rather, the power and wisdom that God has always used to punish sin and overcome evil is the same nonviolent "power and wisdom" he used to punish sin and overcome evil on the cross.

1. A. J. Reimer, "God Is Love but Not a Pacifist," in *Mennonites and Classical Theology: Dogmatic Foundations for Christian Ethics* (Telford, PA: Pandora Press, 2001), 486–92 (491). See also M. Volf, *Exclusion and Embrace: A Theological Exploration of Identity, Otherness, and Reconciliation* (Nashville: Abingdon, 1996), 285, 299–303; and H. Boersma, *Violence, Hospitality, and the Cross: Reappropriating the Atonement Tradition* (Grand Rapids: Baker, 2004), 38–51.

The "Myth of Redemptive Violence"

Christians believe that Jesus stood in our place on the cross and bore the judgment that we deserved. But many Christians assume this means that God the Father needed to vent his wrath toward Jesus by killing him so that he wouldn't need to vent his wrath against us by sending us to hell. This is one version of what's called the *penal substitutionary* view of the atonement. While I firmly believe Jesus died as our substitute, I think this way of understanding how and why Jesus died as our substitute has some insurmountable problems.

Among other things, this view restricts salvation to Jesus's death on the cross, thereby rendering the rest of his life and ministry superfluous in terms of the way Jesus reconciles us to God. In this view, if Herod had succeeded in killing Jesus as an infant, his death would have had essentially the same saving effect. By contrast, I have argued (ch. 3) that the self-sacrificial love that was expressed on the cross weaves together and supremely expresses everything Jesus was about. His whole cross-centered life, from the incarnation to the ascension, reveals God, defeats evil, eradicates the condemnation of sin, reconciles us to God, and restores creation.

On top of this, the penal substitutionary view of the atonement does not make clear how our guilt could be transferred to Jesus, nor how God the Father's decision to pour his wrath on Jesus rather than us is just. Moreover, in this view Jesus doesn't reveal the Father's love (Rom 5:8), he saves us from the Father's wrath. And if Jesus had to die in order to pay the debt that we incurred by sinning against the Father, then the Father never really forgives anyone. Forgiveness means *releasing* a debt, not collecting it from someone else!

***

Perhaps the most significant problem with this view, however, is practical in nature. In the penal substitutionary view, the Father solved the problem of our estrangement from him by raging against and slaying his Son. This understanding is premised on the age-old assumption that violence fixes problems—what has been called "the myth of redemptive violence."

Sadly, the penal substitution view places this destructive myth at the center of history as well as the center of Christian theology. And if this is how the all-wise God solved humanity's ultimate problem, then it just makes sense that Christians should be open to resorting to violence to fix their problems—notwithstanding Jesus's and Paul's strong and clear teachings to the contrary.

Even a cursory survey of church history will make it clear that this is not speculation. It surely is not a coincidence that soon after the "myth of redemptive violence" was introduced into the church's thinking about the atonement in the 11th century, there were five centuries of almost nonstop, church-sanctioned, violence.[2]

Judgment and Abandonment

Prior to the eleventh century, most Christians believed that Jesus died not to free us from the Father's wrath, but to free us from Satan's wrath. This is known as the *Christus Victor* view of the atonement, and in contrast to the penal substitutionary view, this view doesn't implicate God in any violence.

The truth is that, according to the NT, God the Father didn't need to engage in any violence to have Jesus suffer in our place. Jesus certainly suffered a lot of violence, but every bit of it was carried out by wicked humans who were influenced by Satan and other rebel powers.

The only thing God the Father did when Jesus suffered the judgment that we deserved was withdraw his protection to allow other agents who were "bent on destruction" (Isa 51:13) to do what they wanted to do to Jesus. So, for example, Paul says that God did not "spare his own Son" but "*gave him up* for us all" (Rom 8:32, emphasis added), and God "*delivered him over* to death for our sins" (Rom 4:25, emphasis added).

Jesus had already set the pattern for this way of talking about the Father's role in his crucifixion by repeatedly teaching, "the Son of Man will be handed over," or "delivered over," to be crucified.[3] Humans are also spoken of as "handing over" Jesus to be crucified, but in doing this, they were unwittingly playing into God's pre-

2. An excellent book that argues along these lines is A. Bartlett, *Cross Purposes: The Violent Grammar of Christian Atonement* (Harrisburg, PA: Trinity Press International, 2001).
3. Matt 20:18; 26:2; Mark 10:33; Luke 18:32; 24:7.

ordained plan (Acts 2:23; 4:28).[4] Ultimately, it was God the Father who "handed over" Jesus to be crucified.

***

Of course, in the process of withdrawing from Jesus to allow him to suffer, the Father was also abandoning him to bear the full weight of the world's sin and the full terror of the God-forsaken curse that comes with it. And this is why, as Jesus bore our sin and experienced the God-forsaken curse that we deserved, he cried out, "My God, My God, why have you forsaken me?" (Matt 27:46).

As I said earlier, in this moment God experienced *his own antithesis*. He was subjected to the total opposite of the perfect love that is his very essence, and we can be confident that the agony it brought Jesus is beyond anything we could possibly fathom.

This divine abandonment was the cup of God's wrath from which Jesus freely chose to drink (Mark 14:36).[5] In choosing to drink from this cup, Jesus suffered the death-consequences of sin, which included the curse of being separated from God. *This* is the wrath that Jesus experienced, and it involved no anger or violence on God's part.

The Grief Behind the Wrath

In fact, Jesus reveals that God is filled with grief when he sees that he must turn people over to the death-consequences of their sin—that is, when he decides they must experience his wrath. Jesus wept—or perhaps even wailed (*klaiō*)—as he prophesied that Jerusalem was going to be handed over to the Romans because of their persistent sin (Luke 19:41–44).

You can also hear Jesus's grieving heart when he prophesied that

4. "Delivering over" language is applied to Judas (Matt 26:14–15; Luke 22:6) as well as to Jewish authorities (Matt 27:18; Mark 15:1, 10; Luke 20:20). Incidentally, Acts 2:23 and 4:28 say that wicked humans carried out God's preordained plan to have Jesus crucified. But these passages *don't* teach or imply that God preordained which *individuals* would carry out this plan. That would make God the author of evil. See G. Boyd, *Is God to Blame? Beyond Pat Answers to the Problem of Suffering* (Downers Grove, IL: InterVarsity, 2003), 185–86.
5. On the OT background to the "cup of wrath" Jesus's had to drink from, see Jer 25:15–17; 49:12; 51:7; Lam 4:21; Ps 75:8; Zech 12:2–3; Hab 2:16. On discussions on God's wrath as abandonment, see J. Moltmann, *The Crucified God: The Cross as the Criterion and Criticism of Christian Theology* (Minneapolis: Fortress Press, 1993 [orig. German, 1973]), 191–92; 241–46; R. Feldmeier and H. Spieckerman, *God of the Living: A Biblical Theology*, trans. M. Biddle (Waco, TX: Baylor University Press, 2011), 351–52, cf. 378.

God was going to withdraw from the people of Jerusalem and leave the Temple desolate (Matt 23:38). Seeing the dire consequences this would have, Jesus cried out: "Jerusalem, Jerusalem, you who kill the prophets and stone those sent to you, how often I have longed to gather your children together, as a hen gathers her chicks under her wings, and you were not willing" (Matt 23:36–37).

Since Jesus reveals exactly what God is like down to his very essence, we must consider his intense grief over this impending judgment to be indicative of the grief God experiences whenever people come under his wrath. God longs to mercifully protect people from the destructive consequences of their choices, like a hen protects her chicks. But when people are not willing to be protected, and when God sees that his mercy is simply enabling their sin, he has no choice but to "hand them over" to suffer these consequences, just as he did with Jesus. And his heart wails in the process.

***

You can think about it like this. Sin is, at its root, the rejection of God, who is the "fountain of life."[6] So sin, by its very nature, leads to death. As the Lord says in Proverbs, "those who fail to find me harm themselves," and "all who hate me love death" (Prov 8:36). But God is "patient . . . not wanting anyone to perish" (2 Pet 3:9). So God mercifully restrains the death-consequences of sin in the hope that people will turn from their self-destructive behavior.

However, if people become so solidified in their rejection of God that his mercy is enabling their sin, God has no choice but to withdraw his restraining hand and, though it grieves him, to allow people to suffer his wrath.

As was true of Angela, sometimes love has to leave people alone and hope that what they couldn't learn from mercy they will learn by suffering.

***

When read through the looking-glass cross, a number of passages acquire extra significance inasmuch as they confirm that God's heart is grieved whenever he decides he must withdraw and turn people over to suffer the consequences of their decisions. For example, when

6. Ps 36:9; Jer 2:13.

Yahweh considered turning Moab over to the consequences of her sin, he cried out: "I wail over Moab, for all Moab I cry out" (Jer 48:31). So too, after announcing an impending judgment that was coming on Samaria, Yahweh declared: "I will weep and wail; I will go about barefoot and naked. I will howl like a jackal and moan like an owl" (Mic 1:8).

Similarly, you can hear the anguished heart of a loving parent when Yahweh saw that "Ephraim [another name for Israel] [was] joined to idols" and that he had to therefore withdraw and "leave him alone" to suffer at the hands of his enemy, Assyria (Hos 4:17). He cried out: "How can I give you up, Ephraim? How can I hand you over, Israel? . . . My heart is changed within me: all my compassion is aroused" (11:8). Terence Fretheim sums up what God experiences when he decides people must experience his wrath when he says, "Grief is what the godward side of judgment and wrath always look like."[7]

Now, since the ancient Israelites only caught glimpses of the truth, it isn't surprising that biblical authors didn't consistently grasp or express the grief that is behind God's wrath. Indeed, some portraits of God, such as those that echo the savage battling of the Ugarit god Anat that we discussed in the previous chapter, depict God as filled with bloodthirsty rage as he violently smites and even has his sword devour people. But we who know the full truth about God's character through the crucified Christ must be able to look past the culturally conditioned and sin-mirroring surface of these harsh portraits to discern the heavenly missionary stooping to bear the sin of his people.

The portraits of God grieving as he judges people reflect the Spirit of Christ breaking through to provide God's people "glimpses" of the truth. Conversely, portraits of God that resemble Anat reflect the cloudiness of their vision and bear witness to the heavenly missionary's willingness to allow this cloudiness to act upon him and to condition the way he appears in the inspired written witness to his missionary activity.

***

7. T. Fretheim, *Creation Untamed: The Bible, God, and Natural Disasters* (Grand Rapids: Baker Academic, 2010), 60.

Even apart from the biblical confirmations of God's grieving heart, however, the revelation of God in the crucified Christ should be enough to convince us that God experiences intense grief whenever he must judge people. For the cross reveals a God whose love for people is inconceivably greater than the finite and fallen love we have for ourselves and our loved ones. And this entails that the suffering that God experiences when he must turn people over to the death-consequences of their sin must be inconceivably greater than whatever suffering the people themselves experience.

When punishing children, parents sometimes tell them, "This hurts me more than it hurts you." Well, if ever this is true, it is a million times truer of God!

Not only this, but since Jesus suffered the death-consequences of sin for the purpose of redeeming the world, we should conclude that God always aims at redemption when he must allow people to suffer his judgment. And we find this confirmed throughout Scripture. If God strikes Egypt, for example, it is so "they will turn to the Lord, and he will respond to their pleas and heal them" (Isa 19:22).

In this light, I believe we must envision the Father wailing rather than raging, and hopeful rather than vengeful, when he abandoned his Son on the cross to suffer the judgment we deserved. And since the cross reveals what God has always been like, we must envision this same grieving-yet-hopeful posture whenever God sees he has no choice but to abandon people to suffer the destructive consequences of their sin.

***

It's vitally important that readers understand that this does not mean that whenever people suffer it's because they are being judged. I am talking specifically about events that are specifically identified as divine judgments in Scripture: I'm not offering a general explanation for why people suffer.

As I've argued elsewhere, we live in a world in which every decision that every free agent has ever made exerts an ongoing influence on what comes to pass. For this reason, we can't know why things unfold as they do, including why people experience good and evil so randomly.[8] What we can know, however, is that evil originates in

8. G. Boyd, *Is God to Blame? Moving Beyond Pat Answers to the Problem of Suffering* (Downers Grove, IL: InterVarsity, 2003).

the hearts of human or angelic agents, not God. Moreover, we can know that, regardless of the cause of one's suffering, the cross allows us to embrace the truth that God grieves for the sufferer and he is always on the side of healing, restoration, and redemption.

Causing Evil to Self-Destruct

The cross not only reveals that God judges sin by turning people over to the consequences of their sin; it also reveals that this is how God defeats evil. He uses what I call an Aikido-style of judgment. Aikido is a nonviolent school of martial arts in which practitioners never respond to aggressors by using their own aggressive force. Instead they outsmart their opponents by using techniques that turn every aggressive action back on the aggressor. Aggressors thus end up punishing themselves.

This is precisely the method God used to judge the sin of the world and vanquish evil on Calvary. To understand how the cross reveals God's Aikido-style of judgment, we need only connect three dots.

First, the NT indicates that Satan and other fallen powers helped orchestrate the crucifixion. Among other things, John tells us that Satan entered into Judas just before he betrayed Jesus (John 13:2, 27). And Paul informs us that the "rulers of this age" (referring to Satan and other rebel cosmic powers) crucified the "Lord of glory" (1 Cor 2:7–8).

Second, demons readily recognized Jesus as the Son of God, but they were completely mystified as to why he had come to earth.[9]

Third, Paul informs us that, had Satan and the rebel powers who currently reign over the world understood "God's wisdom," they "would not have crucified the Lord of glory" (1 Cor 2:7–8). For it is by means of the crucifixion, which they helped orchestrate, that they are being reduced "to nothing" (1 Cor 2:6). As we read in Colossians, by means of the cross, God "disarmed the powers and authorities" and "made a public spectacle of them" (Col 2:15).

When we connect these three dots, we see that God managed to get the kingdom of darkness to orchestrate the very event that brought about its own demise. And it's not too difficult to understand how God did this.

9. Matt 2:23; 8:29; Mark 1:24; 5:7; Luke 4:34.

***

To the degree that an agent is evil, it can no more understand love than a sociopath can understand empathy. While we aren't given any details, Scripture tells us that Satan and the rebel cosmic powers had made themselves evil by rebelling against God sometime in the distant past.[10]

This explains why the demonic kingdom was mystified when the Son of God came to earth. These evil agents simply could not fathom the possibility that the Son of God loved humans so much that he was willing to set aside his divine advantages to become one of them and to die on their behalf (Phil 2:6–8). For the same reason, these agents could not suspect that there was a love-motivated wise plan in play that would eventually bring them to nothing.

The only thing these evil agents knew was that the Son of God had, for some unknown reason, become mortal and had entered into the domain in which Satan is "ruler" (John 12:32), "god" (2 Cor 4:4), and "the principal ruler of the air" (Eph 2:2). And this meant that the Son of God *could be killed*.

So Satan and the rebel powers influenced people like Judas who had, by their own free choices, made themselves susceptible to their demonic influence, to bring about Jesus's crucifixion. Only too late did these rebel "rulers" realize that, by crucifying the Lord of glory, they had played into the loving and wise plan of God that had been kept hidden throughout the ages.[11]

God knew all along that the self-chosen evil character of Satan and his minions would render them unable to understand why Jesus had become a human. At the same time, God knew that these rebel powers would not be able to pass up this unexpected opportunity to kill his Son.

Only after the deed was done did these rebel powers learn that Jesus was the Father's proverbial Trojan Horse! Satan and the powers thought they had overthrown the Son of God when they got him crucified, but it was by this very crucifixion that Satan's kingdom was disarmed (Col 2:15) and "the prince of this world" was "driven out" (John 12:31). So too, it was by means of this perfect expression of God's self-sacrificial love that God in principle "destroy[ed] the devil's work" (1 John 3:8), broke "the power of him who holds the power of

10. 2 Pet 2:4; Jude 1:6.
11. 1 Cor 2:7; Col 1:26.

death," and thereby freed "those who all their lives were held in slavery by their fear of death" (Heb 2:14).[12]

God wisely used the evil of Satan's loveless heart and inability to understand love to get him to orchestrate the destruction of his own evil kingdom. In other words, *God used evil to vanquish evil*!

This was God's *Aikido strategy* in action. And since the cross reveals what God has always been like, we should assume that this is how the all-wise God has always punished sin and how he continues to vanquish evil.

As we'll see in the following two chapters, it is an assumption that finds a wealth of biblical confirmations.

12. I say *in principle* because, while the kingdom of darkness has been defeated, the world remains under the deception of Satan (Rev 13:14). Hence the victory of the cross and the new creation it brings about will not be *fully manifested* until Jesus brings the whole creation under his Lordship at the end of this age. This is what is known as the "already-not-yet" tension that runs throughout the NT. For a more in-depth discussion of how God defeated the kingdom of darkness on Calvary, see *CWG*, vol. 2, ch. 22.

10

Self-Punishing Sin

Your wickedness will punish you;
your backsliding will rebuke you.
—Jeremiah 2:19

[S]elf-punishment and punishment at God's hands
are not two distinct realities.
—R. Schwager

From Young Rocker to Thief

I have always loved music. I spend an hour or so almost every morning rocking out to music at full volume. I wear headphones with a built-in subwoofer that vibrates to the pulsating bass. I listen mostly to melodic heavy metal, and it just doesn't play well soft! My wife frequently reminds me that this could damage my hearing, but her advice falls on deaf ears. (Sorry, I couldn't resist.) But I've made a deal with her. If at any point my hearing stops being better than hers—because it actually is—I will repent and turn the music down.

Until then, it's full volume—*with subwoofers*!

When I was younger, I was even more of a music addict than I am today. The trouble was, I couldn't afford many albums, and even Led Zeppelin, Iron Butterfly, and The Doors start to grow old if you can't mix in other artists now and then. So at some point I decided to get creative—I started stealing albums. (Note to younger readers: back in the olden days, albums were recorded on twelve-inch circular sheets of plastic and played on ancient devices known as "record players.") At the tender age of twelve, I had become a thief.

At first it was terrifying, but with each theft I grew calmer and more confident. And once I'd acquired a collection that satisfied my hunger, it occurred to me that my creative specialty could provide the money I needed to finally replace the loser drum set I'd been playing with a more professional set. So I increased my nefarious activity and began selling the stolen records.

But after nine months of successful thievery, I got caught. As always, I was wearing my long overcoat with custom-designed lining that allowed me to conceal up to ten albums at a time. This clever coat had served me well all winter long. As I look back on that terrible day, however, I suspect it was this coat, together with my profuse sweating on this 90 degree day in June, that tipped off the undercover cop.

Consider it further proof that the prefrontal lobe, which is the part of the brain responsible for rational decision making, is *significantly* underdeveloped in adolescent boys.

In any event, that was the worst day of my life. After I had received the loudest and most expletive-filled tongue lashing in history, my father took away my record player and grounded me for a month. It was a month from hell, but it worked. I was never tempted to steal again.

The punishment I received from my father is what ethicists call a *judicial* form of punishment. This means that there was no organic connection between my stealing and my being grounded and banned from music. The punishment was simply imposed on me. By contrast, if I were to ever lose my hearing from listening to unreasonably loud heavy metal, that would be what ethicists call an *organic* form of punishment. For in this case my loss of hearing is directly connected to my rebellious refusal to listen to my wife's wise counsel to turn my music down.

Contrary to what many people think, the Bible generally construes God's punishment of sin as *organic* in nature.[1] God doesn't *impose*

1. Two of the many scholars who have demonstrated this are S. Travis, *Christ and the Judgment of God: The Limits of Divine Retribution in New Testament Thought* (Milton Keynes, UK: Paternoster, 2008), and K. Koch, "Is There a Doctrine of Retribution in the Old Testament?" in *Theodicy in the Old Testament*, ed. J. L. Crenshaw (London: SPCK, 1983), 57–87. For a more comprehensive and in-depth review of the material covered in this chapter, see *CWG*, vol. 2, chs. 16–17.

punishments on people. The destructive consequences of sin are *built into the sin itself.* And this is why God only needs to withdraw and let sin run its self-destructive course when he judges people.

Divine Abandonment

With the exception of its violent portraits of God, the Bible *always* describes God's judgments in terms of divine abandonment. For within the biblical worldview, to be separated from God is the worst thing imaginable. God's presence is the source of all that is desirable and it is what the human heart most longs for. As Sarah Richter notes, the "paradise that was Eden, the paradise that is the Holy of Holies," as well as "the coming paradise which the prophets envision, are all characterized by this single concept: YHWH is present."[2]

This is why the Psalmist confesses that the "earth has nothing I desire besides you" (Ps 73:23). Apart from Yahweh's presence he finds "no good thing" (Ps 16:2). To dwell in God's presence and gaze upon his beauty is his all-consuming aspiration (Ps 27:4).[3] So too, the greatest blessing God can give people is his own presence, which is why one of the most common ways OT authors indicate that an individual or group was blessed is to say that *God was with them.*[4] And this is why the very worst thing that could happen is for God to "hide his face" from a person or a group.[5]

But there's another reason God's presence was supremely important to ancient Israelites. They were surrounded by hostile nations, and in their better moments—when they weren't disobediently trusting in their swords or building alliances with other countries—they knew they were completely dependent on Yahweh's protection. The only real security they had was to abide in God's presence and take "refuge in the shelter of [his] wings" (Ps 61:4).

The importance of this divine protection is reflected in the wealth of protective metaphors such as "fortress," "refuge," "rock," and "shield" that get applied to God.[6] It's also reflected in the many

2. S. Richter, *The Deuteronomistic History and the Name Theology: lešakkēn šemô šām in the Bible and the Ancient Near East* (Berlin: Walter de Gruyter, 2002), 11. I should note that "YHWH" is simply a more academic way of referring to "Yahweh," since the original Hebrew contained no vowels.

3. See also Pss 23:6; 61:4.

4. Gen 39:20–21; Num 14:8–9; Hag 2:4.

5. Deut 31:17–18; 32:20; Ps 13:1; 27:9; 44:24; 69:17; 88:14; 102:2; 143:7; Jer 33:5.

6. Ps 91:2–4; Gen 15:1; Deut 33:12; 1 Sam 2:2; 2 Sam 22:2–3, 31–32, 47; Pss 3:3; 7:10; 9:9; 14:6;

passages that depict Yahweh watching over and protecting his people. For example, in Isaiah Yahweh likens his people to "a fruitful vineyard" and declares, "I, the Lord, watch over it; I water it continually. I guard it day and night so that no one may harm it" (Isa 27:3). And if any briers and thorns threaten the field, they will have to "confront me," the Lord says (v. 4).

So, whenever the Israelites found they were falling victim to the hostile aspirations of another nation, they assumed this could only mean that God was no longer with them. Biblical authors often couldn't understand why God had abandoned them as is made clear by the many questions and complaints that are voiced to God throughout the OT. But whether or not they understood why it happened, the prevailing assumption was that God had "hidden his face" in response to their sin.[7] And the destructive consequences that resulted from this abandonment were identified as God's wrath.

***

To illustrate, in 2 Chronicles 12 a prophet warns the elders of Judah of an impending attack by a ruthless Egyptian king named Shishak. Through this prophet the Lord explains: "You have abandoned me; therefore, I now abandon you to Shishak" (v. 5). The elders humbled themselves and repented, so Yahweh rescinded the planned judgment, saying: "My wrath will not be poured out on Jerusalem through Shishak" (v. 7).

It's clear from this passage that Yahweh's "wrath" was nothing other than his abandoning his people to this Egyptian king. In the words of Feldmeier and Spieckerman,

> God hides his countenance and leaves people to themselves. The wrathful God of the Bible is a God who turns away in response to the creature who turns away and who leaves it to itself and its desires and thus ultimately abandons it to death.[8]

18:2, 30–31, 46; 19:14; 28:1, 8; 34:8; 46:7; 64:10; 73:26; 91:2, 9; 92:15; 94:22; 144:1; Isa 26:4; 30:29; 51:1; Hab 1:12.

7. Several good books on this theme are J. S. Burnett, *Where Is God? Divine Absence in the Hebrew Bible* (Minneapolis: Fortress Press, 2010); S. Balentine, *The Hidden God: The Hiding of the Face of God in the Old Testament* (Oxford: Oxford University Press, 1983); R. E. Friedman, *The Disappearance of God: A Divine Mystery* (Boston: Little, Brown, 1995); and S. Terrien, *The Elusive Presence: Toward a New Biblical Theology* (San Francisco: Harper & Row, 1978).
8. R. Feldmeier and H. Spieckerman, *God of the Living: A Biblical Theology*, trans. M. Biddle

But how is it that sin can be punished and evil vanquished merely by God withdrawing his presence? The answer to this question has to do with the kind of world God created.

The Organic Connection between Sin and Punishment

Believe it or not, the OT does not have a distinct word for *punishment*.[9] Instead, the "biblical language for judgment . . . refers to the *effects* of human sin, not [to] a penalty or punishment that God pronounces on the situation or 'sends' on the perpetrators."[10] The Hebrew words for "wickedness" (*ra'ah*), "sin" (*hattā't*), "trespass" (*āwān*), and "corruption" (*sāhat*) have the same root as the words used to describe *the destructive effects* of these sins ("disaster," "trouble," "destruction"). And this indicates that ancient Israelites generally understood the relationship between sin and punishment to be organic, not judicial, in nature.

Related to this, Klaus Koch argues that the phrase that is usually translated "retaliate" or "pay back" (*šlm Pi*) actually means "bringing to completion."[11] Sinners receive the punishment for their sin when their sin is allowed to be brought to completion. The book of James captures this concept well: "Each person is tempted when they are dragged away by their own evil desire and enticed. Then, after desire has conceived, it gives birth to sin; and sin, when it is full-grown, gives birth to death" (Jas 1:14–15).

It's apparent that the relationship between sin and its punishment is as natural and organic as the relationship between the *conception*, *birth*, *adulthood*, and *death* of a person. God doesn't need to punish sinners by killing them, for when their sin becomes "full-grown," it naturally "gives birth to death."

(Waco, TX: Baylor University Press, 2011), 340. All of chapter 11 of this work, titled "Hiddenness and Wrath" (ibid., 339–60), is extremely informative.

9. Koch, "Doctrine of Retribution," 77. The word *paqad* is often translated "to punish," but Koch makes a compelling case that it is better translated as "to visit." So too, Gerhard von Rad, followed by many others, argues that "punish" is never the appropriate translation of this word (*Old Testament Theology*, 2 vols. [New York: Harper & Row, 1962], 1:265, 385). See also T. Fretheim, *Creation Untamed: The Bible, God, and Natural Disasters* (Grand Rapids: Baker Academic, 2010), 51.
10. Fretheim, *Creation Untamed*, 49. For an analysis of the various words used to express sin in the OT, see D. Patrick, "Crimes and Punishments, OT and NT," in *New Interpreter's Dictionary of the Bible*, ed. K. D. Sakenfeld, vol. 1 (Nashville: Abingdon, 2006), 790–802 (790–91).
11. Koch, "Doctrine of Retribution," 60–64.

Along the same lines, numerous passages state that people are judged when they experience "the fruit of their schemes."[12] That is, sin grows into punishment the same way seeds grow to become fruit-bearing trees. As we read in Proverbs, "Whoever sows injustice reaps calamity" (22:8).

It's apparent that the destructive consequences of sin are a "testimony to the way in which God made the world." The organic connection between sin and punishment reflects the "moral order" of God's creation, which is why God need only "hide his face" to allow sinners to come to judgment (Deut 31:17–18).[13]

This is how ancient Israelites *generally* understood sin and punishment. But given that these people were only capable of receiving glimpses of the truth, and given the strong influence their ANE environment had on them, we should not be surprised to learn that this isn't how the Israelites *always* understood sin and judgment. On the contrary, we have seen that the OT contains a number of portraits of Yahweh judicially imposing violent judgments on people, just like other ANE deities did.

Since God didn't impose a violent judgment on Jesus but simply abandoned him to agents who were already bent on destruction, we must understand the organic conception of sin and punishment to be a *direct* God-breathed revelation while assessing the violent portraits of God to be *indirect* God-breathed revelations.

Self-Punishing Nature of Sin

This organic conception of sin and judgment gets expressed in a remarkably diversity of ways throughout the Bible. For example, before I began reading the Bible through the lens of the looking-glass cross, I'd never noticed how frequently biblical authors depict people being punished *by their own sin*. Once I understood how significant this was in light of the cross, I began seeing it everywhere!

For example, using standard ANE warrior imagery, the Psalmist says that Yahweh "will sharpen his sword" and "bend and string his bow" as he prepares "his deadly weapons" and makes "ready his flaming arrows" (Ps 7:12–13). Considered by itself, this imagery would

12. Jer 6:19; 17:10; Hos 10:13.

13. Fretheim, *Creation Untamed*, 49; see also Fretheim, *God and World in the Old Testament* (Nashville: Abingdon, 2005), 19–20, 163–65.

naturally lead us to expect Yahweh to descend from heaven and personally massacre people, and to this extent these verses bear witness to the sin-bearing activity of the heavenly missionary.

But we can discern the Spirit breaking through in the following verses as the author describes *how* this warrior deity swings his "sword" and shoots his "flaming arrows."

> Those who are pregnant with evil
> conceive trouble and give birth to disillusionment.
> Those who dig a hole and scoop it out
> fall into the pit they have made.
> *The trouble they cause recoils on them;*
> *their violence comes down on their own heads.* (vv. 14–16, emphasis added)

While the noncoercive God accommodated the ANE warrior imagery that we find in this passage, the Spirit also managed to completely undermine its violence. It turns out that God's "sharpened sword" and "flaming arrows" are nothing other than the natural self-destructive consequences of people's own behavior!

Notice also the Aikido dimension of this judgment. Violent people eventually find their violence ricocheting back on their heads. As Yahweh says to the king of Babylon, "The violence *you* have done to Lebanon *will overwhelm you.*" He goes on to address the terror that the King had inflicted upon animals by saying, "*your* destruction of animals will *terrify you*" (Hab 2:17, emphasis added).

This same conception is reflected in the passages that teach us that "the wicked are brought down by their own wickedness."[14] And it is reflected as well in the multitude of passages in which people are described as bringing judgment on themselves and harming themselves.[15] *This* is what it looks like when Yahweh wields his sharpened sword and shoots his flaming arrows!

***

Another way the OT reflects the organic conception of divine judgment is by describing sin as inherently self-destructive. To illustrate,

14. Prov 11:5; see also 5:22; 8:36; 21:7; 26:27.
15. According to Fretheim, there are over fifty passages that describe God's judgment in terms of people punishing themselves (Fretheim, *Creation Untamed*, 50n50; Fretheim, *God and World*, 340n25). See, for example, Isa 3:8–9; 59:17–18; 64:5–9; Jer 2:17; 4:18; 6:11, 19; 7:18–20; 21:12–15; 25:7; 44:7–8; 50:10–11, 24–25; Lam 3:64–65.

in response to his grievous sins, Yahweh tells the king of Tyre, "I made a fire *come out from you*, and it consumed you, and I reduced you to ashes on the ground in the sight of all who were watching" (Ezek 28:18, emphasis added). The imagery of a king being consumed by fire that originates within himself suggests that this king was destroyed by his own wickedness.[16]

A particularly fascinating example of this is found in Isaiah 33. In light of an impending judgment, the "terrified . . . sinners in Zion" ask, "Who of us can dwell with the consuming fire? Who of us can dwell with everlasting burning?" (v. 14). Read out of context, one might suppose that Yahweh was planning on burning these sinners alive! But when we place this verse in its broader context, it's clear that this consuming fire resided *within the sinners themselves*, for several verses prior to this one Yahweh says to his people,

> You conceive chaff,
> you give birth to straw;
> your breath is a fire that consumes you.
> The peoples will be burned as if to lime;
> like cut thorn bushes they will be set ablaze. (vv. 11–12)

Consider this interesting mix of metaphors. On the one hand, the wickedness of people is expressed in terms of conceiving "chaff" and giving "birth to straw." On the other hand, their wickedness is conceived of as breathing out fire, and it's by this fire that people are "set ablaze . . . like cut thorn bushes." So this passage is teaching us that people who persistently rebel against God eventually self-destruct.

God's Aikido Response to Evil in the New Testament

As we should expect given the progressive nature of revelation, God's Aikido response to sin is even clearer in the NT.

For starters, what did Jesus do when people didn't want him around? He simply granted them their wish and went away.[17] And when people decided they didn't want to follow him, what did Jesus

16. For example, E. Fisch, *Ezekiel: Hebrew Text & English Translation with an Introduction and Commentary* (London: Soncino, 1950), 193, and M. Greenberg, *Ezekiel 21–37* (New York: Doubleday, 1997), 587. Isaiah 14 also illustrates the self-destructive nature of Satan (as well as of the haughty king of Babylon) when this agent is said to "have destroyed" his own "land" and to "have killed" his own "people" (v. 20).

17. Matt 8:34–9:1; 12:14–15; cf. Mark 3:6–7; John 8:58–59.

do? He simply granted them their wish and let them go, even though it grieved him to do so.[18] Reflecting the noncoercive character of God, Jesus never forced himself on anyone.

Nor did Jesus ever retaliate against those who rejected him. In fact, when some of his disciples wanted to retaliate by replicating Elijah's display of supernatural violence, Jesus rebuked them.[19] If we see the Father when we see Jesus (John 14:7–9), we have to consider Jesus's response to those who rejected him to be reflective of the way the Father has always responded to those who reject him.

***

Another strong confirmation that God judges by withdrawing is found in Jesus's prophecy about the Temple becoming "desolate," cited in the previous chapter (Matt 23:37–38). The word he uses is *erēmos*, and it describes a place that has been vacated. Jesus is here stating that "the divine presence has left the Temple in Jerusalem."[20]

Without its divine protector, the Temple and the entire city of Jerusalem were vulnerable to Roman soldiers who were as "bent on destruction" as anyone could be. And so, just as Jesus prophesied, between 66 and 70 CE Roman soldiers responded to a Jewish rebellion by mercilessly ransacking Jerusalem, inflicting atrocities on its inhabitants, and destroying the Temple (Matt 23:34–39). Anticipating this terrible suffering is what caused Jesus to cry as he rode into Jerusalem (Luke 19:41).

Interestingly enough, Paul explicitly identifies this destruction as an expression of God's wrath (1 Thess 2:14–16). And yet, it was wicked humans, not God, who freely carried out the violence that was involved in this expression of wrath.

***

Along similar lines, in Romans 1 Paul describes the "wrath of God" that is "being revealed from heaven against all the godlessness and wickedness of human beings who suppress the truth by their wickedness" (v. 18). Since the people Paul is speaking about sinned

18. Mark 10:21–22; John 6:60–61, 66.
19. Luke 9:55; cf. 1 Kgs 1:9–12.
20. M. Johnson-DeBaufre, "The Blood Required of This Generation: Interpreting Communal Blame in a Colonial Context," in *Violence in the New Testament*, ed. S. Matthews and E. L. Gibson (New York: T&T Clark, 2005), 22–34 (25).

by rejecting God and worshiping idols (vv. 21–22), God "*gave them over* in the sinful desires of their hearts" (vv. 21–23, emphasis added). Moreover, since they "exchanged the truth about God for a lie . . . God *gave them over* to shameful lusts" (vv. 23–24, emphasis added). And, finally, since "they did not think it worthwhile to retain the knowledge of God . . . God *gave them over* to a depraved mind" (v. 28, emphasis added).

Notice that this passage assumes that God's Spirit had up to this point been mercifully restraining the sinful impulses of these people, hoping that they would repent. But, as the Lord announced prior to the Flood, his "Spirit will not contend with humans forever" (Gen 6:3). When God saw that his mercy had no hope of turning these sinners around, he had no choice but to withdraw his Spirit, thereby allowing people to fall into the inherently self-destructive desires of their heart.

***

God's Aikido strategy is also reflected in Jesus's instructions on how the church is to discipline members. If a person will not repent and be reconciled to someone they've wronged, despite the fact that the church has made every effort to help them, Jesus says the church must "treat them as you would a pagan or a tax collector" (Matt 18:15–17).

Now, this obviously doesn't mean the church should stop loving them, for Jesus loved pagans and tax collectors and, in any case, he commands his disciples to love everyone. Jesus is rather saying that if a person in effect rejects the kingdom community by obstinately refusing to repent and be reconciled, the church should no longer consider this person to be part of the kingdom community.

In other words, the church is to discipline unrepentant members by releasing them to do what they want to do. And the church is to discipline this way because this is how God disciplines.

As a matter of fact, immediately after giving the above instructions, Jesus makes this connection explicit: "Truly I tell you, whatever you bind on earth will be bound in heaven, and whatever you loose on earth will be loosed in heaven. For where two or three come together in my name, there am I with them" (Matt 18:19–20).

In this last sentence, Jesus promises to be with his disciples when they make decisions about releasing someone from the community. So this passage is not only illustrating that the church's Aikido-style of discipline *reflects* God's discipline, it is teaching that God, in the person of Christ, will be *involved in* the church's Aikido-style of discipline. The church's decisions regarding "binding and loosing" members reflect God's own decisions about "binding and loosing."

The same view is advocated by Paul as he confronts the Corinthian church for condoning a sexual relationship that a member was having with his stepmother (1 Cor 5:1–2). Assuming this man remained unrepentant, Paul told the church to assemble, remembering that Christ was present among them, and to "hand this man over to Satan for the destruction of the flesh, so that his spirit may be saved on the day of the Lord" (vv. 3–5).[21]

The assumption behind Paul's instruction is that, to release a person from the kingdom community is to turn them over to Satan, the "destroyer," who reigns everywhere outside the community.[22] So this community was participating in God's Aikido response to sin by withdrawing its protection, thereby allowing this man to suffer the destructive consequences of his sin.

It is also worthing pointing out that it was Satan, *not God*, who destroyed this man's "flesh." Moreover, notice that Paul gave this instruction so that this man "may be saved on the day of the Lord." As we mentioned in the previous chapter, when God sees he must turn people over to suffer the consequences of their sin, he does so with the hope that this tough love will eventually save them.

Three Questions about Divine Aikido

I'm guessing that at this point some readers have some questions that need addressing.

First, if a nation is certain to be judged by God withdrawing his protection, must not God control the agents he uses to bring about this judgment? For example, God judged Israel by allowing Nebuchadnezzar, the king of Babylon, to attack. But what would have happened if Nebuchadnezzar had decided, for whatever reason, not to embark on this military campaign?

In response, the "moral order" of creation that ensures that people's sin recoils back on them has been described by one renowned OT scholar as "a complex, loose causal weave of act and consequences."[23]

21. Similarly, see 1 Tim 1:20.
22. Rev 12:9; see also 2 Cor 4:4; 1 John 5:19.
23. Fretheim, *Creation Untamed*, 49.

The causal weave is loose inasmuch as it is *not rigidly deterministic*. So while it is certain that persistent sin will *eventually* reap destructive consequences, the precise when, where, and how can be affected by any number of variables, including the decisions of free agents, both human and angelic.

The nondeterministic, open-ended nature of this "loose causal weave" is reflected in the fact that some of God's judgments in the Bible did not unfold quite the way God intended, and the attack on Israel by Nebuchadnezzar is a case in point. Scripture tells us that this king and his army went beyond what Yahweh had intended. "I was only a little angry," the Lord said, "but [the Babylonians] added to the calamity" (Zech 1:15).[24] This sort of thing actually happens quite often in the Bible, and each instance makes it clear that God doesn't micromanage the agents he uses to express his judgments.[25]

***

Second, some readers might be worried that the Aikido conception of divine judgment that I've outlined over the last two chapters implies an overly passive God. Am I suggesting that when God withdraws to bring about a judgment, he simply stands back and watches?

Some scholars who embrace this organic understanding of God's judgments hold that, while God withdraws his protective presence when bringing about a judgment, he may nevertheless continue to influence events to keep the judgment on track, as much as this is necessary, and as much as this is possible, given God's commitment to treat all people *as persons* and to therefore work by means of influential, rather than coercive, power. I am in agreement with this perspective *so long as it is granted that God never influences people in a direction that is contrary to his own cruciform character.*

For example, to bring a judgment on Israel, God may have influenced events to make sure nothing prevented the king of Babylon from doing what he wanted to do: namely, to violently subjugate Israel. But it would contradict the cruciform character of God to suppose that God placed the desire to violently subjugate Israel in

24. For an insightful essay on this passage, see T. Fretheim, "I Was Only a Little Angry: Divine Violence in the Prophets," *Interpretation: A Commentary for Preaching and Teaching* 58, no. 4 (October 2004): 365–75.
25. J. Sanders, *The God Who Risks: A Theology of Divine Providence*, 2nd ed. (Downers Grove, IL: InterVarsity, 2007 [1998]), 81–83, 132–39.

this king's heart when he wouldn't have otherwise desired this. This would make God the cause of evil, and this is obviously inconsistent with what we learn about God from the crucified Christ.

So while God is willing to use people (and, we'll later see, cosmic agents) who are already "bent on destruction" to bring about divine judgments, I deny that God would ever *make* a person (or cosmic agent) become "bent on destruction" so that he could use them for this purpose.

***

Finally, some readers may be wondering if the Aikido conception of divine judgment implies that the ultimate reason nations today lose battles or suffer disasters is because God withdrew his protection, and one might wonder this about individual misfortunes as well. In light of the many ill-advised Christians today who think they can discern the hand of God behind the afflictions that nations and/or individuals suffer, I consider this to be an important question.

And my answer to it is an unequivocal and adamant, *No*!

The only reason we know that Babylon's attack on Jerusalem was the result of God turning his people over to the destructive consequences of their sin is because we are told this in Scripture. If we didn't have this information, we'd have no grounds for suspecting this.

Not only this, but Jesus explicitly *rebuked* people who claimed to discern the hand of God behind disasters that came upon various groups (Luke 13:1–5) as well as afflictions that came upon individuals (John 9:1–3).[26] Moreover, while Jesus and the Gospel authors don't completely rule the possibility that an affliction could on occasion reflect a divine judgment (e.g. John 5:14), they uniformly view people's afflictions as the work of Satan and his minions, and Jesus reveals God's will for these people by *healing them*.

In this light, I submit that the default assumption of Christians should be that when groups or individuals suffer misfortune, it simply reflects the fact that God endowed human and angelic agents with free will. And because free will empowers these agents to exert a genuine influence over what comes to pass, for better or for worse, God

26. See G. Boyd, *God at War: The Bible and Spiritual Conflict* (Downers Grove, IL: InterVarsity, 1997), 231–36, where I make the case that, contrary to standard translations, John 9:1–3 does not teach that God caused this man to be born blind.

cannot coercively intervene to prevent the harm they intend toward others.

Of course, the all-good God is always *influentially* working to maximize good and minimize evil. And God has certainly empowered his people to increase this influence through prayer. But however strong this influence is, it stops short of coercively overriding an agent's free will.[27]

As I mentioned in the previous chapter, when agents use their agency to harm others, the God whose essence is perfect love suffers unimaginably more than do the people that are harmed. But the risk that God and others might experience great pain in this world is the price that God, and us, have to be willing to pay to have a creation in which agents are capable of genuine love. And the very fact that all healthy people enter into loving relationships with others, despite the risk, together with the fact that people keep bringing children into the world, suggests that we all agree that love is worth the risk.

***

I was frankly surprised when I first discovered these confirmations of God's Aikido response to sin and evil in the Bible. But what surprised me even more was when I began to discover these sorts of confirmations *in the very narratives that depict God acting in violent ways*! That is, the very narratives that attribute violent actions to God usually provide clues that this violence was actually carried out by other agents who were already bent on violence. Though the authors ascribe the violence involved in a divine judgment to God, the only thing God actually did is precisely what he did on the cross: with a grieving heart and a redemptive motive, he withdrew his presence to allow violent agents to do what they already wanted to do.

To my mind, the material we're about to review in the following chapter provides the strongest confirmation yet of the cross-based interpretation of the OT's violent portraits of God.

27. For an in-depth treatment of issues related to God's providence and free will, see G. Boyd, *Is God to Blame? Moving Beyond Pat Answers to the Problem of Suffering* (Downers Grove, IL: InterVarsity, 2003). For a deeply moving and insightful account of a mother using this model of providence as she wrestles to make sense of the tragic death of her four-year-old son, see J. Kelley, *Lord Willing? Wrestling with God's Role in My Child's Death* (Harrisonburg, VA: Herald Press, 2016).

11

Doing and Allowing

God and God's agents . . .
are often the subject of the same destructive verbs . . .
—T. Fretheim[1]

"*You* Killed My Son!"

For God as well as for us, there's a point where merciful love crosses over into destructive enabling. You will recall from the story that opened chapter 9 that Angela at some point realized that her love for Charlie, her alcoholic husband, had crossed that line. Though it grieved her deeply, she knew she had to take their two children and leave. This was not only for the good of her and her children: it was, Angela believed, the last remaining hope that Charlie would eventually hit bottom and turn his life around.

But in a world where people and angelic agents have real choices, there are no guarantees that every story will have a happy ending. And, unfortunately, Angela's story tragically illustrates this truth.

Charlie's parents, who were classic co-dependent enablers, were enraged when Angela left. Angela told me she had to eventually block their calls because of the many raging and accusatory voice messages they left her. What most angered them was that they had to take over the full task of caring for Charlie. And to make matters worse, in his depression over losing his family, Charlie's downward

1. Terence E. Fretheim, *Creation Untamed: The Bible, God, and Natural Disasters* (Grand Rapids: Baker Academic, 2010), 53.

spiral through alcohol abuse accelerated. Yet, however bad things got, his parents kept trying to shield their beloved son from the pain of his self-destructive decisions.

Charlie's father somehow managed to keep him out of prison after his fourth DWI, even though Charlie had almost killed a pedestrian when he crashed his car into a building. After Charlie was fired from another job and could no longer afford to keep his house, his parents took him in and assumed total responsibility for the sale of his house. And they even looked the other way when it came to the question of how Charlie continued to afford his daily consumption of Jack Daniels. They suspected Charlie had begun selling illegal contraband (which turned out to be true), but they never asked.

This went on for almost a year. Then one night, with a blood alcohol level four times the legal limit, Charlie drove in the wrong direction on a freeway with his headlights turned off. He had a head-on collision with a semi-tractor trailer. The driver of the semi experienced only minor injuries, but Charlie was killed instantly. Some suspected Charlie had committed suicide, though the official report was that it was an alcohol-related accident.

But this story is not quite over. As Angela was walking back to her car with her two children immediately after Charlie's buriel, she was confronted by Charlie's father. She told me that his face was soaked in tears, but his expression was one of pure rage. He planted himself directly in front of Angela and the children, pointed his finger at her and said through clenched teeth: "This is on *you*! *You* abandoned my boy! *You* killed Charlie!"

These were obviously disturbing words, but fortunately Angela was healthy enough to be above believing them. She was able to hear this terrible accusation as nothing more than the cries of an anguished father, and she had compassion on him. And with her heart of compassion, Angela understood that this father felt the need to blame her because he couldn't bear the pain of facing the possibility that he and his wife had actually played a role in Charlie's death.

As I noted in chapter 9, Angela's story illustrates the truth that for God as well as for people, love sometimes requires us to stop mercifully protecting a loved one from the painful consequences of their decisions, in hope that they will learn from pain what they could not learn from mercy. But it also illustrates the truth that sometimes the one who must allow a loved one to fall gets blamed for their falling, especially by those who actually do share some of the blame for their falling.

***

In keeping with their ANE culture, when OT authors attribute violence to God, they usually intend it as an expression of praise. But when the violence they believe God engages in seems unjust, they sometimes respond the way Charlie's father did to Angela.[2] Whether they are crediting or blaming God, however, God is made to look guilty of *having done* what he in fact merely *allowed*, because he had no better option.

Interestingly enough, whether they are crediting or blaming God when they depict him in violent ways, the very narratives in which they do this almost always contain indications that confirm that the violence they ascribe to God was actually carried out by other agents. And even when their own narratives don't provide such confirmations, other aspects of the biblical narratives do.

What follows is a sampling of narratives that illustrate this point.[3]

Who Killed Firstborn Egyptian Males?

To get Pharaoh to let the children of Israel go, Yahweh told Moses, "I will pass through Egypt and strike down every firstborn of both people and animals" (Exod 12:12). Thus far it looks like Yahweh was going to personally kill these doomed people and animals.

Eleven verses later, however, we get quite a different impression when we read, "When the Lord goes through the land to strike down the Egyptians, he will see the blood on the top and sides of the doorframe and will pass over that doorway, and he *will not permit the destroyer* to enter your houses and strike you down" (Exod 12:23, emphasis added).

Note that the first clause of this passage continues to refer to Yahweh as the executioner, yet it does so while clarifying that it would actually be "the destroyer" who would be doing the killing.

2. This is known as the "lament" or "complaint tradition" in Scripture. See S. Balentine, *Prayer in the Hebrew Bible* (Minneapolis: Fortress Press, 1993), and L. S. Flesher, C. J. Dempsey, and M. J. Boda, eds., *Why? . . . How Long? Studies on Voice(s) of Lamentation Rooted in Biblical Hebrew Poetry* (New York: Bloomsbury, 2014).
3. For a more comprehensive and in-depth discussion of this dual speech pattern throughout the Bible, see *CWG*, vol. 2, ch. 17.

The only thing the Lord would do in this judgment is refrain from preventing the destroyer from doing what it wanted to do, a point that is also later emphasized by the author of Hebrews (11:28).

This presupposes that the destroyer was already bent on destruction. There's no indication that God *made him* that way or that he *commanded him* to be that way. And this passage presupposes that this destructive agent *wanted* to kill *whoever he could* but was only able to get at those who were no longer under Yahweh's protection. This is what we should expect from the one the NT identifies as "the destroyer" (Rev 9:11) and whom Jesus describes as "the thief who comes only to kill and to steal and to destroy" (John 10:10). Killing, stealing, and destroying are the only things this cosmic beast ever does!

Since the portrait of God withdrawing protection and thereby leaving people vulnerable to the destroyer is consistent with what we learn about God's Aikido mode of judgment on Calvary, this portrait must be seen as reflecting the Spirit of Christ breaking through the author's culturally conditioned understanding of God to give a *direct* revelation of the cruciform God. But, given the give-and-take nature of God's breathing, discussed in chapter 4, it's not surprising that we find this *direct* revelation right alongside of an *indirect* revelation, when the destroyer's violence is attributed directly to Yahweh. And this is why this narrative depicts Yahweh as simultaneously *doing* and *merely allowing* the same violent actions. I refer to this as Scripture's *dual speech pattern*.

The very fact that this author's own narrative indicates that Yahweh did not actually engage in the violence that he ascribes to Yahweh confirms that his violent portrait of God reflects his fallen and culturally conditioned assumptions about God. It indicates that, at this early stage in God's progressive revelation, this author could only catch glimpses of the radical difference between God and the destroyer.

At the same time, the presence of the portrait of Yahweh as a child-killing deity within the God-breathed witness to God's missionary activity serves as a permanent literary testimony to the truth that Yahweh has always been willing to stoop to accommodate the fallen and culturally conditioned way his covenant people viewed him, for only by this means could he hope to continue to influence them toward more accurate, and more beautiful, understandings of him.

Who Is the Merciless Killer?

Another example of an ancient author who couldn't clearly distinguish between God and Satan is Jeremiah. Prophesying an impending judgment on the people of Judah, Jeremiah depicts Yahweh as declaring, "*I* will smash them one against the other, parents and children alike, declares the Lord. *I* will allow no pity or mercy or compassion to keep *me* from destroying them" (Jer 13:14, emphasis added).

Slaughtering parents and children together is terrible enough, but this portrait goes even further, depicting Yahweh vowing not to allow mercy or compassion to prevent him from destroying them. Set this portrait alongside the story of Jesus refusing to call angels to vanquish his enemies (Matt 26:53) and then praying with his dying breath for mercy to be extended to his own torturers and executioners (Luke 23:24). Quite a contrast!

If we remain confident that the crucified Christ is the exact representation of God's very essence, we can only conclude that this portrait reflects a heavy dose of Jeremiah's fallen and culturally conditioned heart and mind. With a grieving heart, God *said*, "I will judge Judah, and families are going to be mercilessly smashed together." But what Jeremiah *heard* was God, with a raging heart, saying: "I will judge Judah by mercilessly smashing families together."

***

Our cross-centered interpretation of *what else is going on* in Jeremiah's ghoulish portrait of God is confirmed a short while later when Jeremiah recounts the Lord issuing another warning about this same judgment. The Lord says:

> I will give Zedekiah, king of Judah, his officials and the people in this city who survive the plague, sword and famine, *into the hands of Nebuchadnezzar*, king of Babylon, and to their enemies who seek their lives. *He* will put them to the sword; *he* will show them no mercy or pity or compassion. (Jer 21:7, emphasis added)

It turns out that it was Nebuchadnezzar, not God, who showed no mercy or compassion as he slaughtered the families of Judah. Because Jeremiah and other OT authors had a cloudy vision of God that only allowed them to catch glimpses of the truth, they couldn't clearly or consistently distinguish between the God who judges and the violent agents who carry out his judgments.

Indeed, like all other ANE people, the Israelites assumed it was an insult *not* to "credit" God with the violence that resulted from his judgment. And this is reflected in the fact that God and God's agents are frequently made "the subject of the same destructive verbs" in the writings of many biblical authors.[4] In other words, the cloudiness of their vision of God is reflected in their dual speech pattern of depicting God simultaneously *doing* and *merely allowing* the same violent actions.

Yet, if we read their writings through the lens of the looking-glass cross, we can discern times when the noncoercive Spirit of Christ was able to break through their fallen perspective to make it clear that God has always judged people the same way he judged the sin of the world on Calvary. While Jeremiah believed Yahweh was capable of mercilessly smashing families together, the truth is that God, with a grieving heart and with redemptive motives, merely withdrew his protecting presence to allow evil (the violent Babylonians) to punish evil (the idolatrous Israelites). And this is how his people suffered the destructive consequences that were inherent in their sin.

But, like Charlie's father, and like people throughout the ANE, ancient biblical authors mistakenly assumed that the one who merely refused to enable the sinner was the one who actually killed the sinner.

Who Crushes His Virgin Daughter?

A particularly graphic example of this dual speech pattern is found throughout the book of Lamentations. In this book, Jeremiah grieves over the inhabitants of Judah after the Babylonians have ruthlessly vanquished them. Reflecting the same mindset as Charlie's father, Jeremiah attributes all the horrific violence Judah suffered to Yahweh.

For example, Jeremiah portrays Yahweh viciously crushing under foot his "Virgin Daughter Judah" in a "winepress" (Lam 1:15). He depicts Yahweh along the lines of the vicious Ugaritic goddess Anat when he describes him as an enemy who has "swallowed up all the dwellings of Jacob" (2:2, 5). And he then claims that God caused

4. Fretheim, *Creation Untamed,* 53. See the chart of parallel verbs in Fretheim's essay, "Violence and the God of the Old Testament," in *Encountering Violence in the Bible*, ed. M. Zehnder and H. Hagelia (Sheffield: Sheffield Phoenix, 2013), 108–27 (117–18).

everyone to starve and even caused mothers to cannibalize their own children (2:20; cf. 4:4–10).

That's not all. Jeremiah also alleges that Yahweh mercilessly slew all Judah's young men and women. "You have slain them in the day of your anger," he declares, "you have slaughtered them without pity" (2:21–22). Speaking as the representative of Judah, he claims that "the rod of the Lord's wrath" caused him to "walk in darkness rather than light," and then says Yahweh "turned his hand against me again and again, all day long" (3:1–3).

Like Job, this grief-stricken prophet believed God imprisoned Judah, shut out his cries for help, and ripped her to shreds like a vicious lion.[5] And, also like Job, Jeremiah goes so far as to depict Yahweh along the lines of the arrow-shooting Canaanite god, Resheph, and accuses him of using Judah for target practice![6]

I recall how conflicted I used to get when I would read passages like this with the assumption that, since this is part of the inspired word of God, I had to accept that Jeremiah's ugly view of God was accurate. What a relief it has been to be able to understand how these hideous sin-mirroring portraits of God are divinely inspired for the purpose of bearing witness to the hideous sin-mirroring cross! And what a joy it has been to be able to discern in the depths of these portraits the same loving, humble, sin-bearing God we discern in the depths of the cross!

***

Interestingly enough, this cross-centered interpretation is confirmed in Jeremiah's own writings, for other passages in Lamentations make it clear that, as a matter of fact, the only action God took to bring about this judgment was to withdraw his protective presence, just as he did on Calvary.

For example, just after accusing Yahweh of acting like the ferocious Anat, Jeremiah says that Yahweh "*has withdrawn* his right hand at the approach of the enemy" (2:3, emphasis added). Jeremiah then

5. Lam 3:7–11; see also Job 3:23; 19:6, 7–8.

6. Lam 3:12; see also Job 6:4; 7:20. On the allusion to *Resheph* in Jeremiah and Job, see R. S. Fyall, *Now My Eyes Have Seen You: Images of Creation and Evil in the Book of Job* (Downers Grove, IL: InterVarsity, 2002), 118. I have elsewhere argued that a central point of the book of Job is to refute the assumption of Job and his friends that God was behind Job's suffering. See Boyd, *Is God to Blame?*, 85–111; Boyd, *Satan and the Problem of Evil: Constructing a Trinitarian Warfare Theodicy* (Downers Grove, IL: IVP Academic, 2001), 209–26.

reiterates that "the Lord *has rejected* his altar and *abandoned* his sanctuary" (2:7).

Since the sanctuary was believed to be Yahweh's home among his people, for Yahweh to abandon his sanctuary meant that Yahweh had abandoned his people. And, as Jeremiah makes clear, this means that the Lord "*has given* the walls of her palaces *into the hands* of the enemy" (2:7, emphasis added). Every act of violence that the people of Judah suffered came from this "enemy," which was the Babylonians, not God.

A number of other passages in Lamentations make the same point. Jeremiah at one point complains that "the punishment of [God's] people is greater than that of Sodom, which was overthrown in a moment *without a hand to help her*" (Lam 4:6, emphasis added). As was true of Sodom, Jeremiah declares that, once her protector (Yahweh) had "forsaken us," Judah "fell into enemy hands" and "there was no one to help her."[7] The result was that "she saw pagan nations enter the sanctuary," which, as we just saw, had now been vacated by God (1:10).

These passages reflect more of the Spirit breaking through to reveal what *actually* happened when Judah experienced the wrath of God. And they confirm that the atrocious portraits of God that fill Lamentations reflect Jeremiah's own ANE *interpretation* of how God was involved in this judgment, not the way God was actually involved.

God did not in fact viciously crush his Virgin Daughter Judah in a winepress. Nor did God ever act like the ferocious Ugaritic god, Anat, by swallowing up all the dwellings of Jacob. Nor would the true God revealed in the crucified Christ ever cause mothers to cannibalize their children or mercilessly slay Judah's young men and women or act like the arrow-shooting Canaanite deity, Resheph, who uses people for target practice!

What the true God actually did was refuse to allow his mercy to further damage people by enabling them to become further and further entrenched in their self-destructive sin. What the true God actually did was grieve as he withdrew his Spirit to allow his beloved people to suffer the terrible fate they had brought on themselves. And what the true God actually did was stoop to bear the sinful and culturally conditioned way Jeremiah and others viewed him, thereby

7. Lam 1:7; see also 2:7; 5:20.

taking on an appearance in the written witness to his missionary activity that reflects their ugly conception of him.

In short, what the true God actually did was humbly allow himself to appear guilty of things he in fact merely allowed.

Yet, we will only be able to see this if we fully trust that the true God is supremely revealed in the crucified Christ and, therefore, that the true God would never be capable of crushing people like grapes in a winepress, or swallowing up people with their dwellings, or causing mothers to cannibalize their children, or using people as target practice.

Other Examples of Scripture's Dual Speech Pattern

This dual speech pattern permeates the OT. To give you a sense of how widespread it is, I'll briefly review five more representative illustrations.

First, after laying out the blessings and curses of the first covenant, Moses says to the Israelites, "Just as it pleased the Lord to make you prosper and increase in number" when you obeyed him, "so it will please him to ruin and destroy you" if you are disobedient (Deut 28:63). Moses apparently believed Yahweh was just as pleased to personally afflict his people as a violent warrior as he was to personally bless them as a benevolent provider.

We get a very different impression, however, when Yahweh later speaks with Moses face to face as his friend.[8] In this context the Lord laments that his people "will forsake me and break the covenant I made with them," for this meant that he would have to forsake them and hide his face from them. As a result, the Lord adds, "Many disasters and calamities will come on them, and in that day they will ask, 'Have not these disasters come on us because *our God is not with us*?'" (Deut 31:16–18, emphasis added).

This more intimate portrait of God makes it clear that the disasters and calamities that came upon God's people were not the result of Yahweh being present among his people as a violent divine warrior. They were rather the result of Yahweh being *absent* from his people as a protector against violent warriors.

***

8. Deut 34:10; see also Exod 33:11; Num 12:8.

Second, Jeremiah draws on ghoulish imagery that we earlier saw was used for the Ugaritic god Anat. He depicts Yahweh declaring that the houses and palaces of Jerusalem "will be filled with the dead bodies of the people *I* will slay in my anger and wrath" (Jer 33:5, emphasis added). Yet, immediately following this we can discern the Spirit of Christ breaking through this ghoulish Anat imagery to make it clear that, unlike Anat, Yahweh never actually kills anyone. For here Yahweh restates this impending judgment by saying: "I will *hide my face* from this city" (Jer 33:5, emphasis added) and, still later, "I am about *to give this city into the hands* of the king of Babylon, and he will burn it down" (Jer 34:2).

The people of Judah had wanted to be free from Yahweh, and Yahweh was now granting them their wish, albeit reluctantly. But in a context in which you're surrounded by nations and cosmic forces that are bent on destruction, freedom from God amounts to nothing more than the "freedom to fall by the sword, plague and famine" (Jer 34:17).

Jeremiah couldn't clearly and consistently distinguish between violence that God allows with a grieving heart, and violence that a deity like Anat perpetrates with a raging heart. But when the Spirit managed to break through, Jeremiah's own writings make this distinction clear. And this confirms the interpretation of these portraits that we arrive at through the looking-glass cross. This horrific Anat imagery bears witness to just how low the heavenly missionary had to be willing to stoop to remain in covenantal solidarity with his fallen and culturally conditioned people and to continue to further his purposes through them.

***

Third, Ezekiel depicts Yahweh vowing to the people of Judah: "I will pour out my wrath on you and breathe out my fiery anger against you" (Ezek 21:31a). This common ANE imagery of a deity as a fire-breathing dragon gives the impression that Yahweh was going to personally burn people alive with his fiery breath. In the very next sentence, however, this violent imagery is subverted by the Spirit, for the Lord goes on to say, "I will *deliver you into* the hands of brutal men, men skilled in destruction" (21:31b, emphasis added).[9]

9. See also Ezek 25:7; 2 Chron 36:16–20; Ezra 5:12.

Clearly, when God breathes out his "fiery anger," it amounts to nothing more than God withdrawing protection to deliver people into the hands of their enemies. While the ANE dragon imagery reflects Ezekiel's culturally conditioned perspective, the subversion of its violence reflects the Spirit of Christ breaking through. And the fact that these are juxtaposed reflects the give-and-take nature of the cross-based conception of God's breathing.

***

Fourth, in a particularly macabre passage that echoes the warrior cannibalism found in Ugaritic portraits of Anat, Jeremiah depicts Yahweh as an enraged and ferocious warrior who hates his own people (Jer 12:8) and who therefore declares that his sword will "devour from one end of the land to the other" (v. 12). Yet, the actual way the sword of the Lord devours the land is made clear when, in this same context, Jeremiah recounts the Lord declaring, "I will forsake my house" and "abandon my inheritance." And in doing this, he adds, "I will give the one I love into the hands of her enemies" (v. 7).

Related to this, Jeremiah also depicts Yahweh vowing to destroy his house the same way he destroyed the tabernacle at Shiloh.[10] Significantly enough, the only thing the Lord did to destroy the tabernacle at Shiloh was withdraw his protection, thereby giving "his people over to the sword" (Ps 78:59–61). He "thrust [his people] from [his] presence, just as [he] did . . . the people of Ephraim."[11] Here again we see the Spirit breaking through, as much as possible, to subvert Jeremiah's Anat-like conception of Yahweh.

When a sword devoured Yahweh's people, it *did* reflect a terrible divine judgment. But clearly, Yahweh wasn't the agent who wielded this sword.

***

My final example also comes from Jeremiah. In typical ANE fashion, Jeremiah shows Yahweh as a warrior deity who declares: "The Lord will roar from on high . . . he will bring judgment on all humankind and put the wicked to the sword." The result will be that "those slain

10. Jer 7:12, 14; see also 26:9.
11. Jer 7:15; see also Hos 4:17.

by the Lord will be everywhere" (Jer 25:30–31, 33). It certainly looks like Yahweh is going to personally slaughter the wicked everywhere.

We get a very different impression, however, when this same judgment is expressed several verses later as Jeremiah compares Yahweh to a lion that abandons its lair. Just as the cubs would be vulnerable to predators once they were abandoned, so too the land of God's people would "certainly be laid waste by the warfare of the oppressive nation" once Yahweh abandoned them (Jer 25:38, NET).

It is apparent that, despite Jeremiah's fallen and culturally conditioned divine warrior imagery, the "fierce anger of the Lord" amounts to nothing more than the terrible "horrors of war" (Jer 25:38, GNB) that happen whenever people push away the One who alone can preserve peace (cf. Luke 19:42–44). For when God "leaves humans to their own devices, they begin to destroy one another."[12]

And *that* is what it means to come under the wrath of God—which, not coincidentally, is precisely what the supreme revelation of God on the cross leads us to expect.

***

Over the last three chapters we've seen that while God was always willing to humbly accommodate the violent, culturally conditioned ways his ancient people viewed him, his Spirit was also always at work to reveal as much truth as they were capable of receiving. And this is why we find a curious mix of portraits of Yahweh *doing* and *merely allowing* the same violent activity.

Moreover, while OT authors thought they were exalting God by crediting him with all the violence that was involved in divine judgments, the looking-glass cross enables us to see that God was actually allowing sin to punish sin and evil to vanquish evil. And when interpreted through the looking-glass cross, all such episodes can be seen as signs that point to God's ultimate Aikido judgment of sin and victory over evil on Calvary.

***

Thus far we've seen that violent portraits of Yahweh bear witness to the cross when this violence is carried out *by humans*. But what are we

12. R. Schwager, *Must There Be Scapegoats? Violence and Redemption in the Bible*, 3rd ed. (New York: Crossroad, 2000), 67.

to do with OT portraits of Yahweh carrying out violence *when violent humans are not involved?* We clearly can't appeal to humans "bent on destruction" to account for events like the Flood, the destruction of Sodom and Gomorrah, or the drowning of Pharaoh's army. Yet these portraits, which we must also accept as divinely inspired, are as contrary to the character of God revealed on the cross as those that we've already discussed.

It is time, once again, to sit at the foot of the cross and let it teach us.

PART IV

Seeing *Something Else* through the Looking-Glass Cross

12

Cosmic War

There is no neutral ground in the universe;
every square inch, every split second,
is claimed by God and counterclaimed by Satan.
—C. S. Lewis[1]

Discovering *What Else Was Going On*

I'd like to once again return to the story about Shelley's apparently cruel treatment of the panhandler that I told in the Introduction. Suppose that, after meandering downtown in a state of bewilderment for a while, I decide to return home, hoping that Shelley has done the same so I could finally find out what on earth was going on. I walk through the front door and am shocked to find Shelley with a couple dozen men and women dressed in black suits, laughing and shouting out toasts to one another with champagne glasses! Everyone laughs when they notice the completely baffled look on my face. Then Shelley sits me down in our living room to finally explain what I had earlier witnessed.

It turns out this apparent panhandler was the point person in a terrorist plot to blow up a downtown governmental building! Strategically situated across from this building, he was pretending to be a disabled beggar as a cover for his terrorist activity. The Department of Homeland Security (DHS) had learned that

1. C. S. Lewis, "Christianity and Culture," in *Christian Reflections*, ed. W. Hooper (Grand Rapids: Eerdmans, 1967), 33.

this terrorist was coordinating the preparations for this attack from his spot on the corner through a transmitter in his cap—which, as you may recall, explains why he appeared to talk to himself and why he guarded his cap so closely.

The DHS had been tracking this man's terrorist cell for some time and had planned a sting operation to take place on this very day. For it to succeed, however, they needed to get this man's transmitter and create a scene to distract the other terrorists just long enough to gain the decisive upper hand when they made their sting. They needed to find someone this pretend beggar would be comfortable enough with to let his guard down.

Enter my lovely wife! After weeks of close observation, the DHS had concluded that Shelley was perfect for the job. She had been the only regular passerby who consistently demonstrated compassion toward this man and who took the time to befriend him. Sometimes the man even allowed Shelley to give him a goodbye hug. If he ever let his guard down, it was when this kind lady stopped to talk to him each day. The DHS had therefore recruited Shelley earlier in the day and had instructed her to behave the way she did. The fact that I happened to be downtown when all this went down was purely coincidental.

As a result of Shelley's brave and highly distracting behavior, the terrorist plot had been successfully thwarted and the terrorists had all been captured. Hundreds of lives had probably been saved! My wife, it turns out, was the new Jack Bauer!

So you see, Shelley's behavior only made sense once I could interpret it against the backdrop of the much larger story of what was *actually* going on. (Scholars refer to a larger story that interprets a smaller story as a *metanarrative.*) Now that I knew the metanarrative of what was going on, I could understand how Shelley's apparently cruel behavior was actually perfectly consistent with the character of the woman I'd come to know from thirty-seven years of marriage.

And having learned this, I would be so glad that I had continued to trust her character, despite the uncharacteristic behavior I had witnessed.

***

We've been filling out aspects of the biblical metanarrative since chapter 5. We've seen that the cross teaches us that at the center of the story of *what else is going on* in the OT's violent portraits of God is the truth that Yahweh is a humble sin-bearing God and that God brings about judgments by withdrawing his restraining Spirit to allow sin to punish sin and evil to vanquish evil. And we've seen that when we interpret the OT through this lens, we find strong confirmations of these truths throughout Scripture.

We're now going to turn to a third aspect of God's revelation on the cross that helps further fill out this metanarrative. It's centered on the fact that the NT construes Jesus's crucifixion as the decisive battle in an age-long conflict between God and Satan. To interpret the OT through the lens of the cross, therefore, we must interpret it within a metanarrative of cosmic conflict.

In this and the following two chapters, we're going to find that this third aspect of the looking-glass cross discloses *what else is going on* when God is depicted as *directly* engaging in violence. That is, when the violence that an author ascribes to God can't be attributed to humans, it must be attributed to violent cosmic agents. And we're going to see that this cross-centered interpretation finds a wealth of surprising confirming evidence in the narratives that contain these portraits.

Before embarking on this, however, I need to set the stage by discussing the remarkable authority that Jesus and the authors of the NT ascribe to Satan and other rebel powers, for the metanarrative of cosmic conflict only makes sense when this authority is fully appreciated.[2]

A World Engulfed in War

I'm sure you've heard Louis Armstrong's song, "What a Wonderful World." He sees "trees of green" and "red roses too," and he thinks to himself, "what a wonderful world." It's a pretty song, and we can all agree that there is much beauty in the world.

But, as much as I hate to rain on the Armstrong-wonderful-world parade, I'm afraid the NT paints a much bleaker view of the world.

2. For a more in-depth and comprehensive overview of the material covered in this chapter, see *CWG*, vol. 2, chs. 21–22.

In fact, it views the world in its present state as being fundamentally evil and ruled by a powerful, diabolic being.[3]

We catch a glimpse of the scope of Satan's reign over the world in Revelation when John represents all the governments of the world as being part of one kingdom that is ruled by Satan (Rev 11:15). And dozens of times in this book we read that Satan and his cohorts are able to deceive and enslave "all the nations" and "all the inhabitants of the earth" as Satan "leads the whole world astray."[4]

The same global authority is ascribed to Satan in the Gospels' temptation narratives. Scripture tells us that Satan owns all the "authority and splendor" of "all the kingdoms of the world," and he is able to "give it to anyone [he] want[s] to."[5] The devil offered this to Jesus, and although Jesus declined, he didn't dispute Satan's claim to ownership!

Reflecting the same understanding, Jesus three times refers to Satan as "the prince of this world."[6] The word translated "prince" (*archōn*) referred to "the highest official in a city or a region in the Greco-Roman world."[7] So while Jesus and his followers believed God was the *ultimate* ruler over creation, these passages assert that Satan is currently the *functional* ruler over the earth.

Even more stunning is John's incredible claim that "the *whole world* is under *the control* of the evil one" (1 John 5:19, emphasis added). And Paul is so bold as to label Satan "the god of this world" (2 Cor 4:4) as well as "the ruler (*archon*) of the power of the air" (Eph 2:2). In the first-century Jewish understanding of the cosmos, *the air* was the domain of authority over the earth. So this was just another way of saying that Satan is the functional ruler of this world.

***

In chapter 9 we saw that OT authors conceived of destructive cosmic forces as a hostile sea that encompasses the earth or as a threatening cosmic monster. Well, the NT refers to these same sinister cosmic powers with titles like "rulers," "principalities," "powers,"

3. Gal 1:4; Eph 5:6. On the remarkable power ascribed to Satan throughout the NT, see G. Boyd, *God at War: The Bible and Spiritual Conflict* (Downers Grove, IL: InterVarsity, 1997), chs. 6–10.
4. Rev 14:8; 13:8; 12:9; see also 13:3, 7–8, 12, 14; 18:3, 23; 20:3, 8.
5. Luke 4:5–6; Matt 4:8–9.
6. John 12:31; 14:30; 16:11.
7. C. Arnold, *Powers of Darkness: Principalities and Powers in Paul's Letters* (Downers Grove, IL: InterVarsity, 1992), 81.

"authorities," "spiritual forces," "world rulers," and "elemental spirits."[8] Taken together, they refer to "diverse manifestations of a seamless web of reality hostile to God," as Thomas Yoder Neufeld has put it.[9]

Within the apocalyptic worldview that was pervasive among Jews in the first century and that is shared by the NT, it was understood that these cosmic agents had originally been given authority over aspects of nature and human society. Once they rebelled against God, however, they use this authority at cross-purposes with God to corrupt nature and society. This is essentially the perspective of the NT, though the NT is unique in its view that these rebel cosmic agents are ruled by Satan.

The ability of Satan and other demonic agents to corrupt aspects of nature is reflected in Peter's teaching that, "God anointed Jesus of Nazareth with the Holy Spirit and power, and . . . he went around doing good and *healing all who were under the power of the devil*" (Acts 10:38, emphasis). This statement implies that a person afflicted with physical infirmities is "under the power of the devil." And this is why the Gospels uniformly attribute afflictions not to the mysterious providence of God, as so many do today, but to the corrupting influence of Satan and demons.[10]

Satan's ability to manipulate nature in destructive ways is also reflected in Paul's instruction to the Corinthians to turn an unrepentant man over "to Satan for the destruction of the flesh" (1 Cor 5:5, ASV). Paul's instruction presupposes that, with the exception of those who are under the protection of Christ, the whole world is under the influence of one "who holds the power of death—that is the devil" (Heb 2:14).[11]

***

The impression we are given in the NT is that our world is saturated with powerful, corrupting, demonic agents. Satan's kingdom is

8. 1 Cor 15:24; Eph 1:21; 2:2; 3:10; 6:12; Col 1:16; 2:10, 15; 1 Pet 3:22. On these titles, see G. Boyd, "Powers and Principalities," in *Dictionary of Scripture and Ethics*, ed. J. Green (Grand Rapids: Zondervan, 2012), 611–13; Boyd, *God at War*, 267–93; C. Arnold, *Powers of Darkness* (Downers Grove, IL: InterVarsity, 1992).

9. Thomas Yoder Neufeld, *Armour of God*, quoted in E. Warren, *Cleansing the Cosmos: A Biblical Model for Conceptualizing and Counteracting Evil* (Eugene, OR: Pickwick, 2012), 219.

10. See Boyd, *God at War*, 180–91.

11. See also 1 Tim 1:20.

depicted as an ever-present force that works to lead people astray.[12] Jesus went so far as to teach that any swearing of oaths, and indeed, "anything beyond" a straightforward "Yes" or "No" answer, "comes from the evil one" (Matt 5:36–37). And Paul taught that even gossipers who move "about from house to house" have "turned away to follow Satan" (1 Tim 5:13–15).

If Satan and/or other demonic agents are directly or indirectly behind every temptation to sin as well as all sickness and disease, we have to conclude that the corrupting kingdom of the one who comes "only to kill, and to steal and to destroy" (John 10:10) is pretty much all-encompassing. C. S. Lewis was on the mark when he claimed, "There is no neutral ground in the universe," for "every square inch, every split second, is claimed by God and counterclaimed by Satan."[13]

Finally, and most importantly, the pervasiveness of Satan's kingdom is supremely expressed in the NT's teaching that Satan and other rebel powers were instrumental in Jesus's crucifixion, as we saw in chapter 9. Yet, "the reason the Son of God appeared was to destroy the devil's work" (1 John 3:8) and "to break the power of him who holds the power of death—that is, the devil" (Heb 2:14).

This is what Jesus accomplished with his life, ministry, and especially with his self-sacrificial death on the cross. For when Jesus chose to bear our sin and suffer our curse, God "canceled the charge of our legal indebtedness, which stood against us and condemned us" by "nailing it to the cross." By means of the perfect love displayed on the cross, God "disarmed" and "triumphed over" the "powers and authorities," thereby making "a public spectacle of them" (Col 2:14–15).

In short, the supreme revelation of God's love on the cross was also his ultimate conflict with, and victory over, the powers of darkness. And this is why God's conflict with Satan and other fallen principalities and powers constitutes the third aspect of our cross-centered approach to the OT.

***

12. For example, Satan and his cohorts are depicted as being involved in temptations (Matt 4:3; 6:13; 1 Thess 3:5; 1 Cor 7:5), lying (Acts 5:3), bitterness (Eph 4:26–27), marital infidelity (1 Cor 7:5), unforgiveness (2 Cor 2:6–11), legalism (Gal 4:7–10; 1 Tim 4:1–5), false teachings (2 Cor 11:3–4, 13–14; 1 Thess 3:5; Col 2:8; 1 John 4:1–6; 2 John 7), as well as idolatrous sacrifices (1 Cor 10:20), deceptive miracles (1 Thess 2:9), spiritual blindness (2 Cor 4:4; cf. Acts 26:18), and the sowing of "weeds" (false believers) within the kingdom (Matt 13:38–39).
13. Lewis, "Christianity and Culture," 33.

If we accept these teachings about the scope and authority of Satan's kingdom, then we have to think of the cosmic agents that persistently pull people and creation toward destruction as operating on a spiritual level along the lines of how gravity works. For a ball to hit the ground, you don't need to throw it down. You simply need to release it.

Similarly, if the world is as engulfed by rebel cosmic agents as Jesus and the authors of the NT claim, then there is no reason why God would ever need to engage in destructive acts to punish people, even if he had a character that was capable of this. Rather, for people to experience the destructive consequences of their sin, God need only *release them*.

In other words, for people to fall under God's judgment, God needn't *do* anything. He needs to only *stop* doing something: namely, preventing the cosmic forces that are bent on destruction from doing what they are perpetually trying to do. And while the fallen and culturally conditioned authors of the OT were not above ascribing destructive acts to God, when we interpret their divinely inspired writings through the looking-glass cross, we will find a surprising amount of evidence that confirms that *this is all God ever did*.

As our first example, let's examine the divine judgment that came upon Korah and his followers in Numbers 16.

The Destroying Angel and Korah's Rebellion

A man named Korah led a large group of "grumblers" in a rebellion against the leadership of Moses and Aaron. As a result, Scripture says that some of them experienced the wrath of God when they went "down alive into the realm of the dead" (Num 16:40) after "the earth opened its mouth and swallowed" them (v. 32). As this was happening, we read that "fire came from the Lord" and consumed 250 others who had joined this rebellion (v. 35; cf. v. 2).

Instead of putting an end to the rebellion, however, this horrific demonstration of divine wrath only intensified it. On the following day, "the whole Israelite community grumbled against Moses and Aaron," accusing them of killing "the Lord's people" (v. 41). Consequently, an ominous cloud appeared over the "tent of meeting" and "wrath [came] out from the Lord" (vv. 42, 46). This wrath took the form of a plague that killed 14,700 people (v. 49). Even more would have been killed were it not for Aaron "making atonement for them" (vv. 47–48).

Now, since this portrait of God engaging in horrendous violence conflicts with the nonviolent, self-sacrificial character of God revealed on the cross, we have to see it as a literary crucifix that bears witness to our heavenly missionary's sin-bearing nature. Moreover, on the basis of the cross, we must conclude that what actually happened was that God, with a grieving heart, allowed evil to punish evil by turning these rebels over to experience the destructive consequences of their sin at the hands of agents who were already bent on violence. And since humans obviously didn't carry out this judgment, we must assume that it came about when God stopped holding back ever-present cosmic forces of destruction, just as he did with his Son on Calvary.

Given the absolute authority the NT tells us to ascribe to the revelation of God in the crucified Christ, I believe we would be justified holding to this cross-centered interpretation *even if* we had no other evidence to support it. But, as a matter of fact, it turns out there is quite a bit of scriptural support of this interpretation.

***

Let's start with the apostle Paul. In the course of drawing lessons from the OT about how Christians should behave, Paul warns his readers not to grumble, as some Israelites did in the wilderness, for they "were killed by *the destroying angel*" (1 Cor 10:10, emphasis added). The most extensive and famous episode of grumblers being judged in the OT is the one we just read, which is why most scholars believe Paul was probably referring to this episode. Curiously enough, however, there is no mention of a destroying angel in Leviticus 16. But neither is there a destroying angel in any other episode of grumblers being judged.

Which raises the question: Why did Paul attribute this judgment to a destructive agent rather than to God?

Let's consider Paul's historical context. Beginning a couple hundred years before Paul, many Jews began to understand that God's character was incompatible with rage and violence. They thus began to explore ways to disassociate God from the rage and violence that the OT sometimes ascribes to him.[14] And one of the most significant

14. E. Seibert, *Disturbing Divine Behavior: Troubling Old Testament Images of God* (Minneapolis:

ways they did this was by ascribing to fallen angels the morally objectionable activities that OT authors sometimes ascribed to God.[15]

In fact, some people during this time went so far as to alter biblical texts so that the violence that an OT author had ascribed to God was now attributed to an evil angel.[16] For example, several times the author of a second-century BCE book titled *Jubilees* replaces "Yahweh" in a biblical narrative with a Satan-like figure named "Mastema." According to this author, it was Mastema, not Yahweh, who tempted Abraham to kill Isaac, who provoked the Egyptians to pursue Israel, and who sought to kill Moses for failing to have his son circumcised.[17]

Another example of this, according to many scholars, is the way the author of 1 Chronicles replaced "Yahweh" with "Satan" as the one who incited David to sin.[18]

There are many indications that Paul was influenced by this movement, and nowhere is this more evident than when he claims that the violence in Numbers 16 was actually carried out by a destroying angel. For it turns out that three other authors prior to Paul had already distanced God from the violence of Numbers 16 by claiming the exact same thing![19] And if these Jewish authors were motivated by a desire to distance God from violence, how much more was Paul, who based his view of God on the crucified Christ?

In this light, it seems that Paul was engaging in precisely the sort of cross-centered reinterpretation of the OT's violent portraits of God that I am proposing in this book!

***

Fortress Press, 2009), 55; J. Charlesworth, "Theodicy in Early Jewish Writings," in *Theodicy in the World of the Bible*, ed. A. Laato and J. C. de Moor (Boston: Brill, 2003), 470–508.

15. For example, while we have seen that the author of Exodus had no qualms attributing the killing of firstborn males in Egypt to Yahweh as well as to "the destroyer" (Exod 12:12, 23), later biblical and nonbiblical writers attribute this exclusively to one or more malevolent angels (*1 Enoch* 53:3; 56:1; 66:1; *Jubilees* 49:2; Heb 11:28).
16. See B. N. Fisk, "Rewritten Bible in Pseudepigrapha and Qumran," in *Dictionary of New Testament Background*, ed. G. A. Evans and S. E. Porter (Downers Grove, IL: InterVarsity, 2000), 947–53.
17. *Jubilees* 17:15–18:13; 48:2, 12. See O. S. Wintermute, "Jubilees: A New Translation and Introduction," in *The Old Testament Pseudepigrapha*, 2 vols., ed. J. H. Charlesworth (New York: Doubleday, 1985), 2:47–48.
18. 2 Sam 24:1; 1 Chron 21:1.
19. "Wisdom of Solomon," 18:25; *4 Macc* 7:11; "Ezekiel the Tragedian," *Fragmenta Pseudepigraphorum . . . Graeca*, 213, line 1.

Beyond Paul's introduction of the destroying angel into the narrative of Numbers 16, there are pieces of evidence in the narrative itself that confirm that Yahweh was not the agent who slaughtered the members of Korah's rebellion.

Before looking at this evidence, however, it's important to remember that we are dealing with material that reflects a worldview that is far removed from our own. I guarantee you that this material is going to strike you as exceedingly weird. But it is this weirdness that the heavenly missionary had to accommodate to remain in communication with his ancient people, so it is this weirdness that we will have to accommodate if we are going to understand this ancient text.

The most important aspect of this weirdness concerns the earlier-mentioned fact that the people of the ANE did not separate the natural and supernatural realms as we do today. So, while some believers today might be comfortable talking about spiritual agents like God or angels *using* aspects of nature to accomplish some purpose, ancient Israelites, along with everybody else in the ANE, usually *identified* the aspect of nature that was used with the spiritual agent that used it. You'll see what I mean in a moment.

As we now closely examine the three judgments that were carried out in Numbers 16 in this light, we will discover things that confirm Paul's view that it was a destroying angel, not God, who acted violently toward the grumblers of Korah's rebellion.

***

Numbers 16 tells us that the first group of grumblers "went down alive into the realm of the dead (*sheol*), with everything they owned" when "the earth opened its mouth and swallowed them."[20] We modern people are naturally inclined to interpret talk about the earth opening its mouth to swallow people metaphorically. But it's unlikely the original audience understood it this way.

In the cosmology of the ANE, it was believed that *sheol*, which was the ancient Hebrew term for the realm of the dead, existed just beneath the surface of the earth. So when the author says people "went down alive . . . together with their possessions" to *sheol*, the original audience would have understood it quite literally (Num 16:32). Not only this, but when the author says the earth opened

20. Num 16:31–33.

its mouth and swallowed people, a number of scholars argue he was reflecting the common ANE belief that the earth was a cosmic monster that sometimes devoured people.[21]

This explains why, after witnessing their peers get swallowed, the surviving Israelites cry out, "The earth is going to swallow us too!" (Num 26:34). They aren't so much afraid of Yahweh as they are the newly unleashed earth monster!

According to some scholars, the author may also be reflecting an ancient Canaanite belief that a demonic god of death named Mot resided under the earth and had jaws that reached up to its surface to devour the dead, and sometimes the living.[22]

We find allusions to Mot as well as to the earth monster in a number of places in the OT. According to Robert Fyall, for example, the book of Job alludes to Mot a number of times. In fact, the further Job sinks into despair throughout this book, the more he speaks of Yahweh in ways that resemble this sinister Canaanite deity (e.g., Job 18:13–14).[23] Some scholars also argue that Mot mythology is echoed in the many passages that describe *sheol* as hungry, strong, and swallowing people alive. Some even assert that some of these depictions are indirect allusions to Mot.[24]

In this light, it's not hard to see why some scholars conclude that the author of Numbers 16 had a malevolent earth monster and/or god of death in mind when he described the earth opening its mouth to swallow people alive. And it seems reasonable to conclude that this

21. M. K. Wakeman, *God's Battle with the Monster: A Study in Biblical Imagery* (Leiden: E. J. Brill, 1973), 108–17, 124; M. Hutter, "Earth," in *Dictionary of Deities and Demons in the Bible*, 2nd edition, ed. K. van der Toorn et al. (Grand Rapids: Eerdmans, 1999), 272–73; N. J. Tromp, *Primitive Conceptions of Death and the Netherworld in the Old Testament* (Rome: Pontificio Istituto Biblico, 1969), 26–27; J. Day, *God's Conflict with the Dragon and the Sea: Echoes of a Canaanite Myth in the Old Testament* (New York: Cambridge University Press, 1985), 84–86. The same holds true for Num 26:10 and Ps 106:17.

22. See J. F. Healey, "Mot," in van der Toorn, *Dictionary of Deities*, 598–603; J. Day, *Yahweh and the Gods and Goddesses of Canaan* (Sheffield: Sheffield Academic, 2000), 185–97; Wakeman, *God's Battle*, 106–8. The most extended ancient account of Mot is found in the Canaanite myth, "Baal and Mot." On this see J. C. L. Gibson, *Canaanite Myths and Legends*, 2nd ed. (Edinburgh: T&T Clark, 1978 [1956]), 68–81.

23. R. Fyall, *Now My Eyes Have Seen You: Images of Creation and Evil in the Book of Job* (Downers Grove, IL: InterVarsity, 2002), 101–5. See also B. Zuckerman, *Job the Silent: A Study in Historical Counterpoint* (Oxford: Oxford University Press, 1991), 118–35.

24. Jer 51:54; cf. 9:21; Isa 5:14; Ps 69:15; Prov 1:12; 27:20; 30:15–16; Hab 2:5. See Day, *Yahweh and the Gods*, 186; Healey, "Mot," 601–2. Some of these passages may also reflect the influence of Anat mythology, which we discussed in chapter 8.

monster was at least one manifestation of the destroying angel Paul wrote about.[25]

While the author of this narrative wanted to credit God with the violence of this judgment (Num 16:30), as any ANE person would, we can see that it wasn't God who opened up the earth to swallow people: they were swallowed by a menacing cosmic beast that is always hungry for someone to devour (1 Pet 5:8). As an act of divine judgment, God merely stopped preventing this cosmic agent from doing what it always wants to do.

I warned you that this was going to be weird!

***

Now, we today must of course assess the ANE idea of the earth as a malevolent deity to be a reflection of the prescientific and culturally conditioned worldview of the biblical author. The same holds true of this author's conception of Mot and the netherworld residing just under the surface of the earth. As such, these conceptions bear witness to the heavenly missionary's willingness to stoop as low as necessary to communicate with his ancient people.

Nevertheless, with the cross as our ultimate criterion, we must conclude that, while these conceptions are mythic, the demonic realities to which they point *are not*. In other words, these mythic conceptions simply reflect the various ways ANE people thought about Satan and other malevolent angelic agents.

But, you may be wondering, if these conceptions are mythic, what actually happened when God turned these rebels over to the destroying angel? I'm sorry to disappoint you, but I believe questions like this are simply unanswerable. We simply have no means of separating the mythic conceptions from the actual events they refer to.

The upside of this, however, is that this unanswerable question is also irrelevant. As I argued in chapter 4, it is the narrative that is divinely inspired, not the narrative's relationship to history. And for this reason, it's the narrative alone that concerns us.

We must therefore be content with knowing that these rebels were judged when a demonic agent that the author identified as an earth

25. To be clear, I am not claiming that Paul was necessarily thinking of this earth monster when he mentioned "the destroying angel." We can't know what exactly Paul was thinking. I am only contending that as *we* explore Numbers 16 with the knowledge that a "destroying angel" rather than God did the killing, we find evidence that warrants identifying this "destroying angel" with the earth that opened up its mouth.

monster, and that Paul identified as "a destroying angel," was allowed to carry out the violence that it had been chomping at the bit to carry out. God was once again allowing evil to punish and vanquish evil, rendering this judgment a sign that points toward his ultimate Aikido-style judgment of evil on the cross.

***

The second group of grumblers in Numbers 16 were destroyed when "fire came out from the Lord" (v. 35). Now, it's possible that this author is conceiving of Yahweh as a malevolent fire-throwing deity, similar to the way warrior deities are commonly depicted in ANE literature. And if we accept this conclusion, it simply means we must assess this portrait to be a reflection of God's willingness to humbly accommodate the fallen and culturally conditioned ways his ancient people sometimes viewed him, as much as this was necessary.[26]

On the other hand, precisely because fire-throwing deities were common throughout the ANE, some scholars argue that this author was actually attributing the incinerating fire to one of these deities. Fyall, for example, believes that the original audience would have understood the grumblers to be devoured by "fire from the netherworld" that originated from the same malevolent deity that swallowed up the first group.[27]

The fact that the netherworld was sometimes associated with fire, and the fact that fire consumed the rebels immediately after the earth opened its mouth—indeed, while people were still screaming in terror as they were being devoured (Num 16:34)—renders Fyall's interpretation plausible.

Moreover, Fyall argues that the consuming fire is said to have come "from the Lord" only in the sense that it was functioning as a "judgment of Yahweh."[28] In his view, this is no different from the way the Lord is said to "send" other nations against Israel. It's not that God *made* these nations want to attack Israel. They were "sent" only in the sense that their attack reflected God's judgment, for it was God who withdrew his restraining hand and thereby allowed these judgments to happen.

26. I would argue along these lines for the destruction of Sodom and Gomorrah (Gen 19:24). See *CWG*, vol. 2, ch. 23.
27. Fyall, *Now My Eyes Have Seen*, 123.
28. Ibid.

We thus have reason to view this fire as a second confirming piece of evidence that it was a destroying angel, not God, that was behind the violence that was directed toward these rebels.

***

Finally, a third group of grumblers were judged when "wrath" came out "from the Lord" in the form of a lethal plague. Here too we have grounds for concluding that this is a portrait of God permitting a malevolent cosmic agent that was bent on destruction to do what it wanted to do. For one thing, we've seen that even in the OT, the concept of God's wrath typically refers to the dire consequences that naturally come about when people live in ways that violate the moral order of God's creation. Hence, for wrath coming "out from the Lord" need only mean that the Lord had decided to allow these people to experience the destructive consequences of their sinful choices.

On top of that, plagues were uniformly identified with various menacing deities throughout the ANE. As I mentioned in the previous chapter, in Canaanite mythology this deity is named Resheph, and we find a number of probable allusions to him throughout the OT.[29] Because of this, some scholars argue that the original audience would have identified this deity to be the agent that expressed God's wrath by bringing about this plague. And, in this case, we have a third confirmation that it was a destroying angel, not Yahweh, who was behind the violence of this judgment.

***

I would like to close by making a final observation about Paul's "destroying angel." While most agree that Paul is referring, or at least *primarily* referring, to the grumblers involved in Korah's rebellion, it's noteworthy that Paul doesn't explicitly state this. And because his reference to grumblers is indefinite, his reference to a destroying angel could justifiably be applied to *all* episodes in the OT in which grumblers are judged—and there are a number of them![30]

29. For a list, see Day, *God's Conflict*, 84–86. See also Day, *Yahweh and the Gods*, 197–208, and P. Xella, "Resheph," in van der Toorn et al., *Dictionary*, 700–703.

30. Num 11:1–10, 31–33; 14:36; 17:5, 10; Pss 78:21; 106:13–15. Several who argue along these lines are A. C. Thiselton, *The First Epistle to the Corinthians: A Commentary on the Greek Text* (Grand Rapids: Eerdmans, 2000), 743, and D. E. Garland, *I Corinthians*, BECNT (Grand Rapids: Baker Academic, 2003), 463.

In fact, even if the cross didn't require this, one could argue that Paul's introduction of a violent cosmic agent as a means of distancing God from violence establishes a warrant for us to assume that destructive cosmic agents were involved in *all* divine judgments that don't involve the use of violent humans. And in making this observation, I am simply claiming that Paul was beginning to interpret the OT's violent portraits of God through the lens of the cross, along the lines I am advocating in this book.

With this in mind, let's explore a cross-centered interpretation of the most destructive judgment recorded in the Bible: the worldwide Flood that destroyed almost every living thing on the planet.

13

Creation Undone

They were carried off before their time,
their foundations washed away by a flood.
They said to God, "Leave us alone!"
—Job 22:16–17

"Didn't God Love *All* the Animals?"

A number of years ago I was approached after a Sunday service by a young, single mother named Susan. She handed me a children's Bible and told me that the night before, she was reading the story of Noah's Ark to her two toddlers. She showed me the colorful cartoon drawing of God (yes, as an old white guy with a white beard!) telling Noah to build a big boat because a long rain was coming and God wanted to save Noah's family along with the animals. The next page had smiling animals marching onto Noah's Ark, two-by-two, being greeted by a radiantly happy Noah and his smiling family.

The following page had a drawing of Noah's Ark on stormy waters with rain coming down. The caption simply said: "It rained forty days and forty nights." Following this was a picture of Noah and his family along with the animals looking out from the top of the Ark with smiling faces on a sunny day. Noah's hands were raised in celebration as a smiling dove flew toward the Ark with a branch in its mouth.

The story ended with Noah and his happy family, together with the pairs of smiling animals, on dry ground with the Ark in the background. The arms of Noah and his family were lifted in praise. The closing line read, "And that is how God saved Noah and all the animals he loves so much."

Susan told me she tucked her children into bed, kissed them good night, and was about to turn off the light when she suddenly heard her precocious four-year-old say, "Mommy?"

"Yes sweetheart," Susan replied.

"What happened to the animals that didn't get invited onto the big boat? Didn't God love them too?"

Susan was soliciting my advice on how she should have answered her child's question. I don't recall exactly what I said, though I do recall stumbling a bit and being struck by how lame my answer sounded.

***

Let's just admit it: This is a brutal story! Some scholars have tried to minimize the violence involved in this story by arguing that, while the author uses global-sounding language, the Flood was actually a regional catastrophe. I actually think a strong case can be made for this perspective, but it unfortunately doesn't lessen the challenge of this narrative.[1] For while the historical event this story is based on may very well have been a regional rather than a global event, the author of this narrative gives it a global, even cosmic, theological interpretation, as we'll see in a moment. And, as I have stated several times, it is *the narrative* that is divinely inspired, regardless of what we think about the historical event it is based on.

So there's no way around it: We have to accept that this author depicts Yahweh wiping out every living thing on the earth except the remnant that was spared on Noah's Ark.[2]

Since the cross reveals God's true character and Aikido way of punishing evil with evil, we must assess the portrait of God directly bringing about this horrendous violence to be a literary crucifix, bearing witness to the accommodating love of our heavenly missionary that was supremely revealed in the crucified Christ. And since we can't attribute the violence of this judgment to humans, our cross-centered reading requires us to assume that Satan and other

1. For two overviews of the debate, see R. F. Youngblood, ed., *The Genesis Debate: Persistent Questions about Creation and Flood* (Grand Rapids: Baker, 1990), 210–28, and D. Young, *The Biblical Flood: A Case Study of the Church's Response to Extrabiblical Evidence* (Grand Rapids: Eerdmans, 1995).
2. Gen 6:7, 13; 7:4; 8:21.

fallen cosmic powers used their God-given authority over aspects of creation to bring about this catastrophe.

What is interesting, however, is that when we interpret this narrative within the metanarrative of cosmic conflict, as the cross requires us to do, we can discern a number of indications within the narrative itself that support this cross-centered interpretation. In what follows I will first review four Scripture-based considerations that lend support to the cross-centered reading of this narrative. I'll then follow this by highlighting two ways in which we can discern the Spirit breaking through by contrasting the biblical Flood story with other flood accounts that we find in the ANE.[3]

As Humans Go, So the Earth and Animal Kingdom Goes

First, it's important to remember that ancient Israelites viewed the world like a sort of "spider web" in which everything was organically related to everything else. This is why the Bible consistently depicts the welfare of humans, the earth, and the animal kingdom as bound together.[4] Whenever humans, whom God entrusted to care for the earth and animal kingdom, push God away with their sin, the land and animals suffer as a result.[5]

Conversely, biblical authors never separate the salvation of humans from the restoration of the earth and animal kingdom. The entire creation groans and "waits in eager expectation for the children of God to be revealed" (Rom 8:19). And when humans are finally reconciled to God and to one another, Isaiah declares, even the desert will bloom, and even the animal kingdom will once again be free of all violence.[6] God is at work in Christ "to reconcile to himself *all things*, whether things on earth or things in heaven, by making peace through his blood, shed on the cross" (Col 1:20, emphasis added).

The organic connection between human behavior and the welfare of creation is reflected in the fact that some biblical depictions of

3. For a more comprehensive and in depth treatment of the Flood narrative, see *CWG*, vol. 2, ch. 23.
4. T. Fretheim, *God and World in the Old Testament* (Nashville: Abingdon, 2005), 97–100; 163–65; 194–98; T. Fretheim, *Creation Untamed: The Bible, God, and Natural Disasters* (Grand Rapids: Baker Academic, 2010), 48–55.
5. Gen 3:17–19; Jer 4:24–25; 9:9–10; 23:10; Isaiah 24; Psalm 72; Hos 4:1–3; Joel 1:8–10.
6. The theme is especially prominent in Isaiah (Isa 11:6–9; 32:15–16; 35:1–2, 6; 41:18–19; 51:3; 65:25).

divine judgment don't even mention God. For example, in the course of describing a divine judgment, Hosea decries:

> . . . the land dries up,
> and all who live in it waste away;
> the beasts of the field, the birds in the sky
> and the fish in the sea are swept away. (Hos 4:1–3)

The land and animal kingdom clearly suffer as a result of this judgment on humans, yet it's not because God is afflicting them. The destruction of land, animals, and people that this judgment brought about is simply what sin looks like when God allows it to become full grown (Jas 1:15). And this already provides some confirmation that we should interpret the Flood narrative not as a judgment that God violently imposed on the earth, but as an extreme example of what collective human sin looks like when God withdraws his merciful restraints to allow it to run its self-destructive course.

From Corruption to Destruction

Second, we can see the organic connection between humans and creation in the way the author of the Flood narrative speaks about the corruption of humans and the destruction of the earth. "God saw how corrupt (*sāhat*) the earth had become," he says, "for all the people on earth had corrupted (*sāhat*) their ways." Because of this corruption, he continues, the Lord said, "I am surely going to destroy (*sāhat*) both them and the earth" (Gen 6:12–13). The same root word (*sāhat*) is used to describe the sinful condition of humans, the effect their sin was having on the earth, and the punishment for this sin, which indicates that all three are organically related. And this means that the Flood was an organic, not a judicial, divine judgment.

This narrative paints a picture of the God-commissioned rulers of the earth spiraling into an abyss of wickedness and violence and taking all that was under their authority down with them (Gen 6:5, 11–13). The same Spirit (*ruach*) that had restrained "the deep" when this present world was created (Gen 1:2) and that would restrain it once again after the Flood (Gen 8:1) had been mercifully striving with humans to prevent their sin from returning the creation to chaos (6:3).[7] But when God saw that his merciful striving had no hope of turning the earth's landlords around, he had no choice but to withdraw his Spirit, thereby allowing *sāhat* ("corruption") to reap its own *sāhat* ("destruction"). As always, God used evil to punish evil.

Eliphaz would later declare that the people in Noah's day had "their foundations washed away by a flood" because they had been saying to God, "Leave us alone!" (Job 22:16–17). Though it grieved his heart, this is precisely what God did. And because the welfare of animals, the earth, and children are inextricably bound up with the welfare of their God-commissioned rulers, they too suffered the destructive consequences of this persistent sin.

The Agents of Destruction

Third, while this author reflects his ANE cultural conditioning by crediting Yahweh with the horrendous violence of this judgment, it is remarkable that he never actually depicts God actively bringing it about. He instead states that "the floodwaters came on the earth" (7:6; cf. 7:10); "all the springs of the great deep burst forth" (7:11); "the floodgates of the heavens were opened" (7:11); "rain fell on the earth forty days" (7:12); and, "the flood kept coming on the earth . . . as the waters increased" (7:17). The actual agents of destruction, we see, were the floodwaters and the springs of the great deep, *not God*.

Remember that in the ANE worldview, when water and flood are talked about in narratives involving divine judgments, they never refer only to physical water. They also, and often exclusively, refer to the menacing cosmic forces that must be held at bay to preserve the order of creation. When Yahweh withdrew his restraining Spirit, therefore, the earth and its inhabitants were "swallowed up in a great abyss," as one ancient author put it (*1 Enoch* 83:4). God was once again using evil to punish evil.

In this light, it should be clear that God's use of the cosmic waters to bring about this judgment was no different from the way he used nations that were "bent on destruction" to judge Israel. Just as God lifted his protective hedge against Babylon, Assyria, and other hostile nations when he judged Israel, so too he lifted his protective hedge against cosmic adversaries to bring this judgment on the human race, and therefore on the earth and animal kingdom that was under their responsible care.

7. The Hebrew word *ruach* that is used in both Gen 1:2 and 8:1 can be translated as "spirit" or "wind."

The "destroyer" who delights in making "the world a wilderness" while destroying land and killing people was allowed to undo creation.[8] Without a stronger power to hold him in check (cf. 2 Thess 2:6–7), the one who holds "the power of death" (Heb 2:14) and who has been "a murderer from the beginning" (John 8:14) was temporarily unleashed, allowing the power of hell to break loose.[9]

In short, the people in Noah's day experienced God's wrath in the same Aikido-like way Jesus did on Calvary.

The Flood and the Undoing of Creation

Finally, it's significant that the language of the Flood narrative parallels, in reverse order, the creation account in Genesis 1. The author is portraying the Flood as the undoing of creation.[10]

In Genesis 1 the creation had become "formless and void" and God's Spirit hovered over the deep (Gen 1:2), possibly to prepare it for the creative acts that were to follow, possibly to constrain it, or possibly to do both. While "the deep" is depersonalized in this passage, many scholars argue that it nevertheless retains the menacing character that it has in the ANE conflict-with-chaos literature.[11]

The land and its environment begin to take shape on the third day when God places a "vault" or "dome" (NRSV) in the midst of the water to separate "the water under the vault from the water above it" (Gen 1:6–7). Understood in its ANE context, it is likely that this vault didn't merely hold back H_2O: it was also a bulwark against the ever-threatening cosmic forces of chaos.[12] The creative acts that follow are all predicated on this fundamental separation of these waters.

This is reversed in the Flood narrative. The separation of the waters above from the waters below is removed. The "springs of the great deep burst forth," and "the floodgates of the heavens were opened"

8. Rev 9:1; Isa 14:17, 20.
9. As in Rev 9:4–5; 20:7.
10. For a list of OT scholars who argue this, see *CWG*, vol. 2, ch. 23, n. 57.
11. See K. Barth, *Church Dogmatics* III/1, *Doctrine of Creation*, ed. and trans. G. W. Bromiley and T. F. Torrance (Edinburgh: T&T Clark, 1981), 81, 102–3, 105, 108; J. Moltmann, *God in Creation*, 2nd ed., trans. M. Kohl (Minneapolis: Fortress Press, 1993), 77; A. König, *New and Greater Things: Re-Evaluating the Biblical Message on Creation* (Pretoria: University of South Africa Press, 1988), 15–18; J. Levenson, *Creation and the Persistence of Evil: The Jewish Drama of Divine Omnipotence* (San Francisco: Harper & Row, 1988), 122–23.
12. S. H. Webb, *The Dome of Eden: A New Solution to the Problem of Creation and Evolution* (Eugene, OR: Cascade, 2010), 165–71. Other creation passages make it clear that these waters refer to Yahweh's cosmic foes (for example, Job 38:8–11; Pss 74:13–17; 104:7–9; Prov 8:29).

(7:11). As a result, "every living thing that moved on the earth perished" (7:21).[13] The humans who were originally supposed to reflect God's image as they partnered with him in "subduing" all remnant forces of chaos on the earth ended up being subdued by this very chaos.[14]

This understanding of the Flood was nicely summed up by one of the greatest OT scholars of the nineteenth century, Gerhard von Rad:

> We must understand the Flood . . . as a catastrophe involving the entire cosmos. When the heavenly ocean breaks forth upon the earth below, and the primeval sea beneath the earth, which is restrained by God, now freed from its bonds, gushes up through yawning chasms onto the earth, then there is a destruction of the entire cosmic system according to biblical cosmology. The two halves of the chaotic primeval sea, separated—the one up, the other below—by God's creative government (1:7–9), are again united; creation begins to sink into chaos.[15]

In short, while God created the present world by constraining the hostile cosmic waters, he now allows the process to be reversed by lifting his restraint, thereby allowing "the deep" to once again cover everything, returning creation to a state of being "formless and void" (Gen 1:2).

***

The identification of the destructive waters with the cosmic forces of chaos is arguably reinforced in the Flood narrative by the fact that Yahweh set his bow in the sky once he caused the destructive waters to recede.[16] The word that is used for "bow" (*qesheth*) usually refers to a warrior's bow, as when Habakkuk describes Yahweh using a bow with many arrows in his conflict with the sea (Hab 3:8–11). By having Yahweh set this weapon in the sky, the author is signifying that Yahweh had just finished waging a successful battle against his cosmic foes.[17]

13. As outlined by D. J. A. Clines, "The Theology of the Flood Narrative," *Faith and Theology* 100 (1972–73): 128–42.
14. On the association of "subdue" with the forces of chaos, see Fretheim, *Creation Untamed*, 13–14; G. Boyd, *God at War: The Bible & Spiritual Conflict* (Downers Grove, IL: InterVarsity, 1997), 106.
15. G. von Rad, *Genesis: A Commentary*, rev. ed. (Philadelphia: Westminster, 1972), 128; cf. C. Westermann, *Genesis 1-11: A Commentary*, trans. J. J. Scullion (Minneapolis: Augsburg, 1984 [1974]), 434.
16. Gen 9:13; cf. 8:1.

Sometimes when Yahweh used a nation as an instrument of judgment, he turned around and judged the nation he had just used for being the kind of violent nation that could be used for this purpose and/or for going beyond what God intended.[18] This, it seems, is what Yahweh did with the forces of chaos in the Flood narrative. After allowing cosmic agents that were bent on destruction to do what they wanted to do, Yahweh reconquered them in order to restore the creation that they had undone, and he then set his bow in the sky.

Further evidence that the author intends us to view the Flood as the undoing of creation at the hands of destructive cosmic forces is that the stages of re-creation after the Flood more or less follow the pattern of the Genesis 1 creation account.[19] Just as God originally caused his *ruach* ("Spirit," "breath," or "wind") to restrain "the deep" (Gen 1:2), so he now caused his *ruach* to push back and restrain it once again (8:1). The separation of the waters above and below the land was reestablished.[20] Plant life then reappears, followed by the reintroduction of animals on the now-dry land and the reissuing of the original creation mandate for humans to multiply on the earth and exercise dominion.[21]

***

In this light, I trust it's clear that the Flood was not the result of something God *did*, but of something God *stopped doing*. God had created the present world out of primordial chaos and had been sustaining it by keeping this chaos at bay. To undo creation God needed to do nothing more than remove his restraint, thereby allowing the forces of chaos to again envelop the earth, returning it to the state of "formless and void," just as we find it in Genesis 1:2.[22] When the One

17. See E. van Wolde, "The Bow in the Clouds in Genesis 9.12-17: When Cognitive Linguistics Meets Visual Criticism," in *A Critical Engagement: Essays on the Hebrew Bible in Honour of J. Cheryl Exum*, ed. D. J. A. Clines and E. van Wolde (Sheffield: Sheffield Phoenix, 2011), 383–92; C. J. L. Kloos, "The Flood on Speaking Terms with God," *Zeitschrift für die alttestamentlich Wissenschaft* 94 (1982): 639–42.
18. Isa 10:5–16; Zech 1:15.
19. See Cline, "Theology of the Flood"; B. F. Batto, *Slaying the Dragon: Mythmaking in the Biblical Tradition* (Louisville: Westminster John Knox, 1992), 87; E. Van Wolde, *Stories of the Beginning: Genesis 1-11 and Other Creation Stories*, trans. J. Bowden (London: SCM, 1996), 121–23.
20. Gen 8:1–5; cf. Gen 1:6–8.
21. Gen 8:6–12, 17; cf. Gen 1:9–13, 22; 9:1–2.
22. On "formless and void" (*tohu wabohu*) reflecting a reversal of creation, see K. A. Matthews, *Genesis 1-11:26*, NAC 1a (Nashville: Broadman & Holman, 1995), 132. I side with those scholars who argue that the "formless and void" state of creation in Genesis 1:2 does not reflect the way

who perpetually restrains hostile cosmic forces as he holds all things together *refrains from these activities*, then, as a matter of course, all hell breaks loose and the creation lapses "back into primeval chaos."[23]

As God's revelation on the cross leads us to expect, God was once again using evil to punish evil as a sign pointing to, and a stepping-stone toward, his ultimate judgment and victory over sin and evil on Calvary.

The Spirit Breaking Through

We possess numerous accounts, from a variety of different cultures, of gods judging the world by sending a flood, including, most importantly, several flood accounts from the ANE. From a biblical perspective, the most plausible explanation for this is that these stories reflect faint memories of the same flood that the biblical Flood account refers to. As different cultures passed this story on from generation to generation, the story was altered in various ways and for different reasons.

In any event, while God stooped to accommodate the biblical author's culturally conditioned assumption that he was complimenting God by crediting him with the violence of this judgment, we can nevertheless discern the Spirit of Christ breaking through by comparing this account with other flood accounts.

First, in nonbiblical flood stories, a god sends a flood in a fit of rage, and usually for petty reasons. For example, in an ancient Mesopotamian work titled *The Epic of Gilgamesh*, a deity named Enlil sent a flood because he was irritated by how noisy humans had become.[24] By contrast, the biblical author captures God's grief in seeing the need to allow this judgment to take place. The author says that the Lord was "grieved (*astab*) in his heart" (Gen 6:6, NAS), "heartbroken" (GWT), "filled with regret" (GNT), or "filled with pain" (NCV)—to the point that he "regretted (*nacham*) that he had made human beings" (6:6).

The fact that this depiction differs so markedly from other flood

God originally created it, but rather reflects creation after it had been engulfed by destructive cosmic powers. In this view, the creation narrative that follows after verse 2 is actually a *re*-creation narrative. See G. Boyd, *God at War*, 102–12.

23. Col 1:17; Heb 1:3. See B. Anderson, *From Creation to New Creation: Old Testament Perspectives* (Minneapolis: Fortress Press, 1994), 7.

24. *Gilgamesh Epic*, xi.181–95.

stories and from the way people have generally thought about gods, combined with the fact that this depiction conforms to the way Jesus responded to the impending judgment of Jerusalem, justifies accepting this depiction of God to be a *direct* revelation.

***

A second way we can discern the Spirit of Christ breaking through in the biblical Flood account concerns God's motive in allowing this judgment to take place. Whereas nonbiblical accounts uniformly attribute a flood to an enraged deity, the biblical account views the Flood as a necessary judgment that God reluctantly allowed only after he had spent centuries striving with humans to prevent it.

Not only this, but the primary purpose of the Flood in the biblical narrative wasn't even to punish sin, but to *rescue God's creation project*.

To see this, first notice that the Flood account is prefaced by the curious story of "the sons of God" having sex with "daughters of men" and begetting hybrid beings known as the Nephilim. The author tells us that these were the legendary heroes of old that can be found, in one form or another, in ancient literature around the world (Gen 6:1–4). The reason this author uses this story as a preface to the Flood account is to explain why Yahweh had to start over, virtually from scratch, with his plans for humans and the world. Not only had humanity sunk to the point that "every inclination of the thoughts of [their] heart" was "evil all the time" (6:5), but the unnatural sexual union of fallen angelic beings and human women was corrupting God's created order in which everything was to reproduce "according to their kinds" (Gen 1:21, 24–25).

Indeed, one could argue that the introduction of the hybrid Nephilim was corrupting the human gene pool, which meant that God's plans for humans to reflect his image and his loving rule over the earth and animals was in jeopardy. In fact, by singling out Noah as the one person who "walked faithfully with God" (6:9), this author is suggesting that God was down to his last man!

This is why Yahweh needed to go to the extreme of withdrawing his Spirit and allowing forces of destruction to revert creation back to a "formless and void" state. So, while the Flood was a grievous judgment on the world, it was even more fundamentally *a rescue operation*. Only by going to this extreme could God preserve his dream for eventually uniting himself to humans and inviting them to share in his triune love and rule forever.

This emphasis is also reflected in the fact that the authors of Hebrews and 1 Peter both emphasize the salvific rather than the punitive nature of the flood.[25] The Flood narrative reflects the truth, found throughout the inspired written record of God's missionary activity, that when God sees he must allow people to suffer a divine judgment, he does it with a grieving heart and with a salvific intention.

***

When we interpret the Flood narrative through the looking-glass cross, its violent portrait of God becomes a literary crucifix, illuminating God's willingness to bear sinful and culturally conditioned views of him that his people were not yet ready to let go of. And whenever we interpret narratives this way, things that otherwise might seem insignificant suddenly become highly significant.

In the case of the Flood narrative, the organic connection between humans, the earth, and animals, together with the fact that the author ascribes all violent verbs to cosmic forces of destruction instead of to God, confirms that the Flood involved God using evil to punish evil, just as he did on the cross. Moreover, the grief and the salvific motive that the author of Genesis ascribes to God becomes significant, for unlike the narrative's violent portrait of God, these portraits reflect the Spirit breaking through to point us directly to the crucified Christ.

***

Having addressed Korah's rebellion and the Flood, I will now turn to the biblical narrative that I initially thought might prove to be the most challenging to the cross-centered approach. To my great surprise, however, it ended up providing more confirmations of this approach than any other OT narrative! I am talking about the story of Yahweh drowning Pharaoh's army in the Red Sea.

25. Heb 11:7; 1 Pet 3:19–20.

14

Dragon-Swallowing-Dragon Warfare

[T]he waters are God's instrument to punish 'the monster' by his own means:
Babylon will be swallowed, as it swallowed (Jer 51:34) . . .
When the sea covered the Egyptians, the tyrant was tyrannized.
—M. K. Wakeman[1]

The Deliverance and Drowning at the Red Sea

You probably know the story, if only from one of the several Hollywood movies. After ten brutal plagues, Pharaoh finally agreed to let his Hebrew slaves go free. But then he had a change of heart, and he sent his army out to recapture them. The Egyptian army caught up to the Israelites just as they came upon the Red Sea, but a pillar of fire prevented them from succeeding in their mission.[2]

While Pharaoh's army was held at bay, Yahweh split apart the Red Sea, allowing the children of Israel to safely walk "through the sea, with a wall of water on their right and on their left" (Exod 14:29). As soon they were safe on the other side, the pillar of fire disappeared, and Pharaoh sent his troops in pursuit. But as his army raced between

1. M. K. Wakeman, *God's Battle with the Monster: A Study in Biblical Imagery* (Leiden: Brill, 1973), 128.
2. A number of scholars argue that the actual location referenced in this episode is the "Reed Sea." Nothing of significance hangs on this, except that I would note that the biblical account presupposes a very large body of water that matches the Red Sea much better than the Reed Sea.

the two enormous walls of water, Yahweh allowed the sea to return "back to its place" (Exod 14:27), thereby drowning Pharaoh's entire army.

Inasmuch as Yahweh fought and won this battle without any human assistance, some scholars argue that it illustrates the way Yahweh would have always preferred to protect the Israelites.[3] I agree that if the Israelites could have trusted him, Yahweh would have fought all of Israel's battles without their participation. But does God need to resort to violence when he fights, as this position assumes?

As we would expect of any ANE author, the person who composed the Red Sea narrative certainly believed this. It was Yahweh, "a man of war" (Exod 15:1, ASV), who drowned Pharaoh's army in the sea.[4] Yet, the cross reveals that God does not engage in violence when he brings judgment on people. So, as with other divinely inspired violent portraits of God, our cross-centered perspective must interpret this author's ascription of violence to God to be a reflection of his own fallen and culturally conditioned theology.

This is confirmed by the fact that, as is true of all the OT's violent portraits of God, this author's view of Yahweh as a "man of war" bears a strong resemblance to other ANE warrior deities. At the same time, the looking-glass cross allows us to see through the ugly sin- mirroring surface of this warrior representation to behold the beautiful sin-bearing love of the crucified God.

Along the same lines, as we interpret this narrative in light of the conviction that the cross reveals God's true character and true Aikido way of judging sin, we are led to expect that the violence involved in this judgment was carried out by agents other than God. And since humans obviously played no role in this judgment, we must assume that destructive cosmic agents were behind its violence.

***

Now, at first glance there doesn't appear to be anything in this narrative that confirms this cross-centered conviction. Throughout Exodus 14 and 15 it appears that Yahweh simply opens up a body of water to allow the Israelites to cross over to the other side and then

3. M. Lind, *Yahweh Is a Warrior: The Theology of Warfare in Israel* (Scottdale, PA: Herald, 1980), 46. See also M. Lind, "Paradigm of Holy War in the Old Testament," *Biblical Research Bulletin* 16 (1971): 17–31.
4. Yahweh is depicted as being behind this violence in Exod 14:8, 13–14, 24–25, 27, 31; 15:1–4, 6–7, 10, 12, 16, 19, 21.

closes this body of water when Pharaoh's army attempts the same thing. However, if we dig a little deeper and understand this narrative within the metanarrative of cosmic conflict, and, more specifically, against the backdrop of the ANE conflict-with-chaos motif, we will find that there's a wealth of evidence that supports our cross-centered interpretation.

To see this, we must again step out of our Western worldview and into the alien worldview of the ANE. Among other things, we need to remember that the people of this time and area considered heavenly and earthly battles to be two sides of the same reality. And we need to remember that things like mighty seas and raging waters in the OT often do not merely refer to H_2O, for they were one of the primary ways ANE people envisioned the anti-creational cosmic forces that threaten the world.[5]

A Victory over a Cosmic Beast

On a hot July morning several years ago, I was doing research for this book with my good friend Paul Eddy in the basement of Bethel Seminary library. I affectionately refer to Paul as my "research hound," because once I give him the general direction of what I am attempting to argue, he has an uncanny ability to pick up the scent of a more specific trail of research. I mean, this guy can spend ten minutes combing through a 500-page tome and determine, with remarkable accuracy, whether it has anything that is relevant to our research project!

It took me ten years to research and write this book, but it would have likely taken much longer if my friend, the hound, hadn't been running ahead of me, narrowing my reading load to those books and essays that I really needed.

On this particular morning I was looking into the ANE background of the Red Sea narrative for possible indications that other cosmic agents were involved in it. Paul had just returned from an hour-long expedition into this library's bookshelves with a huge stack of books and journals that he had surmised could be relevant to this topic.

The first book and first two articles I combed through didn't offer

5. For a more comprehensive and in-depth treatment of this episode, see *CWG*, vol. 2, ch. 24. For a discussion on the meaning of Yahweh hardening Pharaoh's heart, see *CWG*, vol. 2, appendix VI.

much. But my heart began to speed up with excitement as I then read a rather obscure essay by a scholar named Paul Hanson titled "War, Peace and Justice in Early Israel."[6] Hanson made a compelling case that the author of Exodus 15 uses the ANE conflict-with-chaos motif as the framework for telling the story of Yahweh's victory at the Red Sea. He argues that this author interpreted the parting and closing of the Red Sea to be a reenactment of Yahweh's battle with the anti-creational force he defeated when he created the present world. So when Yahweh split the Red Sea, he was engaging in a battle against a cosmic force of destruction, just as the cross-centered interpretation of this narrative predicted.

After I finished taking notes on Hanson's essay I continued to work through the other books and journals that Paul had delivered. My heart rate rarely slowed down the rest of the day because many of these works supported and/or supplemented the conflict-with chaos interpretation of this narrative.[7]

***

The thing that really blew me away was my discovery that almost every subsequent biblical author who refers to the Red Sea crossing gives it this conflict-with-chaos interpretation! For starters, in a classic conflict-with-chaos passage that celebrates Yahweh's victory both at creation and at the Red Sea, the Psalmist exalts Yahweh, saying, "It was you who split open the sea by your power; you broke the heads of the monster in the waters. It was you who crushed the heads of Leviathan" (Ps 74:13–14).[8] By this means, he adds, Yahweh established the "sun and moon," "the boundaries of the earth," and "the summer and winter" (vv. 16–17).

Notice that this author identifies the Red Sea as the many-headed Leviathan, the same cosmic beast whose heads he crushed when he established the order of the present creation. And for this author, it is this victory, not a victory over Pharaoh's army, that makes the crossing of the Red Sea so significant.

Another Psalm celebrates the crossing of the Red Sea by declaring,

6. P. D. Hanson, "War, Peace and Justice in Early Israel," *Bible Review* 3, no. 3 (1987): 32–45.

7. For a list of works that defend this perspective, see *CWG*, vol. 2, ch. 24, n. 61.

8. For several discussions on this important passage, see Wakeman, *God's Battle,* 126; N. Forsyth, *The Old Enemy: Satan and the Combat Myth* (Princeton: Princeton University Press, 1987), 144–45, and J. Levenson, *Creation and the Persistence of Evil: The Jewish Drama of Divine Omnipotence* (San Francisco: Harper & Row, 1988), 18–19.

> The waters saw you, God,
> the waters saw you and writhed;
> the very depths were convulsed . . .
> Your path led through the sea,
> your way through the mighty waters,
> though your footprints were not seen.
> You led your people like a flock
> by the hand of Moses and Aaron.[9]

Yahweh is depicted as Israel's captain leading them through the Red Sea, though his "footprints were not seen." And as with the previous Psalm, Yahweh's victory wasn't first and foremost over Pharaoh's army, it was over the "waters" and "depths" that "writhed" and "convulsed" in fear as he approached. This is how the Psalmist interprets the restraining of the two walls of water that were formed when Leviathan (the Red Sea) was split in two. The waters were pulling back in fear as Yahweh led the Israelites to safety.

Something similar can be found in Psalm 114, which celebrates Israel's deliverance "out of Egypt" (v. 1) by declaring that "the sea looked and fled" (v. 3). So too, the author of Psalm 106 says that Yahweh "rebuked the Red Sea, and it dried up," which is how "he led [the Israelites] through the depths as through a desert" (v. 9).

The conflict-with-chaos way of framing the parting of the Red Sea is not limited to the Psalms. Isaiah identifies the Red Sea with a different well-known ANE cosmic monster, Rahab. He writes:

> Was it not you who cut Rahab to pieces,
> who pierced that monster through?
> Was it not you who dried up the sea,
> the waters of the great deep,
> who made a road in the depths of the sea
> so that the redeemed might cross over? (Isa 51:9–10)[10]

Habakkuk also declares that Yahweh "trampled the sea (*yam*) with [his] horses, churning the great waters" (Hab 3:15). While *yam* is typically translated as "sea," it also happens to be the name of a well-known Canaanite deity associated with chaos. Many OT scholars argue that Habakkuk is here identifying the Red Sea as this chaos deity.[11]

9. Ps 77:15–16, 19–20.
10. See also Ps 89:9–10, which, according to some, also depicts the Red Sea as "Rahab."

By interpreting the parting of the Red Sea within a conflict-with-chaos framework, these authors were fusing "primeval and historical events."[12] That is, Yahweh's historical victory over the Red Sea reenacts his primeval victory over his cosmic foe when he created the present world. In the words of Bruce Waltke, "The historical event of the crossing and the mythological combat" at creation "have become identical." He concludes, "Deep, Rahab, Red Sea—all are parallel forms of the cosmic and historical adversary."[13]

So, as you can see, in my quest to discover indications of other destructive cosmic agents involved in the parting and closing of the Red Sea, I discovered that *the Red Sea itself* was just such a destructive cosmic agent! It was the sea monster, not God, who devoured Pharaoh's army![14]

On top of this, we can discern God's Aikido wisdom at work in the way he rescued the Israelites and vanquished Pharaoh's army. Just as Yahweh restrained Pharaoh's army with a pillar of fire and then removed it to allow Pharaoh to do what he wanted to do, so too God restrained the cosmic monster to allow his people to march to safety, only then to remove his restraint, allowing this monster that was "bent on destruction" to do what it wanted to do: namely, swallow up people (Exod 15:12). With a grieving heart, God was once again allowing evil to vanquish evil as a steppingstone to his ultimate Aikido victory over evil on the cross.

***

All of this confirms our cross-centered understanding of the portrait of Yahweh as a "man of war" who personally drowned Pharaoh's army. Reflecting his ANE worldview, the author of this narrative was invested in "crediting" Yahweh with drowning Pharaoh's army. And the sin-bearing heavenly missionary obviously was not too proud to stoop to accommodate this fallen and culturally conditioned misunderstanding of what it means to praise God.

11. On the Canaanite background to depictions of Yahweh battling *Yam*, see C. Kloos, *Yhwh's Combat with the Sea: A Canaanite Tradition in the Religion of Ancient Israel* (Leiden: Brill, 1986), 127–212.
12. B. Batto, *Slaying the Dragon: Mythmaking in the Biblical Tradition* (Louisville: Westminster John Knox, 1992), 82. See also ibid., 110–11, 116; Forsyth, *Old Enemy*, 104.
13. B. K. Waltke, *An Old Testament Theology: An Exegetical, Canonical and Thematic Approach* (Grand Rapids: Zondervan, 2007), 187.
14. J. F. D. Creach, *Violence in Scripture* (Louisville: Westminster John Knox, 2013), 56.

But we can nevertheless discern the Spirit breaking through when this author, together with multiple other biblical authors, confirms what God's revelation on the cross leads us to expect. It wasn't Yahweh who drowned Pharaoh's soldiers, it was the one known as "Leviathan," "Rahab," "Yam," and "the monster of the sea." And this is the same cosmic beast that would later come to be identified as "Satan" and other "spiritual forces of evil" (Eph 6:12). In fact, it is the same violent beast that we earlier saw Paul identify as "the destroying angel" (1 Cor 10:10).

Now, unlike the ancient Hebrews, most of us probably find it a little hard to identify a body of water like the Red Sea with Satan. So you may be wondering: What *actually* happened when Pharaoh's army drowned in the Red Sea? And, as I said regarding Korah's rebellion, my answer is, *I don't know*. We simply have no way of getting behind the mythic narrative to determine what took place in actual history.

But, as I also said regarding Korah's rebellion, I consider this question irrelevant when we are reading Scripture as the divinely inspired written witness to God's missionary activity. For it is the narrative itself, apart from all questions related to its relationship with actual history, that is God-breathed and that we are seeking to interpret in a way that points to the cross.

I therefore consider my task to be completed when I have disclosed how the violent depictions of God in this narrative are indirect revelations of God's cruciform love and when I have found confirmations that it was a cosmic agent bent on destruction that devoured Pharaoh's army, *not Yahweh*.

The Aikido Dimension of Yahweh's Victory

Once I was clear about the identification of the Red Sea with Yahweh's cosmic foe, and once I realized how God's Aikido strategy was at work in the vanquishing of Pharaoh's army, I began to notice other aspects of this victory that reflect this Aikido strategy.

First, we saw in chapter 8 that biblical authors sometimes viewed Pharaoh and/or Egypt as an anti-creational monster, the same way they identify the Red Sea with an anti-creational cosmic monster.[15]

15. Ezek 29:3–5; 32:2–8; Pss 87:4; 89:10; Isa 27:1; 30:7; Jer 46:7–8. Since we know it is wrong to identify earthly enemies with cosmic enemies (Eph 6:12), we would say that Pharaoh and Egypt

And this means that, from the biblical perspective, Yahweh was allowing one cosmic monster to swallow another when he withdrew his protection to allow Leviathan to swallow Pharaoh's army.

The Egyptian cosmic foe of Yahweh that had boasted, "I will gorge myself" on Yahweh's people became the food on which another cosmic beast gorged itself (Exod 15:9, 12). So this narrative highlights a God who so masters the cosmic forces of chaos that he can play them off against one another to free his people and to further his sovereign purposes.[16]

***

I then noticed that this narrative, which culminates with God using one serpent (the Red Sea) to swallow another (Pharaoh and his army), began with God using Aaron's supernatural serpent to swallow Pharaoh's supernatural serpents (Exod 7:8–13). And there are several indications that the author of this narrative intends these two events to serve as theme-setting bookends for the plague narrative that is sandwiched between them and that culminates with the Red Sea battle.

First, the author of this narrative praises Yahweh for his victory at the Red Sea by proclaiming: "You stretch out your right hand, and the earth swallows (*bāla*) your enemy" (Exod 15:12). One would have expected the author to say that *the sea* rather than the earth swallowed Yahweh's enemies. For this reason, several scholars have argued that this author is fusing together the sea monster with the earth monster, discussed in chapter 12.[17]

In any event, the important thing to note is that the only other place in Exodus where we find one beast swallowing (*bāla*) another is in the episode that launched Yahweh's battle with Pharaoh (Exod 7:12). Moreover, it is significant that both swallowing-up miracles are preceded by a reference to Yahweh stretching out his hand (Exod 7:5; 15:12).

Second, the word for "serpent" (*tannin*) in Exodus 7:12 does not refer to an ordinary snake. It could be translated as "dragon" or "mon-

were *used by* evil powers (ch. 8). But this correction does not affect the Aikido dimension of God's victory in this episode.

16. So argues Creach, *Violence in Scripture*, 82.
17. Wakeman, *God's Battle*, 118–38; F. M. Cross Jr. and D. N. Freedman, "The Song of Miriam," *Journal of Near Eastern Studies* 14 (1955): 225–59 (239).

ster," and it happens to be the word that describes the anti-creational monster that Yahweh split asunder to save his people and overthrow the Egyptian army at the Red Sea (Ps 74:13; Isa 51:9).

When we combine these considerations with the fact that Pharaoh and Egypt were themselves identified as an anti-creational monster, it's apparent that Yahweh's battle with Pharaoh begins and culminates with God "using a dragon to swallow up a dragon."[18] As he did on the cross, God used evil to vanquish evil.

***

But it's not only the beginning and culmination of this battle that reflect God's Aikido way of doing warfare. The dragon-swallowing-dragon beginning and culmination of this battle suggests that every stage of this battle in between, which involved the ten plagues on Egypt, should be understood along similar lines.[19]

Each plague represents an increasingly intensified step toward the undoing of creation, just as we saw in the Flood. It's just that, in this narrative, this undoing happens in slow motion and only in one corner of the creation. Each plague presents creation "out of kilter," as Fretheim puts it, for each of the natural agents used in the plagues "appears in distorted form." Fretheim continues:

> Water, frog, dust and gnats, flies, cattle epidemic, ashes and boils, weather phenomena, locusts, and darkness . . . none of them appear as they were created by God to be. . . . Water is no longer simply water; light and darkness are no longer separate; diseases of people and animals run amok; insects and amphibians swarm out of control.[20]

In each plague, we see "the natural breaking through its created limits, not functioning as God intended." As such, each plague represents an increasingly intense stage of "[t]he world . . . reverting to its

18. T. E. Fretheim, *God and World in the Old Testament: A Relational Theology of Creation* (Nashville: Abingdon, 2005), 115–16.
19. See ibid., 113–20, 394; D. J. McCarthy, "Moses' Dealings with Pharaoh: Ex 7, 8-10, 27," *Catholic Biblical Quarterly* 27 (1965): 336–47; Z. Zevit, "The Priestly Redaction and the Interpretation of the Plague Narrative in Exodus," *Jewish Quarterly Review* 66, no. 4 (1976): 193–211; Creach, *Violence in Scripture*, 82–86; B. Stephens, *Annihilation or Renewal? The Meaning and Function of New Creation in the Book of Revelation* (Tübingen: Mohr Siebeck, 2011), 217–18.
20. Fretheim, *God and World in the Old Testament,* 119–20.

precreation state."[21] And to bring about each plague, Yahweh needed to do nothing more than to stop restraining the forces of destruction.

Several passages even mention the destructive cosmic agents that were behind the plagues on Egypt. We've already seen that the final plague that killed the firstborn throughout Egypt was not the result of something Yahweh *did*, but something he *stopped* doing: namely, preventing "the destroyer" from killing all it wanted to kill (Exod 12:23).

Psalm 78 indicates that similar destroyers were behind other plagues as well. The Psalmist tells us that Yahweh expressed his wrath against Egypt by unleashing "a band of destroying angels" (Ps 78:49). Moreover, using the Aikido language of "giving over" that we've seen is used throughout Scripture, the author declares that by unleashing these destroying angels, Yahweh "gave over their cattle to the pestilence and their flocks to the plague" (v. 48).[22] Finally, the Psalmist writes that God "did not spare [the Egyptians] from death but gave them over to the plague" (v. 50).

It's likely the pestilence and plague referred to in these passages do not merely refer to catastrophes that this band of destroying angels unleashed upon Egypt. They may be the proper names of ANE deities that were among the entourage of "destroying angels" that God turned the Egyptians over to. The same could be argued for the plague and pestilence that Habakkuk says accompanied the Lord when he turned Egypt over to suffer the consequences of its sin (Hab 3:5).[23]

So while the author of the Exodus narrative believes he is exalting Yahweh by attributing the violence involved in each plague to him, these passages provide further confirmation that Yahweh merely permitted a band of cosmic agents that were already bent on destruction to do what they wanted to do. And the one on which they are allowed to carry out their violence is Egypt, itself identified as a cosmic monster.

It's apparent that, from beginning to end, God's judgment of Pharaoh and Egypt did not require God to act violently. He rather merely allowed one evil serpent to swallow another.

21. Ibid., 120.
22. On John Day's emendation of this passage (which I am quoting), see his *Yahweh and the Gods and Goddesses of Canaan* (Sheffield: Sheffield Academic, 2000), 200–201.
23. See, for example, J. Day, *God's Conflict with the Dragon and the Sea: Echoes of a Canaanite Myth in the Old Testament* (New York: Cambridge University Press, 1985), 139; cf. 199–200.

Battling the Gods of Egypt

There is one final Aikido dimension to this narrative that we should investigate. The narrative tells us that Yahweh's conflict was not only with Pharaoh and Egypt, but also with "the gods of Egypt" (Exod 12:23). A compelling case can be made that each of the ten plagues was actually an assault on one or more of these Egyptian gods.[24] For example, when the Nile was turned into blood, this can be understood to represent a victory over Hapi, the god of the Nile, or Khrum, the guardian of the source of the Nile, or Osiris, for the Nile was said to be his bloodstream. Something similar could be argued for each of the other plagues as well.

In this light, it seems that prior to God allowing one cosmic serpent (the Red Sea) to swallow another (Egypt, Pharaoh), God had already allowed one band of destroying agents (the agents behind the ten plagues) to swallow up another band of evil agents (the ten chief gods of Egypt) and to begin to undo creation in the land of Egypt. And this is why God's battle against Egypt and the Pharaoh, understood as yet another cosmic beast, is launched and is culminated with dragon-swallowing-dragon events.

So, while the author of this narrative credits Yahweh with violence, the truth is that God was directly involved in none of it. Rather, from start to finish God fought and overcame evil in this battle using the same Aikido strategy he employed on the cross. Hence, while the surface meaning of the violent warrior portraits of God in this narrative contradict the revelation of God in the crucified Christ, the Aikido way that God used evil to vanquish evil is perfectly consistent with this revelation. When interpreted through the looking-glass cross, therefore, we should assess the former to be *indirect* revelations and the latter to be *direct* revelations of the God whose love and Aikido-wisdom is perfectly revealed on Calvary.

Remembering God's Love for Pharaoh and Egypt

It seems appropriate to bring this chapter to a close by considering once again God's grieving heart in bringing judgments on people. The author of this narrative clearly had no empathy for those who

24. Zevit, "Three Ways"; C. Missler, "The Invisible War: Against the Gods of Egypt," *Koinonia House*, http://www.khouse.org/articles/2000/263/ (accessed 3/5/2016).

suffered as a result of the plagues and the Red Sea drowning. And since ancient Israelites were always inclined to assume that Yahweh was like them, this author's portrait of God displays no concern for the welfare of these sufferers. But surely we who know God as he's fully revealed on the cross must assume a different perspective.

We know that God loved each and every one of the firstborn child that were slain by the Destroyer as well as each and every soldier that was devoured by Leviathan (the Red Sea). Indeed, he loved them more than any human could possibly love them and more than they could possibly love themselves. So, however much people suffered as they experienced the death-consequences of their sin, or however much loved ones grieved for lost loved ones, God grieved inconceivably more. And this sorrow in the heart of God is also one of the ways this and all other divine judgments point us back to the cross.

It's also important to remember that the historical judgment of the Egyptians cannot serve as evidence of their final judgment. Indeed, though we are not told how, Paul indicates that the process of delivering someone over to Satan for "the destruction of their flesh" may result in their "spirit" being "saved on the day of the Lord" (1 Cor 5:5). Moreover, Paul teaches us that love "always hopes" (1 Cor 13:6). So, we should not conclude that all who perished in God's judgment on Egypt, or any other judgment for that matter, are necessarily lost.

To the contrary, because God's love is stronger than death, we should remain confident that the Good Shepherd will continue to search for every single lost sheep, so long as there is any hope of their being found by him, whether in this life or the next.

***

We have thus far addressed divine judgments that involve human and cosmic agents acting violently. But there is one final category of violent divine portraits that we have not yet addressed. What are we to make of Scripture's depictions of God performing violent miracles through servants like Elisha, Elijah, and Samson? To see *what else is going on* in these portraits, we will need to highlight a fourth and final dimension of God's revelation on the cross.

15

Misusing Divine Power

Do you think I cannot call on my Father,
and he will at once put at my disposal
more than twelve legions of angels?
—Matthew 26:53

The spirits of prophets are subject to the control of prophets.
—1 Corinthians 14:32

On March 14, 2012, police officer Randy Trent Harrison of Del City, Oklahoma, witnessed an eighteen-year-old African American man, Dane Scott Jr., selling marijuana from his car near the Del City High School. When Harrison approached Scott's car, Scott took off, leading to a high-speed chase that ended with Scott crashing his car into a tractor-trailer. Harrison apprehended the uninjured Scott and took away a gun he had on him, but Scott somehow managed to break free.

Despite the fact that Harrison knew Scott was unarmed as he was fleeing away, and despite the fact that Scott had his hands raised as he fled, according to several witnesses, Harrison fired at him four times. One of his shots struck Scott in the back and went through his heart, instantly killing him. Officer Harrison was indicted on a manslaughter charge and given the minimum sentence of four years in prison.

I want to go on the record: I believe the vast majority of white police officers make every attempt not to profile people and to only use their weapons when their life or the lives of others are seriously threatened. At the same time, completely unjustified shootings like this one, and especially unjust shootings of unarmed African American men, are far too common. And with the proliferation of smart phones, they are thankfully being caught on camera with increasing frequency.

These videos capture what it looks like when police officers, who are entrusted with exceptional authority to protect people, instead abuse this authority and unjustly kill people. And each one illustrates the central point of this chapter. When exceptional authority is given to someone, there's no guarantee that they will use it the way they should.

We will see that the cross, together with confirming evidence from Scripture, demonstrate that this principle holds true even when the exceptional authority we're talking about is supernatural in nature and is bestowed by God. And this, we will see, significantly reframes our interpretation of biblical narratives that seem to depict God bringing about violence through individuals he's endowed with supernatural power, such as Elisha, Elijah, and Samson.[1]

Fully God and Fully Human

Scripture teaches, and the historic-orthodox church has always confessed, that Jesus is fully God *and fully human.* He wasn't merely God *appearing* as a human. Rather, in Christ, God made himself 100 percent human. "The Word *became* flesh," John writes (John 1:14, emphasis added). So too, the author of Hebrews declares that Jesus "shared in [our] humanity" and was "fully human in every way" (Heb 2:14, 17).

This means that Jesus had a human will that he needed to submit to the Father. Nowhere is this more poignantly illustrated than in the Garden of Gethsemane. Aware of the terrible physical and unthinkable spiritual anguish he was about to endure, Jesus prayed, "My Father, if it is possible, may this cup be taken from me. Yet," he added, "not as I will, but as you will" (Matt 26:39, cf. 42). Jesus had "come down from heaven not to do [his] will but to do the will of him who sent [him]" (John 6:38), and this was the greatest test of this commitment.

The central significance of Jesus's faithful submission to the Father

1. For spatial considerations, I have omitted a discussion of the violent supernatural power of the ark of the covenant. For a discussion of this as well as a more comprehensive and in-depth investigation of the material covered in this chapter, see *CWG*, vol. 2, ch. 25.

is stressed throughout the NT, but it is most emphasized by Paul.[2] And Paul sees Jesus's willingness to die on the cross as the supreme illustration of his submission. For example, Paul declares that Jesus "humbled himself by becoming obedient to death—even death on a cross" (Phil 2:8). And it was because of this obedience that "God exalted him to the highest place and gave him the name that is above every name" (Phil 2:9).

This means that the crucified Christ is not only the supreme revelation of *God's* perfect character, he is also the supreme illustration of a perfect *human* character—the kind of character God created us to have and the kind of character we shall have when we are fully transformed into the image of Jesus Christ. And Christ couldn't have been the perfect revelation of the first if he had failed to be the supreme illustration of the second, which is precisely why Jesus's faithful obedience to the Father receives so much emphasis in the NT.[3]

As a full human being, Jesus was "tempted in every way, just as we are." But unlike us, "he did not sin" (Heb 4:15). And it was only because he "learned obedience from what he suffered" and was thereby "made perfect" that he could be the perfect revelation of God's character and "the source of eternal salvation for all who obey him" (Heb 5:8–9).[4]

The Authority That Was Entrusted to Jesus

John tells us that "the Father had put all things under [Jesus's] power" (John 13:3), and in Matthew, Jesus claims that "[a]ll things have been committed [or "entrusted" (*paradidōmi*)] to me by my Father."[5] These statements imply that the Father had placed his own divine authority under the power of Jesus's fully human will, to be used at

2. R. Hays, *The Faith of Jesus Christ: The Narrative Substructure of Galatians 3:1-4:11*, 2nd ed. (Grand Rapids: Eerdmans, 2002 [1983]); I. Wallis, *The Faith of Jesus Christ in Early Christian Traditions* (Cambridge: Cambridge University Press, 1995).
3. Matt 26:39; John 4:34; 5:19; 6:38; 10:18; 15:10; Rom 5:19; Heb 5:8; Rev 1:5; 3:14; 19:11. Related to this, many NT scholars, including Hays and Wallis, mentioned in the previous footnote, argue that when Paul says we are saved by "faith in Jesus Christ" (for example, Gal 2:16), it should be translated as "the faith [or faithfulness] *of* Jesus Christ."
4. It lies outside the scope of this book to discuss whether or not Jesus could have actually fallen. Suffice it to say that for Jesus's temptations to be experienced as real, Jesus had to at least *believe* he could have fallen, even if the Father knew he would not. A temptation is only genuine if the person undergoing it is not certain of its outcome.
5. Matt 11:27; cf. 28:28. The NLT and HCSB translate *paradidōmi* as "entrusted."

Jesus's discretion. And this further implies that Jesus could have used this authority in ways that conflict with the Father's will.

So, for example, when Jesus rebuked Peter for using his sword to try to prevent his arrest, Jesus told him he could have called "twelve legions of angels" to fight in his defense if he wanted to (Matt 26:53). And Jesus's statement assumes that had he called these angels, they would have come. Yet, had Jesus used his supernatural authority this way, he would have been acting contrary to his Father's will.

Along similar lines, two of the three temptations the devil brought on Jesus in the wilderness involved him using the divine authority that had been entrusted to him in ways that would have been against the Father's will (Matt 4:2–7). These temptations were genuine temptations only because both the devil and Jesus assumed that the divine authority entrusted to Jesus would have worked, even though it would have done so in ways that were contrary to the Father's will.

Misusing Divine Power

Since Jesus never misused the divine authority entrusted to him, the possibility that he could have is merely hypothetical. It's not hypothetical, however, in the life of Moses. Yahweh had entrusted him with the "staff of God," instructing him to "see that you perform before Pharaoh all the wonders I have *given you* the power to do" (Exod 4:20–21, emphasis added). The instruction presupposes that Moses had some say-so over how he would use the supernatural authority that God had given him by means of this staff.

"While God has gifted Moses with power," Fretheim says, "Moses' decision with regard to the *use* of that power is crucial." Hence, he adds, "God's charge to him in Exod 4:21, 'see that you perform,' makes sense only in view of differing possibilities of response on Moses' part."[6]

Moses obediently carried out the "wonders" God wanted him to perform in Egypt by means of his supernaturally endowed staff. But according to the biblical narrative, Moses later struck a rock with his staff out of anger, causing water to gush out of it in order to quench the thirst of the complaining Israelites (Num 20:11). Yahweh was so angry with Moses and Aaron over this outburst that he did not allow

6. T. E. Fretheim, "Issues of Agency in Exodus," in *The Book of Exodus: Composition, Reception, and Interpretation*, ed. T. B. Dozeman, G. A. Evans, and J. N. Lohr (Boston: Brill, 2014), 591–609 (600–601).

them to enter into the Promised Land (v. 12). Yet the supernaturally endowed staff worked, in spite of the fact that it was used in a sinful way!

***

We see the same misuse of divine power in Paul's instructions to the Corinthians on the right and wrong uses of the supernatural gifts of the Spirit. Though Paul confronts the Corinthians' abuse of certain supernatural gifts, he never once doubts that the gifts these Christians were abusing were genuine "manifestations of the Spirit."[7]

Paul explains how it's possible to misuse the gifts of the Spirit when he tells the Corinthians that the way the Spirit is manifested is under the control of the one through whom the Spirit is being manifested (1 Cor 14:32). And this is why the people who possess a particular supernatural gift are responsible for using it in a "fitting and orderly way" (v. 40) that conforms to God's will (v. 33).

This holds true for all prophets in Scripture. As Fretheim notes, while the Spirit of God sometimes "so completely . . . energized" God's prophets that it was "as if God himself were the one now speaking and acting," the prophet nevertheless remained "a distinct personality from God, subject to all the foibles and flaws of any human being."[8] So, just because a person has received exceptional authority from God does not mean that the way they use it agrees with God.

This makes the sinless way Jesus used divine authority all the more praiseworthy. Instead of using divine authority to protect himself and crush his enemies, he allowed himself to be crushed by his enemies, at the hands of his enemies, and out of love for his enemies.

In this light, we must see the cross, understood as the thematic center of everything Jesus was about, as the quintessential witness to God's willingness to entrust divine authority to humans as well as the supreme illustration of the proper use of this divine authority. And, as I said, it's only because Jesus was perfectly obedient that his crucifixion could constitute the supreme revelation of God's self-sacrificial character.

***

7. 1 Cor 14:13–17, 27–32.
8. T. Fretheim, *The Suffering of God: An Old Testament Perspective* (Philadelphia: Fortress Press, 1984), 151, 154.

This is the fourth and final dimension of the looking-glass cross that enables us to see *what else is going on* in certain violent portraits of God in the OT. When certain people whom God has entrusted with supernatural authority bring about supernaturally caused violence, the looking-glass cross allows us to discern that the responsibility for this violence falls on the agent who had been entrusted with this power, not on the God who entrusted the agent with it.

Of course, since the authors of the narratives who recount these episodes only had glimpses of God's true character, we are not surprised to find that they were not usually able to see this. But, from the vantage point given us on Calvary, we can, and we must.

Calling Down Fire from Heaven

It's evident from the many remarkable miracles Elijah performed that he was a man who had been entrusted with a great deal of divine authority. But with the crucified Christ as our criterion, we can see that at least one of the ways he used this divine authority did not reflect the will of God. Twice Elijah had fire fall from heaven to incinerate two different fifty-man battalions of Samaritan messengers who had been sent by King Ahaziah, simply because Elijah mistakenly thought they meant him harm (2 Kgs 1:10–12).

Though the text doesn't say God sent down this fire, one could argue that the author of this narrative assumed this. And if this is correct, we who read Scripture through the looking-glass cross must discern the revelatory content of this portrait of God to reside in its depth. That's where we by faith can discern our heavenly missionary bearing the sin of this author's fallen theological interpretation of a violent supernatural event.

***

Whatever the author's own perspective, however, there are several considerations that confirm that this killing was not God's will. First, Jesus scolded his disciples for wanting to repeat this same lethal miracle on several Samaritan villages that had rejected their message (Luke 7:51–56). Some early manuscripts add that Jesus told his misguided disciples, "You do not know what kind of spirit you are of, for the Son of Man came not to destroy men's lives, but to save them."

Whether or not this sentence belonged to Luke's original

manuscript, it is nevertheless clear that Jesus would not have approved of Elijah's violent and self-protective use of divine authority had he used it this way during Jesus's ministry. Indeed, Elijah would not even have met Jesus's criterion for being considered a child "of [the] Father in heaven," for incinerating enemies is not consistent with "loving," "blessing," and "doing good" to them.[9] It seems that Jesus attributed violent supernatural feats like Elijah's incinerating fire to "the way of the devil, rather than the way of God."[10]

Second, just as the captain of a third battalion pleaded with Elijah to "have respect for my life and the lives of these fifty men" by sparing them, the "angel of the Lord" (who is usually identified with the Lord himself) appeared. He instructed Elijah to "not be afraid" and to allow this captain to take him to king Ahaziah, who happened to be dying of a fatal injury.[11] Once Elijah met the dying king and reiterated an earlier prophecy that this rebellious king was not going to recover, the king died (1 Kgs 1:16–17).

Think about what this short encounter with the angel of the Lord implies. It means that, far from Elijah's murderous supernatural feat being in line with Yahweh's plan, it was actually completely unnecessary and accomplished absolutely nothing! The Lord makes it clear that it was fear—an unnecessary fear at that—that caused Elijah to show no respect for the lives of the first two battalions of men—men who had no ill intent and who were simply following their king's orders. And the very fact that the angel of the Lord wanted Elijah to go with the captain shows that Elijah's self-protective display of supernatural violence was contrary to the Lord's will.

A third confirming piece of evidence is that the Lord had confronted Elijah's fear of authorities just prior to this episode. The Lord gave him a spectacular demonstration of his power against the prophets of Baal that should have caused Elijah to trust Yahweh and not fear rebellious rulers (1 Kgs 19:1–18). The fact that Yahweh had to confront this fear again indicates that, as is true of all the violence carried out by God's people in the OT, Elijah's fear-motivated misuse of divine authority was predicated on a sinful lack of trust in Yahweh.

Fourth, in the context of the ANE, fire falling from the sky was

9. Matt 5:44–45; Luke 6:27–35.

10. D. Flood, *Disarming Scripture: Cherry-Picking Liberals, Violence-Loving Conservatives, and Why We All Need to Learn to Read the Bible Like Jesus Did* (San Francisco: Metanoia, 2014), 42 (cf. 43–44).

11. 2 Kgs 1:15, cf. v. 10. On the identification of the "angel of the Lord" with Yahweh, see Gen 16:7–14; 22:11–15; 31:11–13; Exod 3:2–4; Num 2:22–38; Judg 6:11–23.

often attributed to a malevolent fire-throwing deity. Moreover, Satan is depicted as causing fire to fall from heaven in Job (1:16).[12] And in a passage in Revelation that some argue is intended to associate Elijah's incinerating miracle with demonic activity, we find a beast operating under the authority of Satan that is able to deceive people by "causing fire to come down from heaven" (Rev 13:13).[13]

Since Jesus reveals God to be against violence while Satan does nothing but kill, steal, and destroy (John 10:10), we have good reason to attribute this fire to Satan or some other destroyer in his camp. And we therefore have good reason to conclude that Elijah's fear and lack of trust in Yahweh caused him to unwittingly use his divine authority to unleash a demonic agent on these hundred innocent men whom God wanted him to follow, not incinerate.

A final piece of evidence that lends support to a cross-centered interpretation of this episode comes from a noncanonical fictional work around the time of Jesus titled *The Testament of Abraham*. It contains a story of Abraham wanting to call down fire from heaven to incinerate some sinners, just as Elijah had done and just as James and John wanted to do. And this work makes it clear that fire would have fallen at Abraham's command had God not sent Michael the Archangel to stop him. Through Michael, the Lord rebuked Abraham, saying, "I have made the world and I do not want to destroy any of them."[14]

While this is an uninspired fictional account, it demonstrates that others around the time of Jesus did not assume that the ability to carry out violent supernatural feats—and even the specific ability to make lethal fire rain from the sky—meant that God was involved in, or approved of, this use of divine authority. And this, I submit, is precisely what our looking-class cross perspective leads us to believe about Elijah's violent miracle. When God endows agents with divine authority, "the agents retain the power to make decisions . . . that fly in the face of the will of God."[15]

12. Note that Yahweh had said to Satan, "everything [Job] has is in *your power*" (Job 1:12, emphasis added). It is evident from this that Satan has the power not only to rain down fire from the sky, but also to incite murderous thieves against people (vv. 15, 17) and bring about lethal windstorms (v. 19).

13. See S. Tonstad, *Saving God's Reputation: The Theological Function of* Pistis Iesou *in the Cosmic Narratives of Revelation* (Edinburgh: T&T Clark, 2006), 36–37; S. Tonstad, "The Limits of Power: Revisting Elijah at Horeb," *Scottish Journal of Theology* 19 (2005): 253–66, esp. 265.

14. *Testament of Abraham* 10. See the discussion in D. Allison, "Rejecting Violent Judgment: Luke 9:52–56 and Its Relatives," *Journal of Biblical Literature* 121, no. 3 (2002): 259–78.

Elisha and the Mauling Bears

Our second example of one of God's representatives misusing divine authority comes from a passage of Scripture that has "brought more criticism of the Bible than almost any other narrative."[16] I'm talking about the infamous account of Elisha cursing forty-two boys who were taunting him. The account reads:

> From there Elisha went up to Bethel. As he was walking along the road, some boys came out of the town and jeered at him. "Get out of here, baldy!" they said. "Get out of here, baldy!" He turned around, looked at them and called down a curse on them in the name of the Lord. Then two bears came out of the woods and mauled forty-two of the boys. (2 Kgs 2:23–24)

Allow me three preliminary comments before I address this passage's supernatural violence. First, most OT scholars argue that this passage belongs to the genre of folklore or legend.[17] I have no problem accepting that God could have used the genre of legend in his inspired witness to his missionary activity. But even if we accept this perspective, it would not diminish the need for us to wrestle with the narrative's violence. For, as I have repeatedly said, the divine authority of any biblical narrative is not dependent on its genre or its relationship to history.

Second, the Hebrew words for "boys" that are used in this narrative are *qatan* (v. 23) and *yeled* (v. 24), and they do not necessarily refer to preadolescent children.[18] In fact, both are used of Joseph's brother Benjamin when he was in his twenties (Gen 44:20).

Finally, when these young men mocked Elijah's baldness, they weren't merely trying to wound his ego on the basis of his looks. In the ANE, baldness was often associated with being cursed or mentally challenged. So it seems likely that these young men were

15. T. E. Fretheim, "Issues of Agency," 606.
16. W. C. Kaiser Jr., *Hard Sayings of the Old Testament* (Downers Grove, IL: InterVarsity, 1988), 122.
17. See, e.g., J. F. D. Creach, *Violence in Scripture* (Louisville: Westminster John Knox, 2013), 160; M. A. Sweeney, *I & II Kings: A Commentary*, OTL (Louisville: Westminster John Knox, 2007), 275.
18. P. L. Leithart, *1 & 2 Kings* (Grand Rapids: Brazos, 2006), 175; D. Lamb, *God Behaving Badly: Is the God of the Old Testament Angry, Sexist and Racist?* (Downers Grove, IL: InterVarsity, 2011), 96; Kaiser, *Hard Sayings*, 123–24.

claiming that Elisha was cursed or deranged for preaching his message of exclusive devotion to Yahweh.

***

These preliminary considerations somewhat alleviate the offensiveness of this account, but they do not address the all-important question of whether or not Yahweh sent the mauling bears. There are several indications that confirm that he did not. For one thing, while Elisha cursed these boys "in the name of the Lord" (2 Kgs 2:24), the text does not claim that Yahweh sent the bears. It is the prophet's own powerful word that either "heals and gives life" (cf. 2 Kgs 2:19–22) or that "brings death."[19]

In fact, the narratives about the supernatural exploits of Elisha and Elijah were intended not to highlight God's activity but to highlight the extraordinary supernatural power that resided in these men and that they had at their disposal.[20] For example, divine power so permeated Elisha that we are told that a corpse was resuscitated when it accidentally slipped off a cart and touched his bones (2 Kgs 13:21)! This story illustrates that, "not only was Elisha endowed with restorative powers during his life, but these powers extended beyond his death into the grave."[21] And the remarkable degree to which Elijah was endowed with divine power is illustrated in the fact that it even lingered in his cloak after he had ascended (2 Kgs 2:13–14).

Whether it's legendary or historical in nature, the narrative of Elisha's lethal curse is not intended to hold him up as a model of exemplary behavior but to "express the remarkable divine authority this holy man possessed and to communicate that it is dangerous."[22] Within the ancient Hebraic worldview, any person or object that was endowed with the power of God was understood to be "energy-laden to the highest degree," for better *or for worse*.[23] And it could potentially operate for the worse because its usage was subject to the prophet's own fallible discretion.

It's also significant that some scholars argue that the Hebrew word for "curse" (*qālal*) in this passage has the sense of "to loosen" or "to

19. M. Cogan and H. Tadmor, *II Kings* (Garden City, NY: Doubleday, 1988), 39.
20. Cogan and Tadmor, *II Kings*; Sweeney, *I & II Kings*, 275.
21. Cogan and Tadmor, *II Kings*, 150. See also Sweeney, *I & II Kings*, 360; cf. 2 Kgs 4:8–37.
22. Creach, *Violence in Scripture*, 151.
23. E. Gerstenberger, *Leviticus: A Commentary*, trans. D. W. Stott (Louisville: Westminster John Knox, 1993), 282.

unbind" something.[24] Not only this, but some ANE sources associate curses with removing protection and turning people over to forces of evil.[25]

Moreover, in the OT and broader ANE culture, demonic forces were frequently associated with wild beasts in the desert. In this light, we should probably interpret the two mauling bears in this narrative to represent forces of evil that were unleashed by Elisha's protection-removing curse.[26] This would answer the otherwise unanswerable question of how two ordinary bears could have managed to kill *forty-two* young men!

It thus seems that, in contrast to Jesus who always submitted the authority he had been given to the will of the Father, even to the point of *sacrificing himself* for the sake of others, this story shows Elisha using the authority he had been given to defend himself by *sacrificing others.*[27]

At the same time, when this story is read through the looking-glass cross, it also bears witness to the truth that the one who perfectly submitted his divine authority to the Father also bore the sin of all those who, like Elisha, did not. It thus bears witness not only to God's willingness to risk placing his authority in the hands of free agents who might misuse it, but to bear their sin when they did.

The Supernatural Strength of a Long-Haired Brawler

The final illustration of someone misusing divine authority that we'll discuss is Samson. According to the author of the book of Judges, Samson acquired supernatural strength when the Spirit of the Lord came upon him and/or when his hair grew long.[28] But Samson

24. See E. Spieser, "An Angelic 'Curse': Exodus 14:20," in *Oriental and Biblical Studies: Collected Writings of E. A. Spieser* (Philadelphia: University of Pennsylvania Press, 1967), 106–17.
25. A. M. Kitz, *Cursed Are You! The Phenomenology of Cursing in Cuneform and Hebrew Texts* (Winona Lake, IN: Eisenbrauns, 2014), 179; 238–44; H. C. Brichto, *The Problem of Curse* (Philadelphia: Society of Biblical Literature, 1963), 82–85; J. Pedersen, *Israel, Its Life and Culture*, 2 vols. (Oxford: Oxford University Press, 1926), 1:451–52.
26. B. Naowski, "Wild Beasts," in *Dictionary of Deities and Demons in the Bible*, 2nd ed., ed. K. van der Toorn et al. (Grand Rapids: Eerdmans, 1999), 897–98. On wild animals as agents that carry out curses among other ANE people, see Kitz, *Cursed Are You!*, 188–91.
27. For my cross-centered interpretation of the supernatural deaths of Ananias and Sapphira (Acts 5:1–10), which in some respects parallels the supernatural death of these forty-two young men, see *CWG*, vol. 1, appendix II.
28. Judg 14:6, 19; 15:4; 16:22.

consistently used this strength in remarkably selfish, vengeful, violent, and often foolish ways.

For example, Samson once murdered thirty innocent bystanders simply to steal their clothes and pay off a foolish bet he'd made (Judg 14:12–20). And he once retaliated against the Philistines by tying a lit torch to the conjoined tails of 150 pairs of foxes and then releasing them to burn down the Philistines' grain fields and vineyards (15:3–5). The Philistines responded by burning alive his Philistine wife and his father (15:6), so Samson "attacked them viciously and slaughtered many of them" (15:8). His thirst for revenge wasn't satisfied, however, so he went on to slaughter another 1,000 Philistines with the jawbone of an ass (15:14).

Far from reflecting the nonretaliatory mindset of Jesus and Paul, Samson reflects the vengeful mindset of Lamech, who boasted to his wives:

> I have killed a man for wounding me,
> A young man for injuring me.
> If Cain is avenged seven times,
> Then Lamech seventy-seven times. (Gen 4:23–24)

Since Samson was *supernaturally* strong, we should consider him a sort of Lamech-on-steroids!

Samson's base character and spiritual immaturity is reflected not only in his thirst for vengeance, but in his whining like a toddler (15:18), in his "foolish propensity for women who belonged to or were in the pay of the Philistines," including prostitutes (14:1–3), and in the infantile way he gave in to querulous and manipulative women (14:16–17).[29]

***

Most OT scholars argue that the Samson stories bear the marks of the genre of folklore or legend, and in this case I find it hard to disagree. In fact, these tales repeat common legendary motifs, such as strength and sexual vigor being associated with long hair and a hero being brought down by a conniving loose woman (16:1–22).[30] But

29. P. McDonald, *God & Violence: Biblical Resources for Living in a Small World* (Scottdale, PA: Herald, 2004), 166. See also Judg 16:1–17.
30. On legendary parallels with the Samson story, see J. Frazer, *Folklore in the Old Testament: Studies in Comparative Religion, Legend and Law* (New York: Hart, 1975), 270–82; D. Friedmann, *To*

as I've suggested, this doesn't render these accounts any less divinely inspired, and it thus doesn't lessen the need for Jesus's followers to address their violent depictions of God.

All who read Scripture through the looking-glass cross must interpret the association of Samson's violence with the Spirit of the Lord to be a literary crucifix. When we read the stories of Samson through this lens, we can only marvel at the humility of a God who, out of covenantal love for his people, would stoop to work through legends of a man as infantile and degenerate as Samson. And we must conclude that the immature, immoral, and violent ways Samson used the divine power he'd been given reflect Samson's character and/or the character of the author of these narratives.

At the same time, if we remain confident that God looks as beautiful as he's revealed in the crucified Christ, one thing Samson's violent and immoral exploits do not do is reflect the true charater of God.

The very fact that this narrative depicts divine power working through Samson when he is engaging in obviously immoral and foolish behavior confirms this. Related to this, at no point does the author show Samson seeking God's will about the use of this supernatural power. Nor does the author ever depict Samson aspiring to use this power for the glory of God. Samson rather uses the divine power that was entrusted to him for personal gain and personal retaliation.

Finally, the association of Samson's supernatural strength with the length of his hair suggests that not only was the use of divine power at Samson's discretion, but even whether or not he would continue to be endowed with divine power was at Samson's discretion. So, when Delilah, his Philistine girlfriend, cut Samson's hair after he foolishly disclosed the "secret" of his strength, the divine power left him, allowing the Philistines to imprison him and to gouge out his eyes (16:4–21).

When Samson's hair grew back, his supernatural strength returned, allowing him to end his life and the lives of thousands of others by causing the temple they were in to collapse (16:27–30). By dying in this tragically violent way, Samson's life illustrates the truth that those who live by violence will die by violence (Matt 26:52), even when their violence expressed God's power residing within them.

All of this confirms that, in sharp contrast to Jesus's obedient use

Kill and Take Possession: Law, Morality, and Society in Biblical Stories (Peabody, MA: Hendrickson, 2002), 73.

of his God-given power, Samson's use of God-given power tells us nothing about God's true character. What reveals God's true character is that he remained in relationship with, and continued to further his purposes through, a nation of people who thought the Spirit of the Lord was capable of inspiring an immoral brawler to engage in such violence.

***

With every free agent that God creates, whether human or angelic, God freely gives away a degree of "say-so" regarding what comes to pass. God would rather have a risky creation in which free agents are capable of genuine love than a risk-free creation in which agents are not truly free. Yet the stories of Elijah's descending fire, Elisha's mauling bears, and Samson's infantile violent exploits, confirm what Jesus's cross-centered ministry supremely reveals: God has always been willing to endow certain individuals with even more agency by giving them a degree of his own power. And God has always done this knowing that, because these agents are free, there's no guarantee that they will always use this power the way he desires.

The criterion of the cross makes it clear that these specially endowed individuals did not always use the divine power entrusted to them in ways that reflected God's will. But, most importantly, the fact that God was willing to remain in relationship with these people despite their misuse of divine power, even allowing himself to be represented in the inspired witness to his missionary activity as complicit in their misuse of divine authority, bears witness to the cross.

Interpreted through the looking-glass cross, these violent representations of God become literary crucifixes that bear witness to the truth that Jesus Christ is the same yesterday, today, and forever (Heb 13:8). Read in this fashion, these accounts reveal that the heavenly missionary has always been the humble, nonviolent, noncoercive, self-sacrificial, sin-bearing God that he's supremely revealed to be on Calvary.

16

Commanding Child Sacrifice

The God who had promised [Abraham] a son
now wants him to destroy that son;
the God who commands his people not to murder
has now ordered the father of the Jews
to sacrifice his own child.
—Bart Ehrman[1]

An Insane Command

On May 9, 2003, Deanna Laney, a thirty-nine-year-old mother of three sons, took her fifteen-month-old son out to the backyard and smashed his head with a large rock. Deanna then went back and brought her two older sons outside and did the same to them. She then called the police and told them what she had done. The two older boys, Joshua, who was eight, and Luke, who was six, were pronounced dead on the scene. Aaron, her youngest child, survived her attack, but with significant brain damage and permanently impaired vision.

Why would a mother do such a horrendous thing? She told police she believed God had commanded her to kill her beloved children. Understandably, a jury concluded that Deanna was not guilty by reason of insanity. It was a just verdict, because anyone who sincerely believed God told them to kill their children is clearly insane.

1. B. Ehrman, *God's Problem: How the Bible Fails to Answer Our Most Important Question—Why We Suffer* (New York: HarperOne, 2008), 169.

So what are we to think of the patriarch of our faith, Abraham, who believed he heard Yahweh tell him: "Take your son, your only son, whom you love—Isaac—and go to the region of Moriah. Sacrifice him there as a burnt offering on a mountain I will show you" (Gen 22:2)? Shouldn't we conclude that Abraham was insane? Or, if we're convinced that Abraham heard God correctly, shouldn't we conclude that *God* is insane?

In this light, it's not hard to see how someone might consider this to be "a dreadful story" about a "monstrous test."[2] Some go so far as to call this story "deranged" and "sadistic."[3] And in keeping with this, many scholars have concluded that, while there may be some insights to be retrieved from this narrative, its portrait of God must be rejected as fictitious and dangerous.[4]

The Cross-Centered Interpretation

When I first began wrestling with this narrative in the light of God's supreme revelation on Calvary, I was inclined to agree that the surface meaning of this portrait of God must be rejected. In contrast to these scholars, however, my conviction that all Scripture is divinely inspired for the purpose of pointing to the cross meant that this rejection didn't solve the challenge posed by this passage. I still had to discern how this unacceptable divine portrait pointed to the cross. And I trust it is by now clear how I eventually came to see how this and every other unacceptable portrait of God in the OT performs this all-important function.

As my research continued, I also found some rather compelling arguments in support of this cross-centered interpretation. For example, given how common child sacrifices were throughout the ANE, and given how susceptible ancient Israelites were to being influenced by their surrounding culture, it's hardly surprising that the OT itself testifies that the Israelites were constantly pulled in this direction.[5]

2. J. L. Crenshaw, *A Whirlpool of Torment: Israelite Traditions of God as an Oppressive Presence* (Philadelphia: Fortress Press, 1984), 12.
3. D. N. Fewell and A. M. Gunn, *Gender, Power, and Promise: The Subject of the Bible's First Story* (Nashville: Abingdon, 1993), 98.
4. E. Seibert, *Disturbing Divine Behavior: Troubling Old Testament Images of God* (Minneapolis: Fortress Press, 2009), 26–27, 217. See also E. Curly, "The God of Abraham, Isaac and Jacob," in *Divine Evil?: The Moral Character of the God of Abraham*, ed. M. Bergmann, M. J. Murray, and M. C. Rea (New York: Oxford University Press, 2011), 58–78.
5. 2 Kgs 16:3; 17:17; 21:6; 2 Chron 28:1–4; Jer 7:31; 32:35; Ezek 20:31; Ps 106:37.

Moreover, the very fact that Scripture frequently prohibits sacrificing children confirms that the Israelites were continually tempted to carry out this diabolic ritual.[6] And this proves that God's ancient people sometimes succumbed to the temptation to view Yahweh along the lines of the child-devouring deities worshiped by their pagan neighbors.

In fact, while this will be hard for some to accept, this influence is arguably reflected in at least three biblical passages that seem to represent *Yahweh* commanding his people to sacrifice their firstborn sons (as well as animals) to him.[7] Conservative scholars have made valiant attempts to argue that these passages don't mean what they clearly seem to mean, and I can't blame them because I was once in that camp. But as I mentioned in chapter 1, ten years ago I found I had to give up trying to put the best possible spin on macabre passages like these and to instead embrace them in all their ugliness as part of God's divinely inspired word.

That is when I began to develop the capacity to see that *something else is going on* in the depths of these sin-mirroring passages and that this *something else* is the same thing that is going on in the depths of the sin-mirroring cross. By exercising the same surface-penetrating faith we exercise when we discern the cross to be the definitive revelation of God, horrific portraits of Yahweh demanding child sacrifices become literary crucifixes that permanently bear witness to the remarkable depths to which our non-coercive heavenly missionary has always been willing to go to remain in solidarity with his fallen and culturally conditioned covenant people.

As I said, I initially interpreted the portrait of Yahweh commanding Abraham to sacrifice his son along these lines. In this view, the portrait of Yahweh giving this grisly command is a humble divine accommodation to the Israelites' fallen and culturally conditioned view that Yahweh was no different than other ANE deities in demanding child sacrifices. At the same time, the fact that Yahweh is portrayed as preventing the sacrifice at the last minute while providing his own sacrifice reflects the Spirit of Christ breaking through to

6. Lev 18:21; Deut 12:31; 18:10.

7. Exod 22:29–30; Judg 11:30–39; Ezek 20:25–26. See J. D. Levenson, *The Death and Resurrection of the Beloved Son: The Transformation of Child Sacrifice in Judaism and Christianity* (New Haven: Yale University Press, 1993); K. Finsterbusch, "The First-Born Between Sacrifice and Redemption in the Hebrew Bible," in *Human Sacrifice in Jewish and Christian Tradition*, ed. K. Finsterbusch, A. Lange, and K. F. D. Römheld (Boston: Brill, 2007).

reveal that Yahweh is not, in fact, like other ANE gods who demand child sacrifices. To the contrary, he's a God who would rather provide his own sacrifice than to receive sacrifices from others.

I still consider this to be a perfectly viable interpretation of this narrative. At the same time, the Conservative Hermeneutic Principle, which I spelled out in chapter 4, requires me to depart from the original meaning of passages *only insofar as is necessary*. Hence, if there are ways of plausibly interpreting apparently violent portraits of God that render their surface meaning consistent with the crucified Christ, I feel obliged to try to find it. While I have concluded that this is not possible with most violent depictions of God in the OT, my wrestling with this particular narrative has led me to the tentative conclusion that this *is* possible with its depiction of God.

If the interpretation I am about to propose is deemed compelling, it means the portrait of God contained in this narrative can be interpreted as a *direct* rather than *indirect* revelation of the God who is fully revealed in the crucified Christ. Moreover, if this interpretation is accepted, we will see that Abraham's testing illustrates the challenge that we've been wrestling with throughout this book, namely: What should you do when you are convinced God is loving and faithful but then seem to find him apparently acting in unloving and unfaithful ways?

Copan's Defense of This Narrative

For reasons that will become clear as we proceed, I believe it will prove helpful to develop my interpretation of Abraham's testing in dialogue with Paul Copan's fine defense of this narrative. Copan argues that Abraham's testing was not only about assessing Abraham's willingness to obey Yahweh; it was also, and even more importantly, about assessing Abraham's trust in Yahweh's faithful character. Yahweh had promised Abraham that he would bless him with innumerable descendants, and in this narrative Yahweh is testing him to see if he would trust him to keep his promise, *despite the fact* that he commanded him to sacrifice the very son who would give him these descendants.

So, rather than suggesting that "the God who had promised [Abraham] a son now wants him to destroy that son," as Bart Ehrman claims, Copan argues that Yahweh wanted Abraham to trust that he *would not* need to destroy his son, notwithstanding his command to the contrary.[8]

According to Copan, the very fact that this testing happens after Abraham had walked with Yahweh for many years and had come to know his "faithful—and even tender—character and promises" should lead us to assume that Abraham was "confident God would somehow fulfill his promise to him, however this would be worked out."[9] Copan argues that the gentle tone with which Yahweh gives this command also indicates that Abraham was being asked to trust God's faithfulness in the face of a command that contradicted it.[10]

Closely related to this, Copan argues that by reiterating to Abraham that Isaac is "your son, your only son, whom you love," Yahweh was reassuring him that he was fully aware that "the divine promise can only be fulfilled through Isaac."[11] And finally, Copan argues that this story indicates that Abraham was in fact trusting that he would not have to sacrifice Isaac when he reassured his servants that he and Isaac would both return to them. Referring to himself and Isaac, Abraham tells his servants: "*We* will worship," he says, "and *we* will come back to you" (Gen 22:5, emphasis added). As the author of Hebrews later observed, Abraham trusted that Yahweh would remain true to his promise, even if this meant that he would have to raise Isaac from the dead (Heb 11:17–19).[12]

Challenges to Copan's Interpretation

I find Copan's interpretation largely compelling. However, I think it faces two challenges. First, I frankly don't get the impression that Copan fully appreciates how radically out of character this command is for the God whom the crucified Christ fully discloses. If we are to believe that the God who is fully revealed on Calvary went to the extreme of uttering this barbaric command, we must assume that he had sufficient reason for doing so. And for me, the suggestion that God was merely trying to find out if Abraham trusted him doesn't suffice.

8. See Ehrman, *God's Problem,* 169; P. Copan, *Is God a Moral Monster?: Making Sense of the Old Testament God* (Grand Rapids: Baker, 2011), 47.
9. Copan, *Is God a Moral Monster?*, 47.
10. As Copan notes, Yahweh's command can be translated as, "Please take your son," or even as, "Take, I beg of you, your only son" (*Is God a Moral Monster?*, 47).
11. Copan, *Is God a Moral Monster?*, 48.
12. Ibid.

Second, if Abraham was as confident in Yahweh's character as Copan suggests, why does Yahweh need to test him? Doesn't the very fact that Yahweh felt the need to test Abraham suggest that he knew, or at least suspected, that Abraham *did not* yet fully trust him to keep his divine promise? By overemphasizing Abraham's confidence in Yahweh's faithful character, it seems to me that Copan has unwittingly undermined the genuineness of this test.

Moreover, the very fact that Yahweh declared, "*Now* I know that you fear God" (v. 12, emphasis added) once the test was completed suggests that something *genuinely* hung in the balance with this test. There was something yet unresolved in Abraham's character, and therefore in God's knowledge of Abraham's character, and this test was designed to resolve it.

I am willing to grant that Abraham's decades-long relationship with Yahweh *inclined* him to trust that Yahweh would keep his promise and not make him sacrifice Isaac. And Abraham undoubtedly *hoped* this was the case. But Abraham could not have been *altogether* confident if this was a genuine test. And, as I will argue below, it would hardly be surprising that Abraham had a lingering concern that Yahweh might *actually* want him to sacrifice his firstborn son, given his pagan upbringing in the land of Ur, where sacrificing children to gods was routine.

Moreover, if we examine Yahweh's interactions with Abraham in the narratives leading up to the testing narrative, we are given reason to believe that this grisly test was not merely to *find out* if Abraham trusted Yahweh's faithfulness; it was, more importantly, designed to *help* Abraham fully trust Yahweh's faithfulness. To this end, I will argue, Yahweh stooped to momentarily take on the appearance of a typical ANE child-sacrifice-demanding deity by giving this horrific command.

I'm suggesting that Yahweh didn't merely stoop to *allow* Abraham or others *to believe* he gave this command. In this one instance, the heavenly missionary stooped to *actually give it*! And Yahweh did this to have Abraham undergo a highly emotional paradigm shift in his view of God that removed any doubt that Yahweh might be like other ANE gods who required this ultimate sacrifice. Indeed, far from demanding this sacrifice, Abraham needed to learn that Yahweh is a God who makes sacrifice.[13]

13. The interpretation I am about to offer has been significantly informed by discussions with Ty

A Curious Compliance

I will unpack my proposed interpretation of this narrative in three steps.

First, it is significant that Abraham offers no objection to Yahweh's shocking command. This is especially surprising in light of the strong objection Abraham earlier voiced when he learned about Yahweh's plan to allow Sodom and Gomorrah to be destroyed (Gen 18:16–33). Like so many other biblical heroes, Abraham didn't hesitate to object when Yahweh seemed to be acting out of character. Yet, when Yahweh instructed him to sacrifice his son—the very son Yahweh had supernaturally given him and whom Yahweh promised would give him innumerable descendants—Abraham says nothing!

What explains Abraham's curious silence? As strange as it may seem to us, the most plausible answer is that Yahweh's command to sacrifice Isaac simply didn't shock Abraham the way the announced plan to have Sodom and Gomorrah destroyed did. And here is where Abraham's pagan upbringing becomes relevant.

For the first several decades of his life, Abraham had worshiped other gods in the land of Ur where, as I said, child sacrifices were routine.[14] Moreover, the revelation that Yahweh was actually revolted by child sacrifices was not given until the Sinai covenant, which took place hundreds of years later. And as I noted earlier, even after Yahweh had prohibited this barbaric practice, Abraham's descendants were still tempted to conceive of Yahweh as a typical ANE deity who demanded and delighted in child sacrifices.

If the Israelites were tempted to think Yahweh demanded child sacrifices long after he had explicitly prohibited it, it shouldn't surprise us that Abraham, raised in a pagan culture that routinely practiced child sacrifice, was tempted to conceive of Yahweh along these lines and in these terms.[15] Moreover, we have no account of Yahweh explicitly telling Abraham that he was not like other ANE gods when it came to demanding child sacrifices. The fact that Yahweh had

Gibson as well as by his book, *A God Named Desire: What If You're the Object of an Unstoppable Love?* (Nampa, ID: Pacific Press, 2010), 108–14. For a more extensive discussion that arrives at a similar interpretation, see S. Tonstad, *God of Sense and Traditions of Non-Sense* (Eugene, OR: Wipf & Stock, 2016), 142–62.

14. Gen 11:31; Josh 24:2.

15. For this reason, I think those who argue that this command represents a form of emotional abuse on the part of God are thinking anachronistically (for example, Seibert, *Disturbing Divine Behavior*, 27).

supernaturally given him Isaac would certainly *incline* Abraham to think Yahweh would not want him sacrificed. But it wouldn't altogether rule this possibility out.

These considerations not only explain Abraham's acquiescing silence, they also make clear why this was a genuine test for Abraham and why Yahweh felt the need to put him through it. While God wanted to determine Abraham's level of obedience and trust, he even more importantly needed to remove any lingering suspicion Abraham had that Yahweh might have a side to him that was like the child-devouring gods he had previous worshiped.

The Instructional Strategy of Pushing to the Edge

The second step in developing my claim that Yahweh was testing Abraham in order to have him undergo an emotional paradigm shift in his thinking about God's character is this: when we place this narrative in the broader context of the story of Abraham's dealings with Yahweh, we can see that Yahweh had employed this strategy before.

Have you ever wondered why God allowed Abraham and Sarah to grow too old to bear children before he fulfilled his promise to them? Well, consider how Abraham and Sarah responded to this long delay: they devised a plan to bring about their promised son *on their own* by using Abraham's handmaid, Hagar, as a concubine (Gen 16:1–4). Given their pagan past, this response to Yahweh's delay is almost to be expected, for a uniform aspect of the common theology of the ANE was that deities need humans to do their part in order to receive divine blessings. The long delay in receiving the son that Yahweh had promised apparently led these former pagans to conclude that Yahweh needed their help in delivering on his promise.

So on Sarah's recommendation, Abraham impregnated their servant, Hagar. Their plan, however, was not God's will, and it therefore failed miserably. Out of jealousy, Sarah eventually forced Hagar and her son to leave, though Yahweh mercifully promised to care for them.[16]

Yet, even after this contrived plan failed, Yahweh waited another thirteen years before delivering on his promise![17] Why? It seems Yahweh was taking this couple "to the edge," where they could easily

16. Gen 16:4–14; 17:20.
17. Gen 17:1, 19.

despair of ever receiving their promised son, as a means of freeing them from every last vestige of their pagan assumption that God needed their help. By delaying so long, God was setting them up to learn in dramatic fashion that the promise of the one true God "will be fulfilled not by [their] power, but by HIS power."[18] And for this reason the apostle Paul could later hold up Abraham as the forefather of the covenant that is based on faith, not works.[19]

We can further discern that God was engaging in an "aggressive effort to reconfigure their perception of where the power really lies" in the manner in which God changes their name. Yahweh told Abram, which means "exalted father," that his name would now be Abraham, which means "father of many nations." God explains this change:

> For *I* have made you a father of many nations. *I* will make you very fruitful; *I* will make nations of you, and kings will come from you. *I* will establish my covenant as an everlasting covenant between me and you and your descendants after you for the generations to come, to be your God and the God of your descendants after you. (Gen 17:5–7, emphasis added)

So at least part of the significance of this name change concerned the fact that Abraham would now be the father of many nations, not by being an exalted father who accomplished great things on his own, but simply by trusting in the faithfulness and power of Yahweh.

Along the same lines, God told Abraham that he was changing his wife's name from Sarai to Sarah. It's not clear how this name change signifies her new role, for most scholars agree that both names mean "princess." However, the very fact that Yahweh conferred on her a new name reflects a deepening of their covenantal relationship.

This deepened relationship is reflected in the fact that she is, for the first time, given promises similar to Abraham. Yet, like Abraham, Sarah now knows that she will receive these promises not by carrying out her own schemes, as she had done before, but simply by trusting in the character and power of Yahweh.

The lesson that Abraham and Sarah learned through their long ordeal was not missed by the apostle Paul. He notes that Abraham's first son was by "a slave woman" and was "according to the flesh,"

18. Gibson, *A God Named Desire*, 104.
19. Rom 4:13–22; Gal 3:6–9, 14–18; cf. 4:21–31.

while his second-born son was "by the free woman" and was "born as the result of a divine promise" (Gal 4:23). For Paul, this metaphorically illustrated two very different ways of perceiving our relationship with God. Hagar, the slave woman, represented the "covenant . . . from Mount Sinai" that brings forth "children who are . . . slaves," for they strive to be rightly related to God on their own effort (Gal 4:24). Sarah, by contrast, represented the new covenant that brings forth "children of promise" who are "born of the Spirit" (4:28–29).[20] And this is why Paul understood Abraham to be the "father of all who believe" (Rom 4:11).

Paul's use of this illustration confirms why Yahweh delayed the fulfillment of his promise so long. Had Abraham and Sarah quickly conceived their promised son during their childbearing years and by natural means, the lingering pagan aspects of their view of God would have gone unchallenged. Moreover, the distinction between children born "according to the flesh" and the "children of promise . . . born of the Spirit" would never have been made.

In this light, it's apparent that Yahweh had to bring Abraham and Sarah to a point where it looked as though Yahweh was not going to fulfill his promise, and where no work "according to the flesh" could be of help. And Yahweh did this in order to convince them that, in contrast to the pagan gods of their past, Yahweh is able to fulfill his promises without any human help whatsoever. They needed to learn that receiving God's promises comes by faith alone, apart from all human striving.

Pushing Abraham to the Edge

I believe a similar strategy to purge lingering pagan elements from Abraham's understanding of Yahweh is at work when Yahweh stoops to take on the appearance of an ANE deity who demands child sacrifice, and this is the final step I need to take in unpacking my proposed interpretation.

In Abraham's pagan upbringing, sacrificing one's firstborn child was the ultimate "work" a human could perform to prove their loyalty to a god or to court a god's favor. So if there remained any suspicion that Yahweh was in any respect like other ANE gods, it would be about this. As a means of finally freeing Abraham from

20. See also Gal 3:14.

every remnant of this cursed view of divinity, God humbly stooped to temporarily take on the likeness of this cursed view.

As we've seen throughout this book, God was once again stooping to meet his covenant partner where he was at in order to lead him to where he wanted him to be.[21] The difference, however, is that Yahweh wasn't merely stooping to allow his covenant partners to view him in their fallen and culturally conditioned ways. Out of love for Abraham and a desire to see him set free of his lingering pagan conceptions of him, Yahweh in this one instance *actually* stooped to play this role.[22]

***

To see how this teaching method could be effective, we need to get inside the heart and mind of Abraham as much as possible. By commanding Abraham to offer up his only son, Yahweh was forcing Abraham to confront his lingering pagan suspicion that Yahweh might, after all, be similar to other ANE gods who require this ultimate sacrifice. This all-too-common command placed Abraham's trust in Yahweh's good and faithful character in sharp tension with his now-activated lingering pagan conception of God. It also placed Abraham's trust in God's good character in sharp tension with his commitment to obey God at all costs.

We can easily imagine the turmoil in Abraham's heart and mind as he and Isaac traveled to Moriah. Trying to trust in Yahweh's faithful character, Abraham demonstrated his loyalty by obediently following the command to the very end. And even as the climactic moment approached without any sign of Yahweh's intervention, Abraham tried to remain confident, telling his servants that both he

21. We can discern a similar strategy at work when Jesus tested the faith of a Canaanite woman by momentarily taking on the appearance of an all-too-typical first-century Jew who considered Canaanites to be dogs (Matt 15:21–28).

22. A common apologetic strategy among Evangelicals is to argue this way regarding all violent portraits in the OT. In this view, God was stooping to meet people where they were at when he commanded and engaged in all the violence that OT authors ascribe to him. Against this, I would simply point out that it is not contrary to the character of the crucified Christ for Yahweh to temporarily stoop to play an ugly role that involved no violence in order to free Abraham from any suspicion that he is like that. As was mentioned the previous note, Jesus himself seemed willing to do that (Matt 15:21–28). By contrast, the suggestion that Yahweh commanded his people to engage in genocide, let alone that he did so with the intention of having them carry it out, blatantly contradicts the enemy-loving, non-violent character of God that is revealed in the crucified Christ. On top of this, the common apologetic strategy doesn't disclose how these violent divine portraits point to the cross.

and Isaac would return (Gen 22:5) and reassuring Isaac, "God himself will provide the lamb for the burnt offering" (v. 8).

At the same time, whatever lingering worry Abraham had that Yahweh might in fact require this ultimate sacrifice, it surely hit a fever pitch as he raised the knife to slay his son (v. 10). For the truth is that, in that last moment before the knife was about to be plunged into Isaac, it certainly looked as if Yahweh was exactly like the pagan gods of Abraham's past who demanded child sacrifices.

And then, at the last moment, the Lord intervened and provided Abraham with his own sacrifice (vv. 11–13). Having just experienced the deepest possible emotional anguish arising from his suspicions that Yahweh was like the child-devouring gods of his past, Abraham now experienced the greatest possible emotional relief as he learned the dramatic lesson that Yahweh was not at all like these child-devouring gods. As he had done by long delaying the birth of Abraham's promised son, God once again pushed Abraham to the edge for the purpose of dramatically reframing his conception of him. At "the peak point of horrific clarity," Gibson says, "God crushed the [pagan] image out of existence and introduced a whole new spiritual realization."[23] And the emotional intensity of this moment is precisely what would make the reframing effective and permanent. In this sense, we might think of God's strategy in this testing narrative along the lines of "flooding" or "implosion" therapy, in which patients are made to dramatically confront, and thereby overcome, their worst fears.[24]

Through this testing, Abraham demonstrated the same level of loyalty that the pagan gods demand when they required a child sacrifice. But this dramatic paradigm shift enabled Abraham to understand that his ultimate loyalty was to a God who not only did not *require* child sacrifice, he *provides* the sacrifice. Abraham therefore named the place where he had bound Isaac, "The Lord will provide" (v. 14). And those of us who know God as he is fully revealed in the crucified Christ know more deeply than Abraham possibly could the profundity of this name. For on Calvary we learn that, rather than requiring

23. Gibson, *A God Named Desire*, 115–16. So too, Gibson notes that God was "cleansing Abraham's faith from every lingering trace of the appeasement or salvation-by-works theology with which he was raised in Babylon" (ibid., 109).

24. See A. Boudewyns, *Flooding and Implosive Therapy: Direct Therapeutic Exposure in Clinical Practice* (New York: Plenum, 1983); E. B. Foa and M. J. Kozak, "Emotional Processing of Fear: Exposure to Corrective Information," *Psychology Bulletin* 99 (1986): 20–35.

humans to offer up sacrifices to him, the true God sacrifices himself for all humans.

No wonder Jesus taught that "Abraham rejoiced at the thought of seeing my day; he saw it and was glad" (John 8:58).

The Choice

When I witnessed Shelley seeming to mistreat the panhandler on the other side of the street in the imagined story with which I began this book, I was forced to make a very important choice. Would I allow this shocking episode to compromise my knowledge of Shelley's loving and compassionate character, or would I trust that, after thirty-seven years of marriage, I *really did* know Shelley and thus conclude that *something else must be going on*?

Similarly, when Abraham received the terrible divine command to sacrifice his only son, he had a decision to make. Would he continue to trust that Yahweh was the faithful God he'd come to know over many years of walking with him, or would he instead allow this horrific command to activate his latent fear that Yahweh might turn out to be like other ANE deities who demand a child sacrifice as proof of one's loyalty to them?

In both cases, the test boils down to this: Will we trust God's loving character even when God appears to be acting in ways that contradict this character? This is the question all followers of Jesus must face, and it's the question this book has tried to answer.

When we encounter horrifically violent portraits of God in the written witness to God's missionary activity, will we remain confident that we *really do* know the true God, down to his very essence, in the cross-centered life and ministry of Jesus? Will we therefore assume that *something else is going on* when OT authors depict God in violent ways that contradict this revelation? Or will we instead suspect that the cross doesn't reveal the full truth about God's character and will?

Will we suspect that God might actually be capable of the atrocious violence OT authors sometimes attribute to him, thereby empowering these violent portraits to compromise the beauty of God's character as it is revealed on the cross?

Everything hangs on how we answer this question! If we remain confident that the Son is the very shiningness of God's glory and the perfect expression of his very essence, we will be able to see *what else is going on* when OT authors depict God in horrifically violent ways. And in seeing this, we'll discern how these violent portraits point to the cross.

That is, if we read these violent divine portraits while exercising the same surface-penetrating faith we exercise when we come to embrace the crucified Nazarene as the definitive revelation of God, we'll see how the sin-mirroring ugliness of these literary crucifixes bears witness to the sin-mirroring ugliness of the historical Crucifixion and how the beauty of the sin-bearing God behind these literary crucifixes bears witness to the beauty of the sin-bearing God in the historical Crucifixion.

Conversely, if we refuse to fully trust the revelation of God in the crucified Christ by continuing to suspect that God is actually capable of the horrific violence OT authors sometimes ascribe to him, we will see nothing more in these violent portraits than what their ancient authors saw. We will not suspect, let alone discern, that there is *something else going on* behind the scenes of these portraits.

Unless we fully trust the revelation of God in the crucified Christ, in other words, we will not have the motivation or the capacity to discern how these ugly violent portraits bear witness to the unsurpassable beauty of God revealed in the crucified Christ.

To sum it up, if we choose to fully trust the beauty of the cruciform God revealed on the cross, we will find ourselves empowered to see his beauty reflected in all Scripture, including its most violent portraits of God. If we choose not to fully trust this revelation, however, we will fail to see his beauty in these violent portraits. Indeed, we will in this case be allowing these sub-Christlike portraits to cloud our vision of the beauty of the cruciform God, just as they clouded the vision of the OT authors who initially penned them.

My prayer is that this book has helped readers see that the choice is clear. Never settle for mere glimpses of the truth when God has given us the full revelation of the one who *is* the truth! Never settle for cloudy approximations of God's character when God has given us the one who is the very radiance of God's glory and the exact representation of his innermost essence. Place *all* your trust in the one who perfectly reveals the self-sacrificial, nonviolent, enemy-embracing love that defines God to the core of his being. Dare to believe that God *really is* as beautiful as the cross reveals him to be!

And when you henceforth encounter monstrous portraits of God in the OT, view them through the looking-glass cross so that they serve to remind you just how low God has always been willing to stoop to remain in loving solidarity with his covenant people. For within the inspired witness to God's missionary activity, these monstrous portraits are permanent testaments to the truth that, appearances notwithstanding, Jesus Christ truly is the same today, yesterday, and forever.

Which means, God has always been the humble, loving, self-sacrificial, sin-bearing heavenly missionary that the cross supremely reveals him to be.

Postscript: Four Words of Encouragement

After a message I recently gave on how the OT's violent portraits of God bear witness to the cross, a woman in her mid-sixties approached me with tears streaming down her face. "All my life I've tried to believe God was as beautiful as Jesus reveals him to be," she said, "but I never could *fully* give my heart to him." Her lips quivered and her voice cracked as she continued.

It was like I was courting a man who gave me every reason to believe he would make the greatest husband in the world but whom I knew had once slaughtered a classroom full of little children! Regardless of how wonderful he was to me, just knowing he was ever capable of such an atrocity would prevent me from marrying him. That's how I've always viewed God. I love the God who gave everything for us while we were yet enemies, but I can't love a God who ever demanded that people mercilessly massacre untold numbers of innocent babies!

The passion and pain in this lady's voice indicated how deeply she felt this contradiction. She then looked straight into my eyes and needed to take a couple of intentional deep breaths to speak through the strong emotion that was clearly welling up inside her. "Today," she finally managed to say, "you helped me see that I don't need to believe God ever ordered babies to be massacred! I can finally let myself believe God *really is* as beautiful as the cross reveals him to be! I can finally trust God with my entire heart!"

Then, crying profusely, this woman threw her arms around me

and gave me a tight hug while joyfully crying out, "He didn't do any of those terrible things!"

To me, there is nothing more beautiful than seeing someone like this woman set free from lingering suspicions about God in order to fully embrace the beautiful loving God who is fully revealed on Calvary. Nothing is more beautiful, and nothing could be more important.

As I mentioned in chapter 2, the depth of your passion for God and of your transformation into his likeness will never outrun the beauty of your mental representation of God. As this woman's testimony illustrates, to the extent that you entertain lingering suspicions that OT authors might be right when they ascribe atrocious behaviors and attitudes to God, it can't help but compromise your passion for God and, therefore, the beauty of the person you're becoming.

My hope and prayer is that this book has done for you what that sermon did for that woman. Can you now dare to *completely trust* that God is, to the core of his being, as beautiful as he's revealed to be on Calvary?

But adopting a cross-centered understanding of the OT's violent divine portraits requires a 180-degree paradigm shift, and that's never easy. I know from my own experience that it takes a while, as well as continual concerted effort, for our brains to adjust to a completely new paradigm.

There may be days when you suddenly find you're thinking about God as though the cross did not fully reveal him. On occasion, you may unconsciously slip back into your old way of interpreting the OT's violent divine portraits. There may come other times when you find it hard to discern how certain violent portraits of God point to the crucified Christ. And for some, there may be moments when you forget why you ever accepted the cross-centered interpretation of the OT's violent depictions of God and begin to question the whole thing.

If any of these things begin to happen, I want to encourage you to remember four things.

First, remember that the cross only functions as a looking-glass that enables us to discern *what else is going on* behind the scenes of the OT's violent divine portraits when we remain fully confident that Jesus's cross-centered life and ministry fully reveal what God is like. If you find you are having trouble seeing how various violent portraits of God point to this supreme revelation, it's because, whether you are aware of it or not, you are on some level suspecting that God might actually be capable of engaging in the violence that these portraits ascribe to him. And this means you are not yet, or are no longer, *fully* trusting God's self-revelation in the crucified Christ.

If you find yourself in this position, I encourage you to reread chapters 2 and 3 where I make the case for the crucified Christ being the supreme revelation that culminates and surpasses all previous revelations.[1] This will help you remember that the OT authors merely caught "glimpses of truth," which means their vision was mostly cloudy.

Second, if you were once accustomed to believing in a God who has a dark side, you will likely sometimes find yourself thinking that allowing the cross to completely define your conception of God *feels too good to be true*. If that happens, embrace it as good news! For the truth is that, however beautiful you envision God, he is infinitely *more* beautiful than that! So if the God you're envisioning feels too good to be true, that simply means that you are moving *in the right direction.*

You feel this way because your brain is accustomed to calling God "good" even though the God you envisioned is partly ugly. So envisioning a God who is *truly* good—indeed, better than anything we can imagine—initially feels "off." But if you continue to place your complete trust in the cross, your habitual association of truth with a partly ugly God will gradually fade. As it does, your awareness that humans can never have an accurate conception of God that is "too good to be true" will grow.

Third, when you come across ugly portraits of God in the Bible, remind yourself that this ugliness is a reflection of the ugliness of our sin that Jesus bore on the cross. These ugly pictures are literary testaments to the truth that the heavenly missionary has always been willing to humbly stoop to bear the ugly sin of his people and to thereby take on ugly appearances that mirror that sin.

Finally, and most importantly, if you aren't doing so already, I encourage you to invest a good amount of time cultivating an ever-deepening relationship with the God of self-sacrificial love revealed on Calvary. One of the most powerful ways to do this is to ask the

1. If that does not suffice, you might consider reading *CWG*, vol. 1, chs. 2–5, which offers a more comprehensive and in-depth treatment of this material.

Spirit to help you concretely imagine the one who gave his life for you.

We think with our imaginations.[2] If you doubt this, let me ask you this simple question: What is the color of your bedspread? As you hold the answer in your mind, ask yourself: What did you do just now to access that information? The answer is that you just imagined your bedspread, as though you were right now looking at the bed. This is just how we think. We represent (literally, *re*-present, *make present again*) experiences in our imagination. And the more vivid and real-like the representation is, the more it impacts us.

Here is why this is so important. Even after a person is convinced that God is altogether beautiful and has no non-Christlike streak in him, this view will continue to *feel unreal* so long as our mental picture of God's love is abstract or foggy. But in Christ, God has given us a vivid, concrete, flawless expression of exactly what he is like. So I encourage you to ask the Spirit to help you vividly imagine the beautiful, true God revealed in Christ, and especially in Christ crucified.

It is the Spirit who has removed the veil over our minds so that all of us, "with unveiled faces," can see, in our minds, "the glory of the Lord as though reflected in a mirror." And as we behold "the glory of God in the face of Jesus Christ," we "are being transformed into the same image from one degree of glory to another; for this comes from the Lord, the Spirit."[3]

So I encourage you to regularly take time to surrender your imagination to the Spirit, asking him to help you see God's perfect, infinitely intense love for you in the eyes of Jesus. Hear God's perfect, unwavering love for you in words that Jesus tenderly speaks to you. Sense God's perfect, unsurpassable love for you in the warm embrace of Jesus. And, especially if you are a person for whom this beautiful God yet *feels unreal*, I encourage you to do this *frequently*. For the more vivid and real you experience the crucified God, the more *unreal* the violent portraits of God that conflict with this vision will feel. And the more unreal these portraits feel, the more naturally you will interpret them through the looking-glass cross.

2. On the central role of imagination in our thinking process and why this is extremely important, see G. Boyd and A. Larson, *Escaping the Matrix: Setting Your Mind Free to Experience Real Life in Christ* (Grand Rapids: Baker, 2005). On the importance and power of imaginative prayer, see G. Boyd, *Seeing Is Believing: Experiencing Jesus Through Imaginative Prayer* (Grand Rapids: Baker, 2004).
3. 2 Cor 3:16, 18; 4:6. For the context of these verses, see 2 Cor 3:7–4:6.

It may take time, but I promise you that if you are persistent, you will eventually discern the beauty of the stooping heavenly missionary in the depths of the OT's ugly, sin-bearing portraits of a violent warrior god as naturally as you now discern the beauty of the stooping heavenly missionary in the depths of the ugly, sin-bearing, crucified criminal on Calvary.

Acknowledgments

As I look back on the journey I embarked on ten years ago once I stopped trying to put the best possible spin on the OT's violent portraits of God, I am filled with profound gratitude for the numerous people who have supported, encouraged, assisted, and challenged me along the way. In keeping with the Anabaptist tradition I align myself with, I believe that the Spirit works through community discernment, and I therefore consider the many people and organizations with whom I have had the honor of dialoguing to be my greatest asset.

I first want to thank the entire team at Fortress Press for the enthusiasm they have consistently expressed toward this project, expressed in both an academic (*Crucifixion of the Warrior God*) and non-academic (*Cross Vision*) venue. It has been a joy working with all of you! I also want to express my deep gratitude to Crossroads Church in Cincinnati, led by Brian Tome; the Upper Room in Edina, Minnesota, led by Joe McDonald; East Lake Church in Seattle, led by Ryan Meeks; the faculty of Anabaptist Mennonite Biblical Seminary in Goshen, Indiana; and Michael Bradley and the Association of Renewal Churches. Each of these churches or organizations invited me to share aspects of the cross-centered reinterpretation of violent divine portraits and offered helpful encouragement and feedback. I admire and appreciate your humble and bold willingness to hear what I had to share and to dialogue with me about it.

I also have been greatly encouraged and helped by a multitude of dear friends and colleagues with whom I have discussed various ideas found in this book. I will first mention the "Crux Reformers," a group of young, radical—and radically fun!—future kingdom leaders who met in my living room on a monthly basis for three consecutive years. Our lively discussions over just a wee bit of beer and wine helped shape this book in ways I am sure you do not fully realize. I also have been tremendously helped by the many dialogues I have enjoyed with a number of dear friends, including Jim Beilby, David Clark, Brad Cole, Brian Lowther, Tye Gibson, Bruxy Cavey, Tim Day, Mike and Jean Antonello, Dan and Barbara Kent, and Mark Moore.

I want to make special mention of Alex and Julie Ross and Dave and Terri Churchill, committed lifelong friends of Shelley and myself. Thank you for sharing my excitement over ideas as they were coming into being, and thank you for encouraging me to press on even when none of us were entirely sure of the direction my ideas were taking me.

I also need to express a sincere, heartfelt thank you to Jeremy Jernigan, David Morrow, Vanessa Collins, Scott Boren, and William Barnes who took the time to read through earlier versions of this manuscript and who offered helpful insights about its strengths and weaknesses. I also want to give a shout out to my friend and colleague Di Kistler whose remarkable editing skills contributed greatly to this work.

I want to make special mention of my dear friend Jessica Kelley who read through several versions of this manuscript. It was an unthinkable tragedy that brought us together, Jessica, but how God has been at work to bring good out of this tragedy! Jessica's intellectually and emotionally stirring book, *Lord Willing?*, is a remarkable case in point, and I consider our many helpful discussions about this present project to be another.

Then there is my beloved covenant brother Paul Eddy, a man who has, from the start, contributed more than anyone else to the evolution of my cross-centered approach to violent divine portraits. As I mentioned in this book, over the last ten years Paul has selflessly sacrificed entire days to help me do research on issues surrounding my approach! Paul, you are to me the embodiment of covenantal faithfulness, and I consider myself blessed beyond measure to have been your covenant partner over the last two decades.

As everyone who knows me would acknowledge, I would not be able to do what I do, whether it be writing books, preaching sermons, heading up ReKnew Ministries, pastoring Woodland Hills Church, or just knowing what I am supposed to do day-to-day, were it not for the remarkable patience, the faithful hard work, and the unwavering love and support of my precious wife of thirty-seven years, Shelley Boyd (aka "Beso"). It surely reflects God's providential design that Shelley is strongest in the areas where I am weakest, which happen to include all those practical areas that make life actually work. Shelley, I am as indebted to you as I am in love with you.

And I trust you know that I would *never* believe you capable of being cruel to a disabled panhandler, even if I witnessed you seeming to do so with my own eyes!

Finally, I want to express my profound love and sincere appreciation for the staff and congregation of Woodland Hills Church in Maplewood, Minnesota, which I have had the distinct honor of serving as Senior Pastor and primary teaching pastor for the last twenty-five years. How many Evangelical and/or Anabaptist churches do you know that would allow, let alone encourage, their Senior Pastor to explore, and then publically share, controversial theological ideas such as the nontraditional, cross-centered way of interpreting Scripture's violent portraits of God?

I am fully aware of just how rare this is and, therefore, of how blessed a pastor I am. I will go to my grave being grateful for every moment we have shared together.

With heartfelt love and appreciation, I dedicate this book to you.

Index of Authors and Subjects

Index of Scripture

Revelation